For John,

with thanks,

January 2015

THE LIFE OF
ROMAN
REPUBLICANISM

THE LIFE OF ROMAN REPUBLICANISM

JOY CONNOLLY

PRINCETON UNIVERSITY PRESS
PRINCETON AND OXFORD

Library of Congress Cataloging-in-Publication Data

Connolly, Joy, 1970–
The life of Roman republicanism / Joy Connolly.
pages cm.
Includes bibliographical references and index.
ISBN 978-0-691-16259-1 (alkaline paper)   1. Rome—History—Republic,
510–30 B.C.   2. Republicanism—Rome—History.   3. Political science—Rome—
History.   4. Rome—Politics and government—265–30 B.C.   I. Title.
DG231.C65 2015
937′.02–dc23   2014000095

British Library Cataloging-in-Publication Data is available

This book has been composed in Sabon Next LT Pro, Futura ND and Trajan Pro

Printed on acid-free paper. ∞

Printed in the United States of America

1 3 5 7 9 10 8 6 4 2

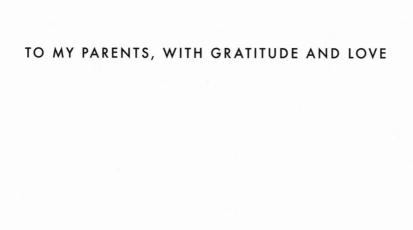

TO MY PARENTS, WITH GRATITUDE AND LOVE

CONTENTS

PREFACE

Democracy risks being reduced to the mere exercise of delegation; we need tools and methodologies to face the challenges of the collective construction of knowledge by citizens, granting them the role they demand of arbiter of life in our cities. . . . This new paradigm entails new values, and it is precisely in the context of culture that we have to understand our work as a motor of new ways of rethinking and making [politics]. . . . The objective of the book you are holding is to become a user's manual for creative practices.[1]

"BY YOUR PERMISSION I lay before you, in a series of letters, the results of my researches. . . ." So Schiller opens his 1794 collection of letters on the aesthetic education of man (*Über die ästhetische Erziehung des Menschen in einer Reihe von Briefen*). He explains that his main inspiration was Kant. I have no single philosophical guide or single hermeneutic model to point to, and because I have written this book in the hope of reaching across disciplines that are each armed with distinctive expectations of what makes a worthwhile book, I want to offer a short account of the conditions of its design here, before I explain its method and approach in the more formal Introduction. As I begin to sketch the troubles and disaffections that have driven my thinking, I recognize that many others—notably political scientists, sociologists, and other social scientists—have tackled them at far greater length, with greater exactness, and using different tools. The volume of work on these problems is far too large to cite. So "by your permission," to quote Schiller one more time, I set the scene, trusting from the evidence—found in everyday encounters with friends, family, colleagues, the newspaper, and the never-ending onslaught of violent movies and television shows portraying crime, corruption, and the apocalyptic destruction of the earth—that the worries I describe here are not mine alone. They are pretty widespread. But reading is widespread too; and if I do not have a single hermeneutic model, I write with the conviction that reading carefully, giving close attention to how artful language works, offers one powerful if not completely reliable way "to break through the crust of conventionalized and routine consciousness," as John Dewey put it—in other words, to think ourselves out of this mess.[2]

1   "La Comunità Inconfessabile," *Venezia, Catalunya*, Venice Biennale 2009.
2   Dewey, The *Public and Its Problems*, 141. He goes on: "Artists have always been the

IX

DEMOCRACY AS WE KNOW IT

On 24 September 2011, New York City police officer Anthony Bologna pepper-sprayed two Occupy Wall Street protesters who had been herded behind flexible orange mesh barriers a few minutes earlier. Several cameras caught the young women frantically swiping their tear-streaked faces, screaming in shock and pain, as the officer strode away (figure 1). One week later, on 1 October, OWS protesters moved down the pedestrian walkways of the Brooklyn Bridge. As their lines grew longer, the marchers began to stream into the road. "The cops watched and did nothing, indeed, seemed to guide us onto the roadway," said one protester.[3] Marchers on the road made it halfway down the bridge—only to find themselves trapped by the NYPD's walls of orange mesh. Seven hundred people were rounded up and taken to precinct stations around the city that day, their arms leashed by prepared zip-ties the officers had at the ready.

Variations on this scene occurred across the country through the autumn of 2011, including on university campuses like UC Berkeley and Santa Monica. It has become a national and a global pattern, one driven by many intertwined factors. This suggests that "public order" is now valued more highly than the public expression of dissent, which tends to be framed as disorderly and thus dangerous by journalists, politicians, and the police. Spaces once viewed in the first instance as gathering places for free political debate, regardless of their formal legal identity as "public" or "private," have been reinvented as spaces for commerce and consumption. (This is itself not an essentially depoliticizing move, since markets are political spaces, as the farmers at my local market on Union Square would strenuously insist—but I am thinking of the frequency with which groups applying for permission to march or meet for political reasons are delayed, moved, or denied access on the grounds that major open public spaces must be in the first instance kept safe for commerce.) Access to the airwaves is distributed on a pay-to-play basis. The university is being transformed into a virtual entity where "relevance" and concrete preparation for work have become primary criteria for the student-consumer's choice of coursework, with minimal counter-advice coming from administrations eager for a reliable cash flow. Airports and government buildings operate as though they are the private

---

real purveyors of news, for it is not the outward happening in itself which is new, but the kindling of it by emotion, perception, and appreciation."

   3   Quoted in the *New York Times*, "Police arrest more than 700 protesters on Brooklyn Bridge," by Al Baker, Colin Moynihan, and Sarah Maslin Nir, October 1.

FIGURE 1 Photo of Occupy Wall Street protesters after being pepper-sprayed.
Photo credit: Jefferson Siegel / *New York Daily News*.

property of the so-called "security" industry, whose employees enforce do-
cility among the populace in the name of public safety and efficiency. Craig
Calhoun notes that these developments encourage the right-wing view that
"private property is natural while public space (and perhaps the public interest) is optional."[4]

Why do so many citizens tolerate the police when they recklessly harm
the harmless, why do they tolerate the entrenched corporate and political
forces squeezing public space? Why are leaders and public opinion-makers
so quick to brush off expressions of dissent as symptoms of disorder? Common sense—as the Catalonian artists and activists who wrote my epigraph
would surely argue—ascribes the tolerance of state interference and the
decay of dissent on the one hand to the fear of change among the complacent well-off and the adherents of established political parties, and on the
other to the alienation of the citizen majority from politics.

The novelist José Saramago sees citizen alienation as a rational if dismal
response to the impossibility of seeing democracies in the developed world

---

4   "Evicting the public" at ssrc.org (11/2011). See David Held and Kevin Young, "Crises
in parallel worlds: the governance of global risks in finance, security, and the environment"
(20–32) and other essays in *The Deepening Crisis*; also other volumes in the *Possible Futures* series
edited by Craig Calhoun and Georgi Derluguian.

as anything but façades: "elections have become the representation of an ab-
surd comedy, shameful, where the participation of the citizen is very weak,
and in which the governments represent the political commissionaires of
economic power."[5] Jacques Rancière argues that democracy is no longer
lived as a choice but as an "ambient milieu" offering egalitarian pleasures
rather than demanding struggle and sacrifice.[6] Other thinkers, following
Jean-Jacques Rousseau and Hannah Arendt, suggest that the fundamental
problem is not citizen apathy as measured by low participation in elections,
but the fact that many citizens of democracies identify their role in politics
primarily with voting. (It is telling that the electoral races with the highest
degree of participation involve federal offices furthest from the citizenry's
local life; in the United States, even these elections draw less than half of
eligible voters.) When the act popularly perceived as central to democratic
citizenship is the silent and unaccountable act of vesting power in others,
something is wrong.

Rousseau argues in the *Social Contract* that in order to be legitimate,
the state must be constituted of citizens who enter into the social contract
of their own free will. "The assumption is always that the state in question
is free; for apart from anything else, a man's family, his property, necessity,
violence, or the lack of asylum may make him continue to reside in a country against his will, and if so, the fact of residence does not of itself entail
consent to the contract" (4.2). Today Rousseau's reference to property raises
troubling questions about the legitimacy of American democracy. Income
inequality in the United States now rivals that of the Gilded Age, with the
richest tenth of the citizenry now controlling two-thirds of the nation's net
worth. Economic opportunity or constraint—depending on perspective—
tugs many citizens from exurb to exurb, city to suburb. Gated communities
"protect" the well-off from the rest.

The effects of inequality are among the many divisive and diverging
consequences of a larger economic picture.[7] The increasingly intense, ever-
present pressure of daily work and sustaining the individual household
pushes concerns about the larger community off the table. A vast array
of leisure options designed to appeal to specific consumer groups drives
deeper wedges among those already divided by class, age, gender, religion,

5   Saramago, *La Lucidité*, quoted in English translation by Erik Swyngedouw, "Where
is the political?" See also Peter Alexander Meyers, *Civic War*, introduction.
6   Rancière, *On the Shores of Politics*, 22.
7   I have learned from Robert Putnam, *Bowling Alone*; Daron Acemoglu and James
A. Robinson, *Why Nations Fail*; and Joseph Stiglitz, *The Price of Inequality: How Today's Divided
Society Endangers Our Future*.

ethnicity, and color. Racial and ethnic minorities defensively turn inward and are implicitly or openly encouraged to do so by the mainstream. Citizens and politicians alike, finding few connections that feel real in local and state communities, discover in religiosity a communal glue and a litmus test for moral character. Working-class and middle-class people flock to megachurches in the suburban sprawl. The less fervent withdraw, their civic faith in common identity weakened by the experience of fanaticism or intolerance.

These developments have aesthetic and epistemological as well as political and moral consequences (if indeed these four terms can be untangled in the first place: this book suggests such an effort is in vain). The world as it is experienced by the poor and middling multitude is disconnected from the world as it experienced by the wealthy few. The world of the few is small and shaped by moneyed interests like banks and the energy industry. But its influence on the worldview of the broader citizenry cannot be underestimated, because the world of the few is the world recreated in political discourse, the world that sets the terms of elections and policy-making. There are links between the two worlds, both real and ideological (in both worlds people pay taxes, worry about the economy, value rights, and so on) but the political processes dominated by the few are beyond the control and the understanding of the many. New media have filled the gap separating the political class from the rest with dramatically amplified partisan and extremist rhetoric, which strengthens the perception—which in some ways is a reality—that different classes inhabit different worlds and literally see the world(s) in different ways.

Together with economic hardship, uprootedness, and auto-identitarian social habits, epistemological alienation nourishes the lack of accountability in government, the rise of unchallenged incumbencies, and weak habits of political judgment. When life as one lives it seems unreflected or irrelevant in the political world seen on TV or the internet, the impulse to embrace unreality is exceptionally strong; it may take the guise of conspiracy theory, or impractical, irresponsible visions of government (lowering taxes and increasing spending while promising to decrease the national debt). Arrogance and hypercertainty are praised; compromise is attacked as "flip-flopping." Ignorance of history, religion, and science breeds paranoia and makes citizens vulnerable to fanaticism and the misplaced passions of resentment and envy. In the United States, this paranoia fuels the national obsession with violent policing: we build walls to keep out "aliens" and wage "war" on terrorism and drugs. Political culture becomes a spectator sport.

So what prevents us from recognizing our present condition as a crisis?

John Dewey described the incapacities of the American union in terms that resonate as powerfully today as they did in 1927:

> We have inherited local town-meeting practices and ideas, but we live and act and have our being in a continental national state. . . . The public seems to be lost; it is certainly bewildered. What is the public under present conditions? . . . What hinders it from finding and identifying itself? . . . Our Babel is not one of tongues but of the signs and symbols without which shared experience is impossible.[8]

Dewey argues that the fault lies in our deep-seated habit of judging democratic life from the liberal standpoint of the individual and individual rights. If we begin from the assumption that government exists for the purpose of preserving individual rights, we grow accustomed to seeing the relations of the individual and the community as antithetical, a knotty problem to be solved. But the relation of the individual to the community, Dewey insists, is not a problem. It is a fact of human life and action, and it is with the consequences of this truth that we must begin our analysis if we wish to bring the democratic community into being.[9] It appears that the liberal tradition alone is unlikely to save us. The question is whether any other tradition can—particularly (given the unparalleled horrors of the past century and a half) any premodern one.

THE PROMISE OF THE REPUBLIC

I began to study the republican tradition in earnest in 2001, at a time when the promise of rescue it offered—by mapping a third way between liberalism and communitarianism, bolstering the study of the past, reclaiming the language of virtue from the right—spoke directly and personally to me and many thinking people as the United States stumbled through an exceptionally difficult time. The Bush administration's imprudence, paranoia, and disregard of democratic values stoked in me an anger equalled only by the disgust I felt at my own and my fellow citizens' inability or unwillingness to stand up to it. The many ways since then in which the Left has fallen short of expectations and shown itself captive to moneyed interests have

8   Dewey, *The Public and Its Problems*, 113, 125, 142.
9   Jodi Dean adds that anyone seeking to improve or regenerate democracy must be wary of the strong influence of the rhetoric of capitalism in what passes for democratic discourse today: free choice, diversity, inclusivity, satisfaction ("Politics without Politics").

intensified my desire to ask questions that might help us respond more intelligently and humanly to the situation in which we find ourselves.

My first book, *The State of Speech*, argued that beliefs about the spoken word lay at the heart of Cicero's ideas about republican citizenship, which reflected, to a certain degree, the thoughtworld of the first century BCE. It engaged in fits and starts with the ideas and arguments articulated in the neo-republican thinkers I was then reading. But I left it to the book you are reading now to explore Roman republicanism in an idiom that could more effectively blend the methods and goals of political theory with those of classical studies.

As I worked, I glimpsed common ground between postmodern political thought and the Roman authors who constituted the core of the early modern Latinate curriculum. I began to understand why the neo-Roman republican revival in political theory that gained momentum from the 1970s through the past decade (on which more below) had mostly ignored Roman writings dating to the republic in favor of allusions to late imperial works like the emperor Justinian's collection of civil law. The republican revivalists' normative, mostly liberal, conceptual, constitutional concerns—akin in some important purposive points to the Greek philosophical tradition— are far from the problems and methods of Roman writers. I also began to understand the degree to which Roman concerns have been simplified and distorted in the conventional treatments of the history of ancient political philosophy. According to handbooks and frequently cited studies by D. C. Earl, Chaim Wirszubski, A. A. Long, Malcolm Schofield, and Maurizio Viroli, when the Romans talk about politics, they talk about virtue: liberty, patriotism, courage, self-control, securing the common good, self-sacrifice, integrity, the preservation of property, and the achieving of martial glory. To read some liberal recuperators of the republican tradition, it seems that their most pressing concern is simply how to adjust the Romans' long list of demanding virtues to the pluralistic, diverse, industrialized, feminist-friendly, less martially-minded outlook of modernity. Alternatively, the solution is to deny the Romans a place in the history of political thought.[10] Both positions arise from the recognition of the massive differences in conceptual and cultural norms between the ancient Mediterranean and the post-industrial modern world—for example, the absence of the modern notion

---

10   So (in very strong terms) Ando, "A dwelling beyond violence"; see also Dagger, *Civic Virtue* (with some hedging, 13–15) and Honahan, *Civic Republicanism*: "Aristotle and Cicero lay out significant elements of two threads in the republican tradition, but they should be regarded as antecedents rather than strictly as republican thinkers" (40).

of rights from the Roman intellectual landscape.

The good news is that virtue theory is only one piece of a much more complicated assemblage of Roman political thinking. Robert Pippin makes the provocative suggestion that modernity is the moment when it is discovered that being a subject is something at which *"we can fail."*[11] Romanists have good reason to object that this stance is not unique to the moderns. The Roman writers discussed at greatest length in this book—Cicero, Sallust, and Horace—are deeply concerned with failure, as well as with fantasy and delusion, self-knowledge and its tragic limits, with irony and the horrors of moral certitude. They see politics as both creating and caught up in the cyclical violence of class conflict and corruption. Though they failed completely to solve the problem of economic inequality (as we are failing today), worry, fear, even horror at its effects exerted a profound effect on Roman moral discourse, and the contours of their avoidance strategies may illuminate our own. Their interest is caught by the imagination's power to propel us into the past and to shape our moral judgments, and by the dynamic intersubjective relations by which we come in a limited way to know ourselves. Veterans of losing sides in civil war, Cicero and Horace in particular are preoccupied with compromise and its attendant frustration and guilt. Though the Hellenophilic nineteenth century purged these texts from philosophy and theory, their topics are relevant and crucially important for the twenty-first century. For these reasons, they deserve recovery.

---

11   Pippin, *The Persistence of Subjectivity*, 21 (his italics). I share Pippin's eloquently described worry about the privileging of failure (23; see also his relevant criticism of Arendt's response to modern atrocities, 162–67).

ACKNOWLEDGMENTS

WRITING A BOOK about Roman political thought that works closely with Roman texts while sustaining a meaningful dialogue with contemporary political thought proved a tougher task than I expected. Even as I bring it to a close, I keenly anticipate writing more.

I'm deeply grateful for the chances I've had to air my arguments as they evolved. Some of the book's main concerns began to take shape at Stanford, where I spent several years as an assistant professor in the early 2000s. It felt right and proper to present this material in the Eitner Memorial Lecture in 2010: I thank the Lecture's endowers Peter and Lindsay Joost, as well as Walter Scheidel and my colleagues at Stanford for the opportunity. Many thanks to Simon Goldhill for the chance to preview my approach to Roman political thought at the Cambridge Triennial conference. Earlier versions of chapter 1 were delivered at the American Political Science Association annual meetings in 2009 and 2010: I would like to thank Arash Abizadeh, Jill Frank, Christina Tarnopolsky, Gary Remer, Ryan Balot, Bryan Garsten, Daniel Kapust, John McCormick, Cary Nederman, and Michelle Zerba for their own contributions and lively discussion. I hope our conversations continue.

Lectures at the University of Toronto, McMaster University, Brown University, and the University of California at Santa Barbara (where I had the honor of giving the J. P. Sullivan Memorial Lecture) helped refine my approach to Horace's *Satires*. Christopher Chinn and his colleagues at Pomona College gave me the chance to think through the connection between Sallust and the Occupy movement. I spent two wonderfully stimulating days in the spring of 2012 at the University of South Carolina, for which I am beyond grateful to Jill Lane, Paul Allen Miller, and their colleagues and students: their sharp, insightful comments on material from two chapters came at a critical moment. A very early version of chapter 4 was delivered at a conference on "contradictory selves" at the University of Chicago organized by Alex Lee, Diana Moser, and Aaron Seider. I learned a great deal from my trips to Northwestern University at the invitation of Dilip Gaonkar and Keith Topper, who along with Bob Hariman made ideal interlocutors on Cicero and advocacy.

By happy accident my first attempts to grapple with the *pro Marcello* occurred in the lovely surroundings of the Veneto. I am grateful to Gianpaolo Urso for organizing "Dicere Laudes," a conference sponsored by the Fondazione Canussio in Friuli, and for assistance later with the permissions process. I thank Giovanni Campolo and Sandra Borghini for permission to print an adapted version of the article as chapter 5. Spencer Cole and the Classics faculty at the University of Minnesota offered useful comments on the speech.

I am lucky to owe a debt to Willy Cingano for his warm hospitality over the years during which I have participated in the Advanced Seminar for the Humanities hosted by Venice International University. Comments from the seminar's graduate students and faculty have whipped my thinking about the paradox of republican panegyric (and other matters) into better shape.

I cannot adequately thank Ineke Sluiter for her generous invitation to work with her research group at the Netherlands Institute for Advanced Study in the spring of 2012. This period of relative peace amid the grassy dunes of the North Sea coast allowed me to finish the bulk of the work on the manuscript. The lively conversation and friendship of the NIAS fellows, especially Ineke herself, Dino Abazovic, Tracy Adams, Tazuko van Berkel, Gianpaolo Corsetti, Maria Koinova, Reif Larsen, Vjekoslav Perica, Saskia Peels, Ianthi Tsimpli, Mitja Velikonja (later my host in Ljubljana), and Kip Williams, were unlooked-for gifts that so far, to my delight, keep giving. I also thank the then rector, Aafke Hulk, for her support.

The experience of writing this book while also taking on demanding administrative work has sharpened my awareness of how heavily I lean on colleagues far and near, especially fellow administrators. I am deeply grateful to Daniel Holub, Trace Jordan, and Vince Renzi in NYU's College Core Curriculum and Kit Frick and Jonathan Lipman in the Office of the Dean for Humanities. Their talents and generosity gave me the breathing space for research and writing even in the busiest seasons of the academic year.

Colleagues and graduate students make the Department of Classics at NYU a rewarding place to work, especially David Levene (who commented on an early version of chapter 2), Danielle La Londe, Inger Kuin, Melanie Subacus, and Osman Umurhan. Michèle Lowrie's work is a source of constant inspiration, and her comments on the manuscript at several stages were invaluable. I owe a great deal to the thoughtful, constructive criticism of Andrew Riggsby and two anonymous readers for Princeton University Press. At the Press itself, I thank editor Rob Tempio for inventing the book's title and for his confidence in the project. Kathleen Cioffi and Ryan Mulligan patiently ushered the manuscript through production. Emma Young was a marvelous copy-editor, quick, smart, and eagle-eyed.

For conversation and other forms of support I thank Alessandro Barchiesi, Tom Carew, Katie Holt, Phillip Mitsis, Ralph Rosen, Alessandro Schiesaro, Iakovos Vasiliou, Elizabeth Wingrove, and Nancy Worman. I am especially grateful to Paul Cartledge and Susanna Braund for originally inviting me to write on Roman republicanism and its reception, and for their understanding as this manuscript grew in unexpected ways. Thanks too to Basil Dufallo, Jim Porter, and Miriam Leonard, whose recent invitations to write papers have helped me reach closure on this book and glimpse the contours of the next one. Like everyone else thanked here they bear no responsibility for the contents of these pages.

Thanks to Phil Magnuson, Bobby Quidone, and the Magnuson family, whose quiet refuge in the White Mountains is the perfect place to write. My sister Jessica Paulson is a fountain of good sense, humor, and perspective. Michael Strevens, my partner in all things for over twenty years, has my thanks for his constant affectionate encouragement and the example of intense intellectual engagement he continues to set.

I cannot begin to describe the extent of what I owe to my parents, source of unstinting support and love. This book is for them.

THE LIFE OF
ROMAN
REPUBLICANISM

INTRODUCTION

The serious writer is obliged to reawaken the reader's numbed sense of the concrete through the administration of linguistic shocks, by restructuring the overfamiliar or by appealing to those deeper layers of the physiological which alone retain a kind of fitful *unnamed* intensity. (Fredric Jameson, *Marxism and Form*, 20–21)

THIS BOOK SEEKS to place Cicero's *Verrines*, Caesarian orations, *Republic*, and *Laws*; Sallust's *Catiline* and *Jugurtha*; and Horace's *Satires* at the center of the republican tradition. In the process, I aim to rewrite the orientation and concerns of that tradition in a different idiom than they are currently understood. I address these writings as the literary texts that they are, not as sources of isolated quotations, and for this reason I proceed through close individual readings. Though I approach each text knowing a good deal about its intended audience and the conditions under which its words were first set down, my ultimate aim is not to make guesses, however highly educated they might be, about what each text could have meant to its readers at the moment of its composition.[1] Nor is my ultimate purpose to discern what these authors intended to convey to their original audience. I agree with Hans Gadamer, who has argued in *Truth and Method* that in seeking to understand the relationship between past text and present reader, we must remember that we are not the direct descendants of the Greeks and the Romans: we never confront the texts in all their freshness as things in themselves, but as things already read, and in the reading, altered.[2] So I balance contextualist knowledge and regard for the words on the page with possible meanings that were not, perhaps because they could not be, expressed openly or given special

---

1   Compare the efforts of Skinner in, e.g., *The Foundations of Modern Political Thought* and *Reason and Rhetoric in the Philosophy of Hobbes* (and many other works) and Pocock ("The reconstruction of discourse: the historiography of political thought") to recover rhetorics, the thick textures of political speech: "I shall seek to give an account of how the historian sets about reconstituting political thought as discourse: that is, as a sequence of speech acts performed by agents within a context furnished ultimately by social structures and historical situations, but also—and in some ways more immediately—by the political languages by means of which the acts are to be performed" (Pocock, 959–60).

2   Miriam Leonard eloquently argues along similar lines (citing Gadamer and Jameson) on behalf of preserving "the trace of the past" in the encounter between modern reader and ancient text, in "The uses of reception," especially 116–19.

emphasis at that originary moment. These are meanings that run just beneath the surface of the text, buttressing its structure, silently helping it cohere. At times, more radically, I treat these texts as prompts that make ideas available for our active use. Being neither for nor of our time, they grant a sense of the past's difference, and in doing so they grant us a perspective of difference and help us see ourselves and our world anew.[3]

In short, I am doing my best to follow the spirit of Hannah Arendt's quotation of Karl Jaspers in the preface to the first edition of *The Origins of Totalitarianism*:

> To fall prey neither to the past nor to the future.
> What matters is to be entirely (in the) present.
>
> Weder dem Vergangenen anheimfallen noch dem Zukünftigen.
> Es kommt darauf an, ganz gegenwärtig zu sein.

A thinker consumed by the unique and urgent challenges of modernity, Arendt insisted on rereading Greek and Latin texts. She explained her method as the quest "to discover the real origins of traditional concepts in order to distill from them anew their original spirit which has so sadly evaporated from the very key words of political language—such as freedom and justice, authority and reason, responsibility and virtue, power and glory—leaving behind empty shells."[4]

Though she compared herself to a pearl diver, bringing up lost meanings from the depths, Arendt was no objective philologist holding a magnifying glass to Greek and Latin terminology. Nor was she a contextualist like the Cambridge School historians J. G. A. Pocock or Quentin Skinner. Arendt placed the recovery of historical words in the context of her belief in the importance of action in the world in the present. In her gracefully emphatic phrase, words are *"something like a frozen thought that thinking must unfreeze."*[5] I take this to mean that recovering the spirit of words' original meanings involves transforming something that first resembled ice, hard and clear, into water, which refracts light at different angles and flows this way and that. The liquid of an idea holds the essence of its icy past: it has the same chemical composition, and certain attributes are identical under the exami-

3   I agree with Saxonhouse on the importance of preserving the practice of reading ancient political thought for more than simply providing an alternative "perspective" on modern beliefs and concepts ("Political theory yesterday," 856).
4   Arendt, *Between Past and Future*, 15.
5   Arendt, "Thinking," in *The Life of the Mind*, 171.

nation of our senses of sight, taste, and touch. If the kind of recovery Arendt has in mind necessarily creates water out of ice, it is also true that in order to process and understand this liquid thought, we must observe and analyze its icy form—the words on the page.

To think about words is not necessarily to define concepts. Try asking the question: what is a republic? Late in life John Adams confessed to his friend Mercy Warren that he had never understood what a republic was, and that "no other man ever did or ever will."[6] Twenty years earlier, Thomas Paine had grumbled that courtiers love "to abuse something which they called republicanism, but what republicanism was, or is, they never attempt to explain." He continued:

> What is called a *republic*, is not any *particular form* of government. It is wholly characteristical of the purport, matter, or object for which government ought to be instituted, and on which it is to be employed, RES-PUBLICA, the public affairs, or the public good; or, literally translated, the *public thing*. It is a word of a good original, referring to what ought to be the character and business of government; and in this sense it is naturally opposed to the word *monarchy*, which has a base original signification.[7]

Paine's stab at defining the republic raises some difficult questions. First, what is the "public good," who defines it, and by what standard? Should we understand it in moral terms, as his use of the phrase "the character . . . of government" implies, or in material or institutional terms related to the "business" of government? Second, once citizens have freed themselves from domination by a king or tyrant and become free to govern themselves—a key element of the *res publica* for Paine and Adams—what motivates them to turn their freedom to the task of self-government? Might citizens end up "*too free* to consult the general good," as the educator and political thinker James Burgh worried in 1774?[8]

Before pursuing the question of definition any further, it is worth recalling that the Romans had no written constitution and, if textual evidence is anything to go by, little interest in defining their government in philosophically rigorous terms. This is why Michel Serres invokes the images of a black

6   Adams to Mercy Warren, 20 July 1807, cited in Wood, *The Creation of the American Republic 1776–1787*, 48–49.
7   Paine, *The Rights of Man*, 279.
8   Burgh, *Political Disquisitions*, 116.

box and dark cave to characterize the Romans' account of themselves: he seeks to capture Roman writers' defiance of the narrativization of certain elements of their history by explicitly or indirectly representing them as non-narratable—*non enarrabile*, as Vergil says of the great shield crowded with violent images of Rome's future that Vulcan makes for Aeneas (8.625).[9] In the Conclusion, I will suggest that living with the fact that our written constitution is constantly under interpretation and reinterpretation retains an important trace of what Jacques Rancière might call the permanent "disagreement" at the core of the Roman civic experience.

In fact, we live with a constitution and with the modern concept of rights.[10] Rather than lament the absence of regime theory and of detailed debate in Latin on the nature of the *res publica*, I will suggest that taking a lesson from Roman thinkers and from Arendt, we can conclude that the most useful response is not to seek to settle on a definition of what the republic was or is or might be, nor to seek the end or purpose of the constitution, as Aristotle did in his *Politics*, nor to construct ideals of civic virtue that exist in denial of the chaotically diverse reality of democratic plurality and embodied life.[11] Instead I explore Roman thinkers' image of the republic as they saw it in past and present action, their emphasis on grasping the action around them, and the complex processes involved in making the judgments we make as citizens, all of which together involve reason, imagination, acknowledgment (specifically, the acknowledgment of limits), sensation, memory, and the emotions, especially hope and despair.

In taking this approach I am directly inspired by John Dewey's call in *The Public and Its Problems* for a series of pragmatic recognitions. First, we must recognize the fact that human beings live in communities, and consequently that each of us is always already part of a plural "we." Second, we must recognize this "we"—a project we are most likely to realize if we create a persuasive common set of terms that we can agree defines the community

9   Serres, *Rome: The Book of Foundations*, 13: "We never get out of texts, turning our backs on the dark origins." (The shield of Aeneas features images of conflict, including a man being torn to pieces by horses.)

10   Here with regard to my presumed audience (the "we") I follow Judith Shklar: "Who are the 'we' of whom I seem to talk so confidently? I have assumed that I live among people who are familiar with the political practices of the United States and who show their adherence to them by discussing them critically, indeed relentlessly" (*Ordinary Vices*, 227).

11   Hammer insightfully discusses the expulsion of Roman texts from the political canon that began with Romantic Hellenocentrism and continues in contemporary ancient history and philosophy, in *Roman Politcal Thought and the Modern Theoretical Imagination*, 13–37.

as it is, as opposed to what we would like it to be. Our common definition need not exclude all elements of the aspirational, but if it is to avoid generating its own tyrannical dogma, we are best served by anchoring it in lived experience. Third, we must recognize that all actions (including thoughts) have consequences, and we should direct our political thinking to the task of maximizing good consequences and minimizing bad ones.[12]

The challenge Dewey pinpoints, to flesh out a point I made very briefly in my earlier quotation from his book, is that while we each think and reflect as individual subjects, we must build ways to live together, together. How do we think across the gap from our selves to ourselves? To gain "the clear consciousness of a communal life [which] constitutes the idea of democracy" Dewey insists that we begin from the acknowledgment that we cannot treat the relations of self and other as oppositional or antithetical.[13] Both terms (Dewey prefers "individual" and "social") are "hopelessly ambiguous." But because social and political analyses treat them as discrete entities existing in opposition, "'society' becomes an unreal abstraction and 'the individual' an equally unreal one," and because it is possible to imagine an individual utterly disassociated from a group, "there develops the unreal question of how individuals come to be united in societies and groups [in the first place]: the individual and the social are now opposed to each other, and there is the problem of 'reconciling' them."[14]

Where modern virtue theorists begin by defining individual virtues and explaining their innate worth and public utility, Roman republican writers tackle the nature of the community and individual agency as interlocked problems that need to be handled together. The claim that I want to make is difficult to express in brief, but I want to suggest that it is in precisely the *different* ways Roman writers think about self and community, or private and public life, or life alone and life with others, that the potential exists for reorienting our habits of thinking about these things. At one point in the long course of writing this book I entertained the thought of dividing it into sections on "self" and "community." Very quickly I realized that a central contribution of Roman political thinking is to prompt reflection on what those terms mean—by which I do not intend to fall back on the familiar mental picture of Romans heroically if horrifyingly subsumed in the rush of patriotism and self-sacrifice for the community's sake. Instead the

12   Dewey, *The Public and Its Problems*, 17.
13   Ibid., 149.
14   Ibid., 186, 191.

book spends roughly equal time on the constitution of the self and of the community. This is a fitting approach to a literature that takes shape in an intellectual milieu where a clear boundary between politics (the rules by which a group lives) and ethics (the rules by which a self lives) is nowhere to be found. Note that I say "live," not "govern" or "rule." For these Roman thinkers, the founding term of politics is not rule. Desire, hope, passion, time, contest, and fantasy drive and guide political life. It is from this truth that the Romans I treat in this book begin to think the political.

As these terms suggest, my approach differs from those adopted in conventional surveys of Roman political thought, such as D. C. Earl's study of Sallust, Chaim Wirszubski's thoughtful book *Libertas*, or the chapters on the Latin historians and Cicero in handbooks such as the *Cambridge History of Greek and Roman Political Thought*. These works tend to define the content of Roman political thought by singling out pre-existing concepts and values—the pivotal terms *res publica* and *libertas*; the virtues of *virtus, fides, gloria, iustitia*, and so forth; or the causes of decline, *lubido, avaritia, ambitio*—and tracing their appearance in a given text or texts, often in consideration of their social and legal context. Instead my intention is to explore what Anthony Pagden has called (borrowing a term from Hobbes) the "registers" in which specific kinds of political propositions may intelligibly be cast.[15] Because these registers of ideas and values are largely constructed in Roman literature not through analytic definition-building, but through a rich variety of rhetorical and literary strategies—the proper instruments for works originally designed to instruct by dramatic example and rhetorical flair as well as by logical argument—my readings adopt the tone and techniques of literary and rhetorical criticism. I want to stage a productive collaboration between literary interpretation and the history of political thought: this is another important way antiquity may interface with modernity.

The thinking behind this collaboration deserves further explanation. J. G. A. Pocock, one of the most learned and sophisticated contemporary readers of the diverse texts that constitute the tradition of Western political thought, has tried to account for the two simultaneous, mutually provocative tendencies he sees at work in it over time: one toward the preservation of tradition and the other toward innovation in theory and practice. For Pocock, the answer lies in the central role literary interpretation plays in the transmission of ideas:

15   Pagden, *The Languages of Political Theory in Early-Modern Europe*, 1; cf. Pocock, "Languages and their implications: the transformation of the study of political thought," esp. 25–26.

Societies exist in time, and conserve images of themselves as continuously so existing.... The fact is that a literate tradition is never a pure tradition, since the authority of written words is not dependent on usage and presumption only. As durable material objects they cut across the processes of transmission and create new patterns of social time; they speak directly to remote generations, whose interpretation of them may differ from that of intervening transmitters of the tradition they express.... [E]very reader is a potential radical; nontraditional interpretations arise, and with them the question of the authority to be employed in reading and interpreting documents; this authority may be thought of as traditional, rational, charismatic or simply mysterious. Books breed sybils to read them.[16]

"Books breed sybils": this may be the most condensed and provocative statement of words' effect on readers that I know. Yet it rings uncannily true. Do we, can we fully understand what happens to a person when that person reads—especially when the person reads a book about political ideas, about the self's relation to others in the public sphere?

In her brilliant book *Ordinary Vices* Judith Shklar makes a strong argument for giving stories a central place in political thought. Those philosophers who avoid stories, preferring to "copy the theologians more closely," she says, have been less than ideally deft at dealing with change and individual character.[17] Her account of the changes storytelling encourages in the reader wavers in its location of agency. First she gives agentic capacity to the text as able to "force us to acknowledge what we already know imperfectly," which she suggests is equivalent to illuminating the world as it is, "things as they are." Next, she echoes Shelley's *Defence of Poetry*, where poetry "purges from our inward sight the film of familiarity which obscures from us the wonder of our being. It compels us to feel that which we perceive, and to imagine that which we know. It creates anew the universe." She invites the reader into the picture:

A great story brings us to that point.... They impose understandings upon us, sooner or later, by removing the covers *we may have put* on the mind's eye.... They do not, in fact, tell us how to think, but what to think about, and make us "see things as they are." [*My emphasis*.][18]

16   Pocock, "Time, institutions and action; an essay on traditions and their understanding," 254–55.

17   Shklar, *Ordinary Vices*, 229.

18   Ibid., 229–30. Shelley, "A defense of poetry."

Here, *we* put the covers on the mind's eye; *we* think about the matters the text recommends. And it is we who, after reading a book, may change—the mystery being that no one, not even we ourselves, can predict whether we will change or not. As Joshua Landy emphasizes, any effect literature may have on us involves our will as well: it is a gift "we are always free to leave unopened."[19] We are sybils—those opaque, unpredictable prophets—even to ourselves.

When Pocock says that every reader is a "potential radical," his words recall Schiller's letters, the text that opened my preface. Like Pocock, Schiller starts from a concern with time. His object is to explain not the evolution of ideas in the collective or public context, but the changes possible in a particular self living in the world. "Since the world is developed in time, or change, the perfection of the faculty that places men in relation with the world will necessarily be the greatest possible mutability and extensiveness."[20] Schiller means the faculty of perceiving the world, that is, the aesthetic faculty. Its task is difficult, because the self that relates to the world has a sense of itself that includes a sense of permanence. So any potential change for the better or the worse in a self stands in tension with its own sense of selfhood. For this reason, Schiller says, though the aesthetic faculty naturally possesses independence and intensity, it requires strengthening over time. He has already observed in the eighth letter that an enriched understanding of the world "only deserves respect" when it affects the character in its fullness of being in the world, that is to say (in true Romantic form) in both the heart and the head. What is needed is "to educate the sensibility, because it is the means, not only to render efficacious in practice the improvement of ideas, but to call this improvement into existence"—to ensure that ideas are put into practice. How can character be improved? Schiller concludes that the instrument of improvement cannot be sought in the state or other external entity. It rests in the self, in the aesthetic faculty. This is and must be enriched by contact with different experiences.

The more the receptivity is developed under manifold aspects, the more it is movable and offers surfaces to phenomena, the larger is the part of the world seized upon by man, and the more virtualities he develops in himself. Again, in proportion as man gains strength and depth, and depth and reason gain in freedom, in that proportion man

19   Landy, "Formative fictions," 199.
20   Schiller, Letter 13.

8

takes in a larger share of the world, and throws out forms outside himself. (Letter 13)

A longer explanation of my belief in the efficacy of literature would require another book.[21] I have tried here to set the stage for showing how my readings of central republican thinkers—Cicero, Sallust, and Horace—should be understood as training in political thinking, in understanding "things as they are," and thus in taking in "a larger share of the world."

WHY ROMAN REPUBLICANISM?

The turn to Rome in political philosophy has a long history. Cicero, Sallust, Horace, Livy, and Tacitus were required reading for most educated people starting in the fifteenth century—the core of the Latin canon taught in virtually every school and college across Europe.[22] Key tenets of republican values begin to color political debates in England up to and through the Civil War. "Democratical Gentlemen" (as Hobbes bitterly called them) cited Cicero and the Twelve Tables to justify their argument for the ultimate authority of Parliament over the king, and poets on the side of Parliament attacked Vergil and Horace as flatterers who played for Augustus while "Roman Liberty was lost." By the late eighteenth century, references to Rome populate political essays, philosophical works, treatises on education, art, architecture, and fashion in Europe and both Americas. John Adams, Thomas Paine, and James Burgh are examples of the passion for republican ideas and images that raged during the eighteenth century age of revolution. Conservatives like William Burke ardently claimed their share of the

21   Joshua Landy has written just such a book about fiction (*Doing Things with Fiction*). He argues there that the efficacy of fiction lies in its "formative" function. Distinguishing this from three other conventional explanations of what fiction does (the exemplary, the affective, and the cognitive), he argues against those who believe that fiction grants us access to knowledge, and that increase in our knowledge is "the very point of our engagement" with fiction. He encourages us to stop talking about what fiction "says" or "means" and to talk instead about "what it does" ("Formative fictions," 183). He reminds us of Dewey's premise that an artwork is not an object but an experience, and suggests that the experience of fiction helps us fine-tune our mental capacities: it equips us with skills, from "emotional control" to "Zen-like detachment" to being "better at handling and producing figurative language" (189). His strikes me as a productive way to read non-fiction (political thought in particular) as well, *mutatis mutandis*; I must pursue further investigation elsewhere.

22   Waquet, *Latin: Or The Empire of a Sign*, 7–39, with rich bibliography; see also chapters on specific authors in Reynolds, *Texts and Transmission*; Grafton and Jardine, "Studied for action"; Pocock, *Barbarism and Religion*, vol. 3.

republican legacy. In the early nineteenth century, European and American thinkers turned to Rome in an effort to redress the weaknesses of liberal democracy as it was taking shape in industrial capitalist society. Pioneering feminist and revolutionary thinker Margaret Fuller, who learned Latin at the age of six, drowned in a shipwreck before she could finish her history of the Roman republic, which she believed would inspire modern revolutions.[23]

Republicanism's popularity as a political idea declined from the middle of the nineteenth century as egalitarianism and democratic populism caught fire, the experience of empire soured, commerce grew in scope, variety, and social consequence, and military virtues disappeared from the index of elite achievement.[24] In the twentieth century, several waves of renewed interest arose in reaction to current political crisis. First the rise of totalitarianism drove émigrés like Leo Strauss and Hannah Arendt to the United States, where they built their midcentury critiques of modernity on classical thought and values. Meanwhile, spurred by the research of John Pocock, particularly his 1975 book *The Machiavellian Moment*, American historians debated the degree to which Locke or republican thinkers had influenced the American founders. Later, after the social, economic, and political tumult of the 1960s and 1970s, interest in the republican tradition among political philosophers reignited once more.

Most neo-republicans today are communitarians or liberal democrats who worry that liberalism, concentrated as it is on the individual and individual rights and freedoms, offers an excessively slender conception of community and civic duty—too low-calorie a diet for the vigorous political lifestyle of the engaged, well-informed citizen idealized by post-1960s theorists of democracy. Others are radical democrats searching for ways to unsettle conventional ideas about democracy. In the republican ideal they find a promising corrective to an impoverished civic life.

Neo-republican arguments tend to develop along two paths. The first, evolving in the modern era from the work of Hannah Arendt and overlapping in some thinkers with communitarian concerns, takes on the fundamental human question "how shall I live?" and offers a powerful if demand-

---

23   On Fuller, see Reynolds, "Subjective vision, romantic history."
24   On the fortunes of republicanism from the seventeenth through the early nineteenth centuries, consult the useful essays in *Republicanism: A Shared European Heritage*, ed. van Gelderen and Skinner. Malamud, *Ancient Rome and Modern America*, traces the evolution of Rome's impact on the United States from an eighteenth century political ideal to a nineteenth century moral symbol—and in the twentieth century, a commercial symbol, the sign of a luxury brand.

ing answer: live well, which is to say live politically, acting—as Rousseau recommends in the *Social Contract*—with a view to the effects our choices will have on our fellows, all part-owners of public affairs (*res publica*). Richard Dagger, Michael Sandel, and Maurizio Viroli (to take a few examples) understand the republican legacy as resting in the ideal of a virtuous collective of engaged citizens bound by agreement about the law and by the common bond of interest strengthened by the affections of patriotic affiliation (a gloss on *coetus multitudinis iuris consensu et utilitatis communione sociatus*, Cicero, *Rep.* 1.39). A second major direction is represented by the philosopher Philip Pettit, who finds in the republican definition of liberty a strong rejection of arbitrary domination and whose liberal goals lead him to concentrate on procedural and constitutional questions.

Attracted by the prospect of somehow constructing a community of virtue, committed to love of country and shared values grounded in collective memory, neo-republicans advocate for the essence of the republican legacy as they see it: in Rome's ideal of a virtuous community bound together by zeal for self-government and the creation of a deliberative consensus regarding the common good. Some of the dreamier propositions demand contributions from citizens that it is difficult to imagine putting into practice. Cullen Murphy goes the furthest in his popular 2007 book *Are We Rome?*, which suggests that the United States should fortify "institutions that promote assimilation" by establishing a national service program for American youth, a modern version of Rome's ancient military.

For all these thinkers, virtue is central. Tightly knit communities and habits of vigorous civic deliberation can't run on air. Their fuel is a *common culture* of civility, generosity, and trust. Here neo-republicans find themselves in a bind. Common culture, by most accounts, arises out of the affective dimension of political life: the sense of belonging, the love citizens feel for their *patria*, exemplified in (for instance) Aeneas' devotion to Anchises and Iulus and his companions. Yet to liberals, in the wake of the nationalist catastrophes of the twentieth century, patriotism is a dangerous romance indeed. These charges are given weight by strident calls from movements like the American Tea Party for the revival of putatively foundational, putatively republican ideals: cultural homogeneity, love of country, and the willingness to sacrifice much (notably economic equity) in exchange for personal freedom from what they perceive as interference by the state. Desire for common ground slides into horror of racial and cultural difference, and passion and prejudice corrode civility.

Philip Pettit responded to this danger with his books *Republicanism* and *A Theory of Freedom*, and most recently, *On the People's Terms*, which argued that the Roman definition of freedom was more robust than the classical liberal definition of freedom as negative freedom, non-interference, freedom *from*.[25] The Romans, he claimed, understood freedom as non-domination: the condition of being free from any threat of domination, real, possible, or imagined, which might limit the scope of free choice and action. Pettit sought to ground his book in the real world of politics and to avoid the "patriotism problem" in his insistence that a strong democratic republic incorporate mechanisms of public accountability, and in the end, he proposes a common culture of civility, generosity, and trust. Here he draws on a very long tradition of republican thought about civic virtue, especially the four canonical virtues of Plato and Cicero: wisdom, justice, courage (especially the kind of courage that cultivates the citizen's readiness to sacrifice herself for the common good), and moderation or self-control.

Keeping in mind that politics in a diverse pluralistic society entails disagreement, Pettit treats this final virtue with special care. To have a democratic politics where a plurality of views can circulate and be taken seriously, but where agreement on action must be reached, everyone has to accustom themselves to losing every once in a while (and perhaps often). Clearly, Pettit concluded, we need norms in place for political opinions and judgments: they must be based not on whim or sentiment, but reasoned deliberation undertaken in a civil mood. (The nature of deliberation and popular politics will be an important theme in this book, though not quite in Pettit's terms.)

To many observers in the academy, despite efforts like Pettit's to reconcile ancient and modern concepts and expectations, the latest turn to Rome was frankly unwelcome.[26] Why bother with this two-thousand-year-old re-

25   Further discussion of Pettit's work below.

26   A sample of well-argued critiques: Robert Goodin, "Folie républicaine"; Don Herzog, "Some questions for republicans"; Anne Phillips, "Feminism and republicanism: is this a plausible alliance?"; Jacques Rancière, "Democracy, republic, representation." Now see John McCormick's excellent *Machiavellian Democracy*, which argues that Pocock's supposed "Machiavellian" moment should be called a "Guicciardinian" one, since Pocock and most neo-republican theorists dwell almost exclusively (unproductively, in his view) on aristocratic, anti-populist republican thinkers. Through a reading of Machiavelli that underlines its popular concerns and goals, he seeks to recover a refreshed version of early modern neo-Roman republicanism, with particular emphasis on its remaking of the tribunate as a tool of public accountability and the people's restraint of governing elites. Note that McCormick places Cicero at the head of the aristocratic (senatorial) republican tradition. My own reading in chapters 1 and 5 acknowledges Cicero's special pleading on behalf of the senatorial order, but I see productive internal contradictions in his writing whose presence McCormick would likely deny or deprecate.

public, except as an exercise in revisionist history or antiquarianism? On the face of things, Rome is a totally unpalatable model for politics. Neither modern theories of rights nor Athenian-style notions of equality existed there. Among the beliefs and practices that serious Roman thinkers endorsed or took for granted were slavery, the disenfranchisement of women, staggering economic inequality, the near-total domination of politics by a rich and self-righteous senatorial elite, popular reverence for entrenched authority, the devotion of resources to warfare on a massive scale, and the adulation of the battlefield and the gladiatorial arena as the natural theater for the performance of *virtus*, manly courage. How can the neo-republicans ignore the Roman bias toward aristocratic warrior values and the preservation of elite wealth and power? Clifford Ando and Janet Coleman have recently argued that the blindness of the Romans to the concepts of equality and individual rights, as well as their passionate defense of massive inequities of property and opportunity, make any contemporary attempt to recover the republican tradition hopelessly blinkered at best, immoral at worst. Coleman dismisses the Roman republic as an evil regime with a "tendency throughout history to excommunicate the deviant.... I have no doubts whatever that a liberal will remain completely unconvinced of the virtues, either of the mythic or the real republic."[27]

It is one of the ironies of the history of political thought that Roman republicans are condemned both for advocating an excessively demanding model of active citizenship and for passively bearing witness to the republic's death throes. D. C. Earl, the author of a book on Sallust that is still commonly cited in contemporary scholarship and reflects the current picture of Roman thinking, concludes that Sallust's political thought "centres on a concept of *virtus* as the functioning of *ingenium* [talent] to achieve *egregia facinora* [great and glorious deeds] and thus to win *gloria*, through *bonae artes [good or honorable skills]*..." To Earl, Sallust's principal innovation is his reconception of aristocratic *virtus* as "inclusive of all men of whatever class of society and engaged in whatever activity."[28] Critics also complain that the Romans' moralistic critique of republican decline is not matched by meaningful prescriptions for reform. To Quentin Skinner, tracing the

---

27   Janet Coleman, "El concepto de república: continuidad mitica y continuidad real" (I quote from the text of an English version delivered at NYU in 2009); Clifford Ando, "A dwelling beyond violence: the uses and disadvantages of history for contemporary republicans." In chapter 1 I will treat in more detail Patchen Markell's insightful critique of Pettit's theory of freedom, which Markell places in the context of class and colonialism, "The insufficiency of non-domination."

28   Earl, *The Political Thought of Sallust*, 111.

influence of Sallust on Machiavelli's *Discourses on Livy*, James Harrington's *Commonwealth of Oceana*, and Marchamont Nedham's *Excellency of a Free State*, the Romans' signature contribution to the republican tradition is like a snake swallowing its own tail: their belief that a free state is best adapted to attaining glory and greatness is cancelled out by their fear that the vicious byproducts of glory and greatness will ultimately destroy the state.[29]

In his magisterial survey of the historiography of Rome, J.G.A. Pocock argues that the escalating nihilism of the struggle for power in the late republic was something the Romans' highly stylized historical narratives allowed to act as its own explanation; it was a cycle of competition no one knew how to stop.[30] Eric Nelson echoes Skinner and Pocock when he cites Jacob Burckhardt's comments on the Roman preoccupation with glory to support his contention that the Romans recognized the causes of republican doom but, blinded by their nostalgia for archaic civic values and by their conservative reverence for the past, they believed that "there was nothing the republic could legitimately do about it."[31] Worst of the Romans' intellectual failures was their inability, even in theory, to reconcile their commitment to the common good with their refusal to address gross fundamental inequalities in their society and economy—a charge most often levelled at Cicero, who is taken to be the spokesman of conservative aristocratic privilege.[32]

As for the Roman preoccupation with self-sacrifice for the common good idealized in artworks like Jacques-Louis David's *Oath of the Horatii*, Benjamin Constant raised perhaps the most famous objections. In his 1816

29 Skinner, *Liberty Before Liberalism*, 61–64.

30 Pocock, *Barbarism and Religion* vol. 3, 48–49. In this work, and in his *Machiavellian Moment*, Pocock combines the Greek (especially Aristotelian) and Roman (especially Ciceronian) traditions of active citizenship: the *vita activa*. Building on and critiquing Pocock's work, Quentin Skinner appeals to the rhetorical studies of the Italian humanists of the twelfth through the fourteenth centuries, which, he argues, were worked out within the frame of a neo-Roman ethics that drew on Sallust, Cicero, Livy, Valerius Maximus, Tacitus, and Justinian's late antique Codex. The result, as Skinner sees it, was a notion of liberty as the opposite of slavery, or as non-domination, and a commitment to a participatory ideal of civic virtue through which citizens agreed and were attentive to justice and the common good (Cicero, *Rep*. 1). Writing in the context of an aristocratic court culture, and seeking ways in which the non-nobility might participate in its own government, these very early modern rhetorical treatises became the new models of citizenship, and a transformed *vita activa* of public speech, advice-giving, and voting became the new ideal. Gaining honor and glory for oneself and one's family was imagined as part of gaining honor and glory for the *civitas*: it was the natural offshoot of fulfilling one's moral obligations and duties (*officia*) to friends and relations.

31 Nelson, *The Greek Tradition of Republican Thought*, 74; see also 8–10.

32 Wood, *Cicero's Social and Political Thought*, esp. 105ff.

lecture on "The liberty of the ancients compared with that of the moderns," Constant compellingly described the conditions of modern life: the enormous size of modern states, the abolition of slavery, the "vivid love of independence" satisfied by commerce, and the "infinite multiplication" of the means of happiness created by the diversity of private pursuits. All these things place the "active and constant participation in collective power" that for Constant is the central characteristic of classical politics beyond serious consideration for us moderns, whose freedom consists of "peaceful enjoyment and private independence." The message here is that the Romans have little to teach us today.

Finally, critics point out that democratic politics may give due regard to cultural and individual diversity, particularly competing ideas about vice and virtue, only so long as it sustains public faith in, and standards of, deliberative reason. Here too, thanks to its emphasis on a common notion of civic virtue and affective attachments that trump reason, the republican tradition strikes many as falling short. Its rhetorical practices are manipulative and used to incite violence as much as to contain it; its concentration on emotion over logical argument encourages demagoguery. Instead of recuperating this dangerous junk, critics conclude, we had better recognize that the useful elements of recuperated republicanism are in essence liberal arguments and attempt to reform liberalism (Don Herzog), or invent a new politics of the extraordinary (Andreas Kalyvas), or reinvent radical democracy from the ground up (Jacques Rancière, Ernesto Laclau, Chantal Mouffe).[33]

From a historical point of view, looking to Rome for help in thinking through the challenges of citizenship in a liberal democracy, especially the tragically pressing predicaments of poverty, exclusion, and apathy, certainly seems intuitively unpromising at first. Parts of the Roman electoral system were sharply skewed to favor the rich; elite and masses alike revered the ancestral *nobilitas*, returning members of ancient families to magistricial office year after year; it was illegal for a private citizen to address a public assembly without an invitation from an elected magistrate; and nearly all the elected magistrates who conceived and passed legislation were very well-off.[34] To be a citizen meant to be free: the quality of being a *liber*, a free man,

---

33   For Herzog and Rancière, see note 26; also, Andreas Kalyvas, *Democracy and the Politics of the Extraordinary*, 254–90, on Arendtian politics. Kalyvas has revised (with Ira Katznelson) the conventional opposition between republicanism and liberalism in the history of political thought in *Liberal Beginnings: Making a Republic for the Moderns*.
34   Lintott, *Constitution of the Roman Republic*, 199–207.

was defined by not being a slave—a foundational opposition in the Roman conceptualization of *libertas*.[35] The Stoics' indifference to external goods, though it may seem at first a likely jumping-off point for these lines of thought, engendered neither a critique of property ownership nor a theory of property redistribution. Cicero, the leading Roman theorist of republican government, is not above voicing contempt for the populace when he is not seeking its favor for politically expedient reasons, and his ardent defense of property rights corresponds with his firm conviction that the landed wealthy provide the most prudent political leadership for the republic. If he views the republic as a partnership (*societas*) between senate and people, it is quite clear which, to Cicero, is the senior partner.

Yet as I see it, these are precisely the reasons why Rome is relevant to contemporary experience. The array of resemblances between the ideological and material conditions of Roman and modern politics is striking and suggestive. Like us, the Romans faced the challenges of severe economic inequality, corruption, and deeply rooted civil distrust, manifested most prominently today in voter apathy. Like most of us, they placed a high value on individual liberty, the freedom from arbitrary interference from government; they hated tyrannical domination and the forces of corruption that feed it. And like us, they struggled with questions that the republican commitment to liberty raises about various forms of inequality, especially economic equality. But my reason for rereading Roman thought reaches beyond these resemblances.

It is because elitism, racism, sexism, slavery, and nativism have been and to a degree remain institutionalized in the exclusionary and discriminatory laws and practices of modern democracy that the Romans are still useful to us.[36] Contemporary democratic citizens continue to define their communities against outsiders—including constructed "outsiders" who live within the community, such as queer people, people of color, immigrants, those suffering from disease, and the poor. We need to understand how these prejudices can live alongside the belief that the republic is free and just, and further, how that belief is preserved and strengthened (consciously or not) by prejudice.[37] It is because money still holds immense power to silence and mislead modern citizenries that Roman writing about the consequences of corruption retains significance today. It is because liberal democrats are un-

---

35   Brunt, "*Libertas.*"

36   This is the reasoning behind Shklar's consideration of the historical impact of slavery on attitudes toward citizenship in the United States: *American Citizenship*, 13.

37   I am grateful to Andrew Riggsby for pressing me to think harder about the relationship between Roman slavery and liberty and the problematic implications for my project.

willing, for the most part, to make radical property redistribution the solution to economic inequality that Roman explorations of political solutions to economic problems, and the ways in which they at once recognize and evade economic inequity as destructive of politics, are directly relevant to our ongoing efforts to minimize poverty and pull down the psychological and social barriers dividing the poor from the rest of the citizenry.[38]

Contradictorily dedicated to liberty and to the reverent preservation of social and economic hierarchies, to popular consent and elite authority, to persuasive eloquence and strict limits on popular deliberation, the Romans hold up a mirror to our political weak spots and our deepest sources of silent social discomfort. They force us to acknowledge values and dispositions we might prefer to disregard, as we do when we devote ourselves, say, to the recuperation of Athenian democracy and its commitment to equal participation, its eradication of political inequality, its inspiring language of civic friendship and popular consensus. This is not to dismiss the study of Athens, of course, but to stress that hierarchical, class-divided, patriotic Rome brings to the theoretical table certain issues that Athenian participatory democracy does not.

But this brings us back to the question: what is the republic? And what counts as republican political thought? The ideal of a free, unified, cohesive, neighbor- and nation-loving deliberative collective whose aim is *concordia* under the rule of law and whose defenders are staunch exempla of sovereign, self-knowing, self-governing virtue is one important part of the republican tradition. This tradition includes the philosophical works of Aristotle and Cicero, Machiavelli's study of an expansionist, militaristic Rome in his *Discorsi*, Guicciardini's treatment of republican virtue for early sixteenth century *ottimati*, Venetian thinkers on the optimal form of *governo misto*, English agrarian disputes of the seventeenth and eighteenth centuries, and the early American belief in a "natural aristocracy."[39] Knotting together these strands are certain normative concepts, especially freedom and the rule of law, congenial to modern political analysis.[40]

38   Though redistribution is still very much on the table in liberal thought, from the work of Amartya Sen and John Rawls to the recognition vs. redistribution debate: see, e.g., Benhabib, "From recognition to redistribution? The paradigm change in contemporary politics," in *The Claims of Culture*.

39   See J. G. A. Pocock's influential account in *The Machiavellian Moment*; Philip Pettit, *Republicanism*; Quentin Skinner, *Liberty Before Liberalism*; Elizabeth Asmis, "A new kind of model: Cicero's Roman constitution in *de republica*."

40   On the much-studied question of how concepts get articulated in the field of discourse over time through changing idioms and rhetorics, which I cannot treat in detail here, see the essays in *Modern European Intellectual History: Reappraisals and New Perspectives*, ed.

Neither defenders nor critics of this version of republicanism are entirely wrong. But they are arguing over just one strand of Roman republican filiation. (This is what Richard Rorty has called the "calamity" of intellectual history: that most historians "know in advance what their chapter headings are going to be" and thus fail to question their categories.[41]) This book ventures a different approach.

THE ROMAN SCENE AND ITS RELEVANCE

Picture the Roman political scene: a rich and righteous senatorial elite versus an impecunious People whose identity was bound up in the memory of repeatedly having fought and overcome that elite for the sake of liberty.[42] The Roman republic was a polity shaped by the collective experience of almost nonstop war, intense if often corrupt electoral competition, and above all by a tense class conflict fueled by massive economic inequality, elite exploitation, and a social hierarchy with sharply limited permeability. Traditional animosity across socioeconomic lines was intensified by a political system that baldly translated economic status into political power and influence. In its public discourse, moral values and ideology were closely intertwined. The urgent political questions of the early and late republic revolved around which individuals and groups had voices and who could make voice translate into property and power—early on, in the establishment of the tribunate and the legislative powers of the people's assembly; later, in agrarian reform, the conflict over control of the judicial system, and the granting of emergency powers. By the lifetimes of Cicero and Caesar, the status quo was frequently interrupted by violence.[43] Such are the un-

---

Dominick LaCapra and Steven L. Kaplan; Pocock, "The concept of a language and the *métier d'historien*: some considerations on practice" in *The Languages of Political Theory in Early Modern Europe*. Paul Patton provides an overview of the twentieth-century paradigm shift in political thought in "After the linguistic turn: post-structuralist and liberal pragmatist political theory," in the *Oxford Handbook of Political Theory*.

41   Rorty, "The historiography of philosophy: four genres," 70.

42   Yavetz, *Plebs and Princeps*, 136. T. P. Wiseman quotes this passage, recalling Sallust's tribune-hero Licinius Macer telling a crowd in the Forum to remember what their *maiores* (ancestors) had achieved (Sallust, *Histories* 3.48.1, 6, 12, 15), *Remembering the Roman People* (3).

43   Side note: my thinking about Rome has been influenced by the work of the brilliant Africanist Achille Mbembe, and especially his comments on his own field of study: "we must speak of Africa only as a chimera on which we all work blindly, a nightmare that we produce and from which we make a living—and which we sometimes enjoy, but which somewhere deeply repels us, to the point that we may evince toward it the kind of disgust we feel on seeing a cadaver.... What we designate by the term 'Africa' exists only as a series of disconnections, superimpositions, colors, costumes, gestures and appearances, sounds and rhythms,

stable political conditions out of which republican self-understanding emerges. These belie the abstract discussion of liberty and civic virtue that has so far dominated the republican revival.

In the critical preoccupation with concepts and constitutions dominant in liberal thought today, what is lost is Roman writers' attention to the deep contradictions at the core of their own thinking, the prominent elements of fantasy in their representations of the *res publica*, the central role of passion and action (especially speech), and above all, their attention to the complex social and psychological elements of self-constitution and what the sociologist Zygmunt Bauman calls the "waywardness of constitutive agencies."[44]

My approach rests on two propositions. First, I draw a distinction between what I want to call "republican thought" and the particular values espoused by the Roman governing class. It is easy to misinterpret the existing evidence into a neatly uniform set of dispositions, by defining "Roman ideology," as A. A. Long does, as "the system of values expressed by such terms as *virtus, dignitas, honestas, splendor, decus*, and above all, *laus* and *gloria*."[45] He proceeds to admit that these are values that a noble Roman "would give his life for," but a broader view of Roman ideology must take into account the high value the Romans placed on justice, popular liberty, equity, self-sacrifice, and the rule of law, and the complex interconnections that link each to the rest. It is true that senatorial *libertas* and *dignitas* are interdependent in Cicero's philosophical and epistolary writings and elsewhere in elite literature, but as historians Nicholas Horsfall and P. A. Brunt point out, this is only half the story.[46] Tacitus saw disempowerment, not moral corruption, as the cause for the Roman people's willingness to yield up their traditional rights of legislation and election (*Ann.* 1.2). Cicero himself believed that the development of popular *libertas* was powered by economic unrest engendered by debt-bondage (*Rep.* 2.59).

Second, I will approach these texts with particular contemporary questions in mind, from the extent of individual participation required from citizens of modern democracies to the relationship between poverty and political apathy. The particular relevance of Sallust and Cicero and Horace to these questions will emerge in due course, but I want to declare immedi-

---

ellipses, hyperboles, parables, misconnections, and imagined, remembered, and forgotten things, bits of spaces, syncopes . . ." (from the conclusion to *On the Post-Colony*, 241–42).

44 Quotations from Zygmunt Bauman, *Intimations of Postmodernity*, 39, 42; see also the critique of Alain Touraine, "Is sociology still the study of society?" *Thesis Eleven* 23.

45 Long, "The politics of Cicero's *de Officiis*," 216.

46 Horsfall, *The Culture of the Roman Plebs*, 26–30; Brunt, "*Libertas*," 330, 348.

ately what this book does *not* advocate: a defense of the classic *vita activa*, the ideal of life fully engaged with civic affairs, which is regularly understood in contemporary political theory as the core of classical republican thought. I identify priorities, above all attention to economic inequity, around which Roman writers build a strident moralistic tradition that fortifies itself against change even in the act of calling for it (itself a strategy worth exploring and understanding). I articulate a set of dispositions, habits of reading the world that empower citizens to live in a state of uneasy balance between security in the law and the understanding that laws alone are insufficient to guarantee everyone's freedom, and carrying on from that, the understanding that laws must be resistible. This understanding comes, I think, from the habits of perceiving the world from a standpoint divided and not one's own, and of sustaining ironical self-awareness of one's own investments and assumptions—not least about oneself.

OVERVIEW

I begin with Cicero's dialogue *de Republica*, where I examine the roles of antagonism, consensus, and institutionalization in republic politics. For Roman citizens, contest and strife were daily features of their lives, from energetic verbal and physical abuse to the emphasis on competition in political discourse. Struggle characterized the relations within the governing elite, between senate and tribunes, between senate and popular assemblies, and among familial and economic interest groups. Chapter 1 presents Cicero as a thinker concerned with a collective of antagonists and competing interests, against conventional portrayals of his ideal republic as a homogeneous, unified, harmonious community.

Chapter 2, "Justice in the World: The Execution of *Jugurtha*," turns to questions of justice and ends with a close reading of Sallust's *Jugurtha* (and to a lesser extent, his *Catiline*). Sallust organizes his history of Jugurtha's war against the Romans in the North African kingdom of Numidia around the themes of justice and corruption; he ends by abruptly cutting off the conclusion of his story, the execution of Jugurtha. I argue that Sallust's withholding of judgment at the end of *Jugurtha* signifies the ways in which agents in the decaying republic withhold justice on a larger scale. The silence at the ending caps a narrative pattern of repetition and deferral, creating a fundamental dislocation of consequentiality, the notion of an essential relation between intention and action. The civil conflicts that traverse the republican order, together with the desire for power that corrupts political leaders, Sallust suggests, deform civic judgment, the execution of justice, and the passage of time itself. His text proposes that along with calling leaders to account and demanding transparency in the exercise of power, citizens must form habits of orienting themselves in the political world and of assessing the structural violence of that world, in order to defend themselves from the tyranny of domination. Meanwhile, his fine-grained attention to bodies, especially bodies in states of extremity, draws our attention to the corporeal aspect of political life, including a kind of knowledge of the world that only bodies can give us.

With the third chapter I continue the theme of judgment as it is addressed in the poetic genre devoted to passing judgment on one's fellows: satire. Here, as I read Horace's first book of *Satires*, my main question is the influence of others over the subject, and the degree to which the subject's desire for, or fantasy of, autonomy is interrupted by his reliance on, and pleasure in, the influence of those around him. The satiric narrator is a complex subject, mercurial, self-divided, and self-critical, highly attentive to his own faults and suspicious of his capacity to render judgment even in the act of doing so. The divided self is the subject of the short fourth chapter, which takes up several orations of Cicero in their historical context. It reflects on the Roman preoccupation with faces, situations, the mutability of selfhood, and the degree to which the divided self mirrors the division of the polity. Both chapters seek to suture the false opposition between authenticity and artfulness. In Horace and in Cicero, a person's persona is something he refines—a work of art. We too put forward appearances to the world. What does the Roman attention to appearance—how we look to others and how they look to us—teach us about our capacities for moral judgment and our sense of obligation to others?

With the advent of Julius Caesar come the end times of the republic, and the final chapter thus turns to one of Cicero's Caesarian orations. Several key themes from previous chapters come together: responsibility to the other, the significance of imagination and recognition, the politics of irony, the limits of self-sovereignty. Interwoven with these themes is an emphasis on the necessity of speech, speech that may retain some element of resistibility even in the face of tyrannical domination. By including in a book about republican political thought a speech that is commonly taken as the starting point of imperial panegyric, I also intend to foreground the fact that all the texts under consideration here emerge in conditions of disruptive and disrupted politics. It is the shock of the repeat experience of autocracy (after the "decisive rift" created by Marius' seven consulships in the late second century) that distills the republican vision at the heart of Cicero's speech on behalf of the exile Marcellus.[47]

I call this a book about the life of republicanism because it examines aspects of lived self-awareness to which the Roman writers treated here draw special attention, and that I take to be key to contemporary life as well. In his book *The Ethos of the Late Modern Citizen*, Stephen White warns against dismissing too quickly "the subtle but significant role that certain dispositions and actions may have for the enhancement of democratic life."[48] We had better be concerned with a notion of citizenship that grants a certain standing to citizens, a certain sense of self-worth, and that embodies a strong sense of obligation to others and others' opinions. We too should see economic inequity as the central danger to the republic—even if we must look beyond the ancient political canon for solutions to our problems. We must guard against the hubris that comes with uncritical certainty and confidence in our ability to know and master ourselves. And we must learn to live with antagonism as a fundamental condition of politics, and choose our political priorities accordingly—giving first place to the preservation of speech from all quarters of society, including those that we forget to count in the census and in our imaginations.

47   Flower, *Roman Republics*, 27–29.
48   White, *The Ethos of the Late Modern Citizen*, connects his projects to Michel Foucault's recovery of the word *ethos* (4). Like Landy, who emphasizes the voluntary element in his account of fiction's power to mold and enhance our mental capacities, White insists that "the depth of one's commitment [to the ethical stance he describes] does not translate immediately into absoluteness of conviction"—an unsatisfying but honest observation.

1

WHERE POLITICS BEGINS

CICERO'S REPUBLIC

I N HIS FAMOUS 1967 essay "Art and Objecthood" Michael Fried argues that minimalist, or as he calls it, "literalist" art is an art of theatrical-
ity; that in its promise of interpretative endlessness—offered by Donald
Judd's boxes in figure 2, for example, which thematize the seriality of
return—it fosters solipistic emptyheadedness; and that, banking on its
anthropomorphic, dramatically powerful presence, it greets the viewer as a
subject and panders to that subjectivity.[1] Pieces like Tony Smith's black-
painted steel box and Carl André's figure-eight stack of rough cedar logs
evade art's primary responsibility and pleasure by dumping the job of creating the art onto the viewer. By contrast, the art Fried favors—Jackson Pol-
lock, Frank Stella, and Anthony Caro, for instance—presents itself in all the
glory of its presentness. Proclaiming its identity as art, it transcends the
merely theatrical (as Fried would say); it compels the viewer to step out of
herself, to contemplate the composition of the piece, to judge the relationship of its various elements, to feel their structural tension, to think in a dialogic relation to the material. The viewer is a free agent, but an agent whose
thinking and acting, at least for the moment, takes shape and finds meaning
in the space between herself and the composition before her. This relation
between viewer and artwork is dynamic but also, in a crucial sense, constrained by the material existence of the composition.

The sensation of composition, of structure, is a theme I will take up
again in my discussion of Sallust's histories in chapter 2. For now, though, I
want to single out one concern underlying Fried's objections to minimalist
art in this essay, a concern he pursued often elsewhere in his criticism. "The
effect is literally irresistible," he wrote of Larry Poons' first show in early
1963, "and it is this characteristic which finally seems to me to limit Poons'
achievement, maybe severely." Fried glimpsed an "element of coercion" in
Poons' canvases "that runs counter to art, or at any rate to even the barest

---

1   "Art and objecthood," reprinted in a book of the same name (148–72).

FIGURE 2   Donald Judd, Untitled (Stack), 1967. Lacquer on galvanized iron, Twelve units, each 9 × 40 × 31", installed vertically with 9" intervals. Helen Acheson Bequest (by exchange) and gift of Joseph Helman. The Museum of Modern Art, New York, NY, USA. Art © Judd Foundation. Licensed by VAGA, New York, NY. Digital Image © The Museum of Modern Art / Licensed by SCALA / Art Resource, NY.

notion of individual sensibility."[2] Set aside the question of whether or not Fried's evaluation of Poons is persuasive (I happen to like Poons, so I disagree with Fried): the point I want to take away from his discussion is the sensation he describes of being in the presence of the "literally irresistible."

The specific effect that leads Fried to criticize Poons' art in these terms is that every viewer of Poons' work is bound to suffer the optical illusion of the dots' flickering and flaring under the bright lights of the gallery. The paintings resemble scientific experiments, with Poons the scientist scheming to bring about a specific effect in all his subjects. Poons' paintings will have this effect on each and every viewer, and the biological design of the human eye means that they cannot escape. This bothers Fried the most: the artist has made a work of art that is designed to push viewers around, to dominate them. Their agency lost, viewers become objects of force.

Fried has more in mind, I think: the viewer of a Poons dots painting confronts a rectangle of canvas covered with paint applied with care (the dots are discrete and of a limited number of colors against a single-color background) but no discernible order or system beyond a roughly even distribution in space. No dot or set of dots draws attention to itself, just as no box in a Judd stack draws attention to itself; the relation of each dot to the other carries no particular hint of a meaning—there are no sites of perceptible tension, no special interaction between the dots and the edge of the piece. The viewer receives no direction: no figuration to concentrate on, no point of energy to start from, no swirls or patterns to follow, scarcely even the trace of the human hand dragging a brush to track. There is energy, but no entry-point. In the case of the Judd boxes, the evocation of the column or the ladder leads in no particular direction. The viewer is suspended; exactly where depends on the viewer—perhaps in the attempt to create meaning, in the enjoyment of symmetry, in the curious search for flaws in the metal. There is no point of focus, no over-balancing or lunge toward an edge—the kind of aesthetic gesture that gives the viewer a place to stand, something to push back against. It is not that the art lacks power, specifically the power to engage: it is simply irresistible.

Fried's reaction must be understood in the context of his famous (and controversial) view of modernist art, abstract art in particular. He argues that the "chief function of the dialectic of modernism" has been to furnish a "principle" by which painting can be seen and see itself as a tradition, and by which it may transform and renew that tradition. Approvingly citing Merleau-Ponty on fecundity (he has since re-evaluated his heavy reliance on

2   Fried, "New York letter: Kelly, Poons," in *Art and Objecthood* (310–11).

this citation), he sees modern artists as intimately engaged with one another's work: specifically, as solving formal problems posed by earlier artworks. Fried sees this engagement with other artists, again controversially, in moral terms. Modernist painting may seem to have abandoned lived reality and its material concerns, he concludes, but the "actual dialectic by which it is made"—the relation of artist to artist, work to work—has assumed "more and more of the denseness, structure, and complexity of moral experience—that is, of life itself, but life as few are inclined to live it: in a state of continuous intellectual and moral alertness."[3] To make an artwork that transforms the viewer into an experimental subject who has the same experience as all other subjects, that transforms the idealized dynamic exchange between viewer and artwork into an oppressive act, that reduces the experience of the new into the sensation of having been worked upon: for Fried this breaches the implicit moral code by which he judges modern art.

The themes of coercion and resistibility and the creation of the new are important to this chapter: part of my argument is that it is impossible to discuss republican politics without them. The other part takes up the importance of preserving the conditions of resistibility and novelty in politics. Consider for a moment the political community as a work of art: using Fried's terms, the community needs to preserve not just the condition of potential disagreement or dissent, but discernible entry-points into disagreement, sites in which dissenting citizens can not only stand but push back and create new ways of thinking and doing politics.

Liberty and concord—agreement on what constitutes the common good—are commonly understood as core republican political values. I argue here for a new approach to these concepts in Cicero's theoretical writings, mainly his *Republic*. My aim is not to redefine these two concepts from top to bottom but to examine what his account of both reveals about the conditions of a republican politics.

Three themes will be centrally important and will recur in different ways: 1) the place of the people; 2) the formation of concord and consensus; and 3) the role of aesthetics in Cicero's conception of the constitution at the republic's foundation. In the course of handling these, I rebut two common claims: first, that Cicero's thought holds as the main goal of politics the common good as articulated through a consensus made possible in conditions of concord; and second, that the conditions through which consensus is achieved in this vision confirm the irrelevancy of the Roman political experience for today. Proponents of the latter view either argue that the

3   Quotations from Fried, "Three American painters: Noland, Olitski, Stella," 218, 219.

creation of consensus through public assemblies and the like demanded a high level of active participation in politics that is not sustainable under the conditions of modernity (Benjamin Constant's point), or they claim that Roman consensus was the creation of a senatorial elite with little or no investment in popular interests.

By putting the practices of Roman politics in a head-to-head comparison with modern politics, both judgments miss the significance of Cicero's reflections on the republic. Universal freedom and popular participation in politics, by the modern measuring sticks of human rights, ballots, democratic representation, and popular influence on political discourse, are not bedrock values of Roman republican thought, and any attempt to claim otherwise is bound to run into trouble. In its exposure of fundamental tensions at the heart of politics, Cicero's treatment of liberty and concord prompts us to think about what kind of civic experience we had better value. We will see that matters are more complicated than dismissive judgments of elitism allow: Cicero's unmistakable bias toward the domination of the senatorial order does not prevent him from illuminating the conditions of political conflict or from identifying practices of politics that may transcend the conventional familiarities of our own postdemocratic moment.[4] Chantal Mouffe's agonistic politics, Andreas Kalyvas' "politics of the extraordinary," Jacques Rancière's notion of dissensus, and Nadia Urbinati's work on democratic representation are important interlocutors in my account of the Ciceronian vision of politics and how it bears on contemporary experience.

LIBERTY AND CONCORD

In his influential books *Republicanism* and *A Theory of Freedom*, Philip Pettit has defended a tradition of political thought he calls "Roman in origin and character" that emerged in tandem with the institutions and practices of fourth through first century BCE Rome.[5] Roman writers of this period, Pettit argues, conceived of the freedom of the citizen as that which distinguished the free from the slave: the capacity to live not *in potestate domini*,

4 Making the twentieth-century argument that Rome is an oligarchy, Syme, *The Roman Revolution* (7); for arguments against this view, Fergus Millar, *Crowd in the Roman Republic* (1–12), and Wiseman, *Remembering the Roman People* (5–16). For a sophisticated modified picture of a Rome where power lies in the hands of the senatorial elite whose legitimacy is continually upheld by performance in public, see Robert Morstein-Marx, *Mass Oratory and Political Power in the Late Roman Republic*.

5 Pettit, *Republicanism*, 283.

not "in the power of a master," but free from even the possibility of domination by another. Pettit concludes that the three axial "Roman" ideas are the conception of freedom as non-domination, the claim that this sort of freedom requires a body of law under which the polity aims to guarantee the common good, and the belief that institutions are a necessary element in the constitution.

Non-domination involves more than just being free from actual interference by other people at any given moment in time. It means being free from even the possibility of arbitrary interference by others. This is Cicero's point when he says that "freedom consists not in having a just master, but in having none" (*Rep.* 2.43). Pettit defends his neo-Roman conception of freedom on the grounds that it captures the breadth and depth of the injustice of various forms of unfreedom, including slavery, better than the liberal definition of freedom as non-interference. The republican theory of freedom as non-domination proposes that slaves are unjustly, unacceptably unfree regardless of whether their masters are in fact benevolent or cruel, because even the slave of a non-interfering master lives according to the master's arbitrary whim.[6] From this paradigmatic example, Pettit expands the ideal of non-domination to a range of other unfree relationships: the worker fearful of losing his job, the wife submissively obeying her dominating husband, the impoverished person subjected to the petty, intrusive supervision of a welfare worker.

Patchen Markell rightly identifies a problem in Philip Pettit's overarching claims on behalf of non-domination as the heart of the republican account of freedom: that "in seeking to account for the injustice even of rule-bound and norm-governed subordination, we have recourse to a notion of 'common avowable interest' understood as the result of a demanding process through which caprice is purified or educated toward universality."[7] Concerned with "the possible unintended consequences of framing an engagement with [imperial power] exclusively around the problem of arbitrary power" (both in the sense of power exercised by whim and without reference to the good of the interferee), Markell suggests that we should concern ourselves not with domination but with the stultifying, "world-narrowing" effect on relations and experience caused by domination that successfully justifies itself with arguments that its interfering action is benevolent—motivated, for example, by the desire to improve or liberate a

6   Ibid, 31–35. See further Kapust, *Republicanism*, 11–13.
7   Patchen Markell, "The insufficiency of non-domination," 16.

people. Drawing on the history of European imperialistic interventions around the world, Markell calls this effect "usurpation."[8]

I share his concerns about what Pettit's conception of freedom as non-domination leaves out. With regard to thinking about our Roman sources, however, I see this not so much as a matter of properly defining concepts as it is a problem of understanding where politics begins and in what it consists. In Pettit's republican polity no one can interfere with another like a master does a slave, and in cases where representatives of institutions, like tax-collectors or army draft officers, must and do interfere, their interference must "track" the people's "common, recognizable interests." Pettit himself admits that the belief that consent is a necessary element in the legitimacy of any government "has spawned dubious doctrines of implied or virtual or tacit consent."[9]

To avoid such doctrines, he argues that in order to meet the standard of non-arbitrariness, the exercise of a given power (such as tax-collecting) requires neither ongoing participation nor actual consent but "the permanent possibility of effectively contesting it." Some element of "contestability" is required to stop the *imperium* of government from coming to represent an insidious form of domination. "The non-arbitrariness of public decisions comes of their meeting, not the condition of having originated or emerged according to some consensual process, but the condition of being such that if they conflict with the perceived interests and ideas of the citizens, then the citizens can effectively contest them. What matters is ... [the decisions'] modal or counterfactual responsiveness to the possibility of contestation."[10]

Throughout his discussion of contestability or contestation (terms he uses more or less interchangeably), Pettit buttresses his argument with appeals to contemporary democratic theory: Iris Young's inclusive politics of difference, Anne Phillips' politics of presence, Cass Sunstein's deliberative republic of reasons, and Joshua Cohen's deliberative democracy. Rome and Roman writers are notable for their absence. Pettit here limits his citation of the neo-Roman tradition, which he is elsewhere at pains to reconstruct, to Quentin Skinner's work on the classical and humanist tradition of arguing *in utramque partem*, which he claims provides a republican pedigree for

---

8   Ibid., 26. Markell appeals to the Latin word *usurpare* as it is used in Livy and Cicero's speech against Rullus.

9   Pettit, *Republicanism*, 63.

10   Ibid., 184, 185.

deliberative democracy: "the appropriate model will always be that of a dialogue, the appropriate stance a willingness to negotiate over rival institutions concerning the applicability of evaluative terms."[11] The clinical tone of Skinner's description is matched by Pettit's conclusion that "even if there is no imminent consensus ... it remains the case that effective contestability requires that the decisions should be made on the basis of reasoned deliberation."[12] To guarantee contestation, Pettit focuses on procedures that regulate the interactions of already existing groups of people: for example, ensuring the inclusion of minorities via elected representation in the legislative process, perhaps by allocating a percentage of representatives to minorities or the historically disempowered; or legislating compulsory registration or compulsory voting. Outside the legislature, he approves of mandated diversity on juries and government agencies.

Pettit has little to say about contestation outside of the law and the formal procedures and institutions of government. He does acknowledge that Roman thinkers take democratic control to be important, not because of any "definitional connection with liberty but from the fact that it is a means of furthering liberty."[13] In his discussion of the institutionalization of contestability in republican forms of government, he suggests that citizens desiring to contest domination or its threat must be able to exercise their rights of free speech in the act of protesting, writing letters to Congress, and the like. This is voluntary action: the burden of actively participating in checking the actions of government is theirs to carry only if they are so inclined. For the government's part, it must be responsive to citizen complaints, and Pettit sketches a number of institutional and procedural solutions to ensure that responsiveness. As one neo-republican theorist comments about Pettit's theory, "the power of *contesting* political decisions is more important than *contributing* to them."[14]

Along similar lines, when John Maynor attempts to tackle what the republican version of pluralistic public reasoning would look like, he argues for the state establishment of training that will "help to provide the necessary skills and technologies that are available to all and serve as essential

---

11   Skinner, *Reason and Rhetoric in the Philosophy of Hobbes* (15–16), quoted in Pettit, *Republicanism*, 189. Gary Remer, in "Cicero and the ethics of deliberative rhetoric," discusses the moral limits of *in utramque partem*, drawing out the distinctly different consequences of its deployment in philosophical conversation *versus* deliberative oratory (143–46).

12   Pettit, *Republicanism*, 190.

13   Ibid., 30. This instrumental position is often emphasized by neo-republican theorists seeking to find ways to defend a minimal version of active participation in politics.

14   Holohan, *Civic Republicanism*, 216 (her italics), citing Pettit, *Republicanism*, 185.

components in effective dialogue. These questions, it is argued, should be settled through open and inclusive discussions utilizing the necessary skills and forums of the republic that hold out the promise of a substantial degree of consensus."[15] Maynor does not explain who decides what skills are necessary or what constitutes "effective dialogue," where the forums should be held, or how to cope with individuals or groups who do not fit into the consensus. He places his trust in the state's organization of contestation, from Green Papers and campaign finance reform to enforced quotas for women and minority groups and compulsory voting.

Minimizing disturbance and unpredictability and maximizing stability are the overarching goals of these theorists' procedural politics. Establishing formal, routinized procedures of protest and accountability has the virtue of containing what Pettit calls the "tumult of informal, popular protest," and further, it usefully helps to depoliticize difficult issues where popular opinion may intimidate elected representatives into ignoring empirical evidence. Pettit appeals to criminal justice law as a revealing example of how popular fear and outrage leads to unjust and ineffective legislation. When one criminal let out on parole commits a crime, public outrage pushes politicians to sound "tough on crime" and make bad laws that raise incarceration rates and punish prisoners more severely. Only "autonomous, professionally informed bodies that are not exposed to the glare and pressure of public debate" will solve complex problems like crime. Here, "contestatory democracy requires that the *demos* and the legislative representatives of the demos generally tie their hands and gag their mouths."[16]

One might defend Pettit's reticence regarding conflict and popular power by appealing to his effort to displace the "standard" reading of republican thought popularized by Benjamin Constant and Isaiah Berlin "as a tradition that prizes positive liberty above all else, in particular the liberty of democratic participation." The problem with the Constant/Berlin "positive" account of republican politics, Pettit says, citing Hanna Pitkin and Quentin Skinner, is that Roman republican writers represent a people mainly concerned with freedom from interference, especially from magistrates. "The Roman plebs struggled not for democracy but for protection, not for public power but for private security": they valued active participation but their liberty was primarily "passive" and "defensive."[17]

---

15   Maynor, *Republicanism in the Modern World*, 107, discussing David Miller, "Citizenship and pluralism." Maynor summarizes his approach to "contestatory" politics on 158–68.
16   Pettit, *Republicanism*, 196–97.
17   Ibid., 29.

This account has virtues, as Peter Brunt would agree.[18] But it is partial and misleading. Accurate understanding of Roman ideas about liberty and consensus requires examining the concepts as they are presented in Roman writers—and here another meaningful silence in Pettit's work on republicanism makes itself heard. As other readers have noted, there is one historical example of domination in the republican tradition about which Pettit says almost nothing, namely, the domination of the elite: in the Roman case, the domination of the senatorial order.[19]

The domination of the senatorial elite and the resistance of the people are mutually constitutive forces in Roman politics. When Romans talk about freedom, it is always coupled with conflict, usually the conflict between the people's *libertas* and the senate's *dignitas*, the "worthy" status that places them in a position of power over the people: in Livy's phrase, *contentio libertatis dignitatisque* (4.6.11). "The crucial problem of *libertas* at Rome was how to make the fitting adjustment between the equality of the fundamental rights of all and the supremacy of some."[20] Romans consistently examine agency and will in the context of socioeconomic and political inequality, inquiring into the degree to which the agent is capable of resistance, whether he can modulate or refuse demands. The underlying assumption is that freedom must be fought for on the battlefield of social interaction as well as the law courts and the public assembly: that citizens, individually or *en masse*, protect their rights (*libertas, ius*) with an aggressive defense against the offenses of the wealthy senatorial elite. The existence of a "free republic" and "equal laws" rests on this, that "each order hold on to its own rights and its own *maiestas*" in an antagonistic and suspicious scrutiny of the other (3.63.10).[21] As a senator in Livy's early history of Rome concludes, the liberty of the people is constituted in popular resistance to senatorial authority: "in not obeying the senate, the magistrates, the laws, the customs of the ancestors, the institutions of our fathers, and the discipline of the military"

18   Brunt, "*Libertas*," 298–308.
19   McCormick, "Machiavelli against republicanism: on the Cambridge School's 'Guicciardinian Moments,'" 633–34. On the limits of Pettit's approach in cases of imperialism and slavery, see Markell, "The insufficiency of non-domination," 26–30.
20   Wirszubski, Libertas *as a Political Idea at Rome*, 17. His language underscores the aggressive tone of the Roman conception: "The Roman citizen sought to assert and safeguard his rights, not against the overriding authority of the State, or the tyranny of the majority, as it is sometimes called, but against other citizens who were stronger than himself, or against the officers of the State who, in the pursuit of their own private interests, might encroach upon his rights, abusing the power that had been entrusted to them" (16–17). We will examine a different angle on *libertas* and social relations in Horatian satire (chapter 4).
21   This also holds true for the freedom of states, which are represented as having to fight for their freedom (Sallust, *Hist*. 1.55).

(5.6.16–17). Even *auctoritas*, the time-honored authority belonging to all notable Romans and claimed by all senators, was understood to be "sinister if it demanded simple submission."[22]

Republican writers thus view freedom as a possession to be defended against inevitable aggression, and therefore the crucial capacity of the citizen, a social group, or class is the capacity to resist. Further, and more radically, in Cicero's theoretical writing the establishment of a republic—a government of laws passed by free men rather than a government of men themselves—emerges from the struggle between the nobility and the people, when the people interrupt the rich nobles' "natural" tendency to dominate them.

Rather than purify power of its arbitrary elements, as Pettit seeks to do, I suggest we see freedom in the terms set by Cicero, Sallust, Livy, and Tacitus, where it is not the formation of consensus but its opposite, the division of the community into parts, that is the common ground of the community. In their representation of the republic's past, freedom emerges in tandem with the establishment of republican politics, which is a field of antagonism, of over-reach and resistance. Politics thus begins not with contestation from all known quarters of society but with the differentiation of political parts or parties in the first place.[23] When antagonism is the institution of politics, the capacity of resistibility is fundamental.

Leaving out the key fact that these writers view antagonism as a form of political foundation allows Pettit to claim Roman precedent for his habits of flattening political practice into rational processes of deliberation and of minimizing the role of the people as direct (as opposed to representative) agents in politics. His "contestation" is a term that implies the pre-existence of groups and the necessity for the less powerful one to summon up the wherewithal to compete with the dominant one. My term "resistibility" suggests a capacity, not a predetermined situation inhabited by predetermined groups. Resistibility presumes that incursions by the powerful are inevitable, that the *sine qua non* of freedom is the capacity to fight back, and that this conflict rests on the very field where freedom itself is constituted: the public field of antagonism between the haves and have-nots, which manifests itself both inside conventional procedures of deliberation and in the relatively unpoliced territory of protest or mass action. Consider situations where the less powerful agent may not even be acknowledged as an agent:

22 Brunt, "*Libertas*," 329.
23 Pettit, *Republicanism*, 185; though he now acknowledges an "antagonistic" element in politics, *On the People's Terms*, 226.

CHAPTER 1

by the view of politics I want to defend, the agent's interruption of the conventional order to demand a part in the field of antagonism *is* politics.

Antagonism plays a central role in the picture of Roman politics in the theoretical writings of Cicero, who is usually understood as a more or less straightforward champion of the senatorial elite.[24] In his *Republic* and *Laws*, two works composed in the late 50s as experiments in transposing Greek political thought into a Roman idiom, Cicero champions a politics of the common good reached through *consensus* shaped and dominated by leading senators. His terminology in both treatises picks up on language used in a range of earlier orations, from his speech of 66 BCE in defense of Cluentius, which was the first to use the phrase *concordia ordinum* ("the harmony of the orders") explicitly to refer to a goodwill alliance between senators and knights, to the broader notion of *consensus bonorum omnium* ("the agreement of all good men") laid out in the 56 BCE speech *pro Sestio*.[25]

I will first examine Cicero's *Republic* 1 and 2, turning next to his views on advocacy set forth in *Laws* and several speeches. As I see it, Cicero's account of politics as antagonism forces a reorientation of neo-republican tendencies to minimize popular action in republican politics and to overemphasize the negative and passive aspects of republican liberty. The unpredictable, turbulent popular voice emerges in Cicero as a *sine qua non* of republican politics. The challenge for him is to preserve it as a *political* force, that is, without enabling its (always latent) transmutation into violence. Violence, because of its imperviousness to resistibility, represents for Cicero the end of politics. We will see that the institutionalization of resistance introduces two contradictory positions in Cicero's text. First, it provides Cicero with the (to most modern readers, unsavory) grounds on which to justify elite domination of the political process—the very overweening control that he warns against elsewhere in the *Republic*. It also leads him to make a

24   Morstein-Marx provides the most perceptive and fine-grained account of Cicero as a politician with limited sympathies for popular interests as they are articulated in tribunician oratory of the period (viz. his description of "the rich" as his "army" of political supporters, *exercitus locupletium, Att.* 1.19.4) but who was also an expert in *popularis* oratory in a world where speaking in public to the people gathered in a *contio* was by definition and necessity "popular" (*Mass Oratory*, 212ff.)

25   In his recent commentary on the speech, Robert Kaster vigorously denies that it accurately represents Cicero's political thinking, arguing that the famous discursus on political ideology represents nothing but a "tendentious and deceptive" effort to win his case (35). *Contra* Kaster I assume that there is no "political thought" anywhere in Cicero that is free from tendentiousness, because his understanding of discourse and politics excludes the possibility of theory free from practice and contingency. While he sketches a space apart for the work of theorizing (most frequently the holiday villa where his interlocutors gather), he consistently links their debate back to goings-on in the *curia* and the Forum.

34

provocative argument about the role of advocacy in unsettling institutions so that they do *not* become unyielding fortresses of elite domination.

One further word on the thinker under discussion. Cicero is the founder of Roman rhetoric's discursivity. That is, he is not just the author of his own works on rhetoric and political thought but an originator of "possibilities and rules for the formation of other texts"; as Foucault said of Freud, "he has made possible a number of divergences—with respect to his own texts, concepts, and hypotheses" about public speech and politics.[26] He belongs in that category of thinkers who are at once committed to the normative and keenly attuned to the inevitable failure of norms. To say this about a canonical thinker has become something of a truism these days, but Cicero makes the attunement to failure a stylistic and a political priority; it perceptibly shapes his expression and defense of norms. He understands and exploits the dynamic power of mass politics but also cultivates suspicion of the unpredictability, ignorance, and violence of crowds; he is committed to conserving the past, but a past that is repeatedly remade in order to suit the demands of the present.

He does not, of course, fit the mold of the Roman politician as he was normally envisioned in the early first century BCE. Cicero was a *novus homo* or "new man" from the town of Arpinum, seventy miles south of Rome. Thus he lacks the pantheon of ancestors devoted to public life, commemorated on coins and inscriptions and statues, in which nearly all of his senatorial colleagues rejoiced. His Arpino-Roman identity permits him, early in his career, to exploit a kind of cultural "archaism of the periphery"; like the elder Cato a century earlier, he crafts a political voice that chastises the *Romans* amidst the Romans, exhorting them to adhere to the virtue of their forefathers that is better preserved in Rome's outskirts than the city. His suburban identity also transforms him (and his texts) into a site from which alternative ethical and political possibilities are generated.[27]

One reader of Hannah Arendt recently commented that she holds "the agonistic and consensual moments of political life in a common, if tension-filled frame."[28] In Cicero's *corpus*—influential texts that knit together productive instabilities where the parts usually fail to cohere—the drive to achieve *concordia* or *consensus* thrives only within a framing of politics as

26   Foucault, "What is an author?" 115.

27   This is true of "Roman culture" in general, which is produced by almost no actual Romans (Julius Caesar being the most famous exception) but rather by Italians, Africans, and Gallic and especially Spanish provincials.

28   Kimberley Curtis, "Aesthetic foundations of democratic politics in the work of Hannah Arendt," 30.

antagonism, where the political leader is conceived as a virtuosic speaker of and to an acknowledged multiplicity, and where the patterns of thought and action modeled by oratory reflect in microcosm the ideal operation of deliberative and judicial institutions—alive, responsive, dynamic, and self-aware.

CONCORDIA AND CONSENSUS

> The struggle between rich and poor is not social reality, which politics then has to deal with. It is the actual institution of politics itself. . . . Politics exists when the natural order of domination is interrupted by the institution of a part of those who have no part. . . . It defines the common of the community as a political community, in other words, as divided, as based on a wrong that escapes the arithmetic of exchange and reparation. Beyond this set-up there is no politics. There is only the order of domination or the disorder of revolt.[29]

In his *Republic* of 54–51 BCE, Cicero prioritizes the notion of concord by introducing it very early in the dialogue, as he sets the scene: the villa of Scipio Aemilianus, leading politician and an emblem of Roman imperial violence, who stamped out bloody revolt in Spain and razed Carthage in the Third Punic War. Concord is marked as a practical proposal for Roman politics and as a symbol of a Roman rejection of Greek theorizing.[30] But in a typically ironic Ciceronian foreshadowing, the manner of its appearance in the first passionate argument in the dialogue couples it with themes of conflict and resistance.

Scipio's friends arrive one by one, starting with the young Tubero, who asks Scipio's opinion about the recent unsettling appearance of two suns appearing simultaneously in the sky. As Tubero and Scipio debate the utility of the study of astronomy, more guests arrive, including Scipio's closest friend Laelius. Informed about the topic of conversation, Laelius angrily objects that his friends are finding doubles in all the wrong places:

> I will speak out, by the gods, and maybe you'll criticize me, since it was you who asked Scipio about these celestial goings-on in the first

---

29   Rancière, *Disagreement*, 11.

30   Cicero remarks that Greek philosophers dispute in corners over abstractions (*Orat.* 1.57), and the theme is carried over into *de Republica*, where Laelius praises Scipio's Romanized, historicized version of Plato's theory.

place, but speaking for myself, I think that we should examine instead the things that are seen to exist in front of our own eyes. How can it be that the grandson of Lucius Paulus, the nephew of Scipio here, born into the most noble of families and in such a great republic, asks how two suns may be seen, but doesn't ask why in a single republic there are two senates and practically two peoples? ... Don't worry about the second sun, young men: either it doesn't exist or it does [and we can't do anything about it]! ... But to have a united senate and people—this is possible, and if it doesn't happen, it will be very dangerous. (*Rep.* 1.31–32)

dicam mehercule et contemnar a te fortasse, cum tu ista caelestia de Scipione quaesieris, ego autem haec quae videntur ante oculos esse magis putem quaerenda. quid enim mihi L. Pauli nepos, hoc avunculo, nobilissima in familia atque in hac tam clara re publica natus, quaerit quo modo duo soles visi sint, non quaerit cur in una re publica duo senatus et duo paene iam populi sint? ... quam ob rem si me audietis adulescentes, solem alterum ne metueritis; aut enim nullus esse potest, aut sit sane ut visus est.... senatum vero et populum ut unum habeamus et fieri potest, et permolestum est nisi fit.

Laelius' exhortation to heal the divided state proleptically argues on behalf of Scipio's theory of *concordia ordinum*, which defines the republic as a mutually beneficial, unified partnership in which *senatus* guides *populus*.[31] Cicero elaborates in book 2:

Just as in the case of string instruments or flutes or singing, a certain harmony (*concentus*) must be maintained out of distinct sounds, the interruption or violation of which is not to be borne by trained ears, and this harmony, arising out of a blending of very dissimilar notes, is nonetheless made concordant and in agreement, so a *civitas* is made harmonious by the common agreement (*consensu*) of the most dissimilar elements through a blending of the highest, lowest, and intermediate orders (*ordines*) as if they were musical notes. What the musicians call harmony in a song is concord in the state, the tightest and

---

31   On *concordia*: Arnaldo Momigliano, "Camillus and concord"; H. Strasburger, *Concordia Ordinum*; Henry Boren, "Cicero's *concordia* in historical perspective"; Bernard Combet-Farnoux, "Fabius Pictor et les origines du thème de la concordia ordinum dans l'historiographie romaine"; Kapust, *Republicanism*, 83–101.

best bond of safety in a state, and it can in no way exist without justice.

> ut enim in fidibus aut tibiis atque ut in cantu ipso ac vocibus concentus est quidam tenendus ex distinctis sonis, quem inmutatum aut discrepantem aures eruditae ferre non possunt, isque concentus ex dissimillimarum vocum moderatione concors tamen efficitur et congruens, sic ex summis et infimis et mediis interiectis ordinibus ut sonis moderata ratione civitas consensu dissimillorum concinit; et quae harmonia a musicis dicitur in cantu, ea est in civitate concordia, artissimum atque optimum omni re publica vinculum incolumitatis, eaque sine iustitia nullo pacto esse potest. (2.69)[32]

This modification of Plato's tripartite account of the soul divides the Roman republic into a tripartite hierarchy of *ordines*: the senate, knights (wealthy and well-born non-senators), and the multitude. "Common agreement," Elizabeth Asmis optimistically argues, "does not consist in an agreement of the people to be ruled by senators. . . . It consists of a hierarchical blending of wills, in which the two highest classes are viewed as leading the rest. Constituting a tiny fraction of the citizen body, the topmost classes are given a hugely disproportionate voice in the harmony of the whole; yet they must also attune their will to that of the other classes."[33] A more suspicious Peter Brunt contends that there is a troubling arbitrariness to Cicero's theory, which appears to minimize popular freedom in favor of senatorial power.[34]

What these and other readings miss is context. First, the notion of concord lands on the theoretical table in a dialogue that, itself a contest, thematizes conflict among a group of like-minded men. Over the course of the dialogue, the interlocutors create a miniature law court where each speaker contends with learning and wit for the group's approval. As in the dialogue *de Oratore*, where Marcus Crassus and his friends converse under a plane tree they compare to Socrates' tree in Plato's *Phaedrus*, the *Republic* plays out

---

32   At *civitas con[sensu]*. . . there is a lacuna: the rest of the sentence is supplied from Augustine *de Civitate Dei* 2.21.

33   I have adapted Asmis' eloquent translation from "A new kind of model," 404–405.

34   Brunt, "Fall of the Roman republic," glosses Cicero thus: "there can be no stability in a state except where every man is firmly fixed in his own social and political grade (*Rep*. 1.69) . . . . Admittedly the true statesman would aim at harmony between all orders for the sake of political stability (*Rep*. 2.69) and in *pro Sestio* (137) he declares it to be the senate's duty to conserve and augment the liberty and interests of the people, but this is a task to be fulfilled at the senate's own discretion" (57). Brunt is clearly influenced by Cicero's dismissive references to the people (e.g., notoriously as "the dregs of the city," *faex urbis*, *Att*. 1.16).

on a stage metatheatrically set for another scene in the ongoing Ciceronian contest with Greek intellectual history.

More important is the historical account that clarifies the manner of concord's emergence. At the end of book 1, Scipio ends his lecture on Greek-style constitutional theory, and in a style he describes as more appropriate for men sitting together engaged in collective deliberation (1.70), he recounts the historical formation of the Roman constitution, which Christian Meier called "organic" as opposed to "foundational."[35] The subsequent foundation narrative, which occupies most of the second book, is an intervention into what had become by Cicero's lifetime a highly contested ideological field, with a pro-nobility tradition celebrating the achievements of the patricians countering a plebeian tradition featuring noble arrogance and incompetence.[36] Scipio, by representing Rome as a machine of conflict and reconstitution through the struggle between the haves and the have-nots, makes antagonism the normative frame of republican politics.

This is also a story with imperial implications, of course. For Cicero, as for Sallust and Livy, the consequences of empire are twofold: on the one hand, empire enjoys the grand common narrative of exemplary victory (also recorded in monuments around the empire, especially in the city itself); on the other, empire trembles at the ever-present threat of the collapse of community, a collapse it brings ever closer with each new conquest, each new injection of destabilizing diversity, each new act of repression, each new importation of pillaged wealth.

Rome's constitutional evolution as Scipio describes it is a series of conflicts where the powerful minority seeks to maximize its power and the people staunchly resist. In the first stage, Romulus founds a city that mingles shepherds and wild men with the civilized subjects of the kingly rule Romulus had violently overthrown, anticipating his republican descendants. He is succeeded by a number of kings who stabilize Roman civic practice through a series of reconstitutions that are bloodless, but not without conflict. Romulus' mysterious death inaugurates popular confusion and

---

35   Hölkeskamp, *Reconstructing the Roman Republic*, 15, notes that Meier recognized that "certain peculiarities of this state were actually strengths and that they in fact provided the basis of its remarkable and fascinating stability, flexibility, and ability to adapt to dynamically changing conditions over the course of several centuries."

36   For extensive discussion of the historical problems with early Roman history and especially the "Conflict of the Orders" see, in Raaflaub (ed.), *Social Struggles in Archaic Rome*: Mitchell (128–55), arguing that the struggle is an invention of second and first century historians, and Raaflaub's judicious response (185ff.). See also Wiseman, "Romulus' Rome of equals," (81–99); he explores the patrician creation of the virtuous Furius Camillus and the competing history featuring prudent plebeians (an episode dating to the 390s) in *Myths of Rome*, 124–30.

disagreement. The dark suggestion of senatorial domination and its further-ance by compulsion and propaganda emerges: because the people suspect that Romulus was murdered by his own council (the predecessors of the senate in Scipio's account), the council members pressure a poor peasant to pretend that Romulus appeared to him in a vision, announcing that he had been transformed into a god named Quirinus (2.20). Briefly pacified by this tale, the people nonetheless immediately resist when the council members attempt to set themselves up as the permanent rulers after Romulus ("the people did not put up with it," *populus id non tulit*, 2.23). The people collec-tively choose a foreign king with no ties to the native nobility.

In what will become a key move in the ongoing antagonistic relation between senate and people, the proto-senatorial council transforms crowd action into law, by which process it simultaneously assents to and contains popular will. The council institutionalizes the people's act for future times with the invention of the *interregnum*, a temporary office designed to sup-plement the people's choice of king and prevent violence after the rupture caused by the king's death. Each of the kings in turn (with one exception, Servius Tullius) follow the senate's turn to law, formally legitimating their choice by the people by requesting self-authorizing legislation to be passed in the popular assembly.

The antagonism between senate and people is displaced to Rome's bor-ders in the *fort-da* activity of Romulus' successors. The second king, Numa Pompilius, sets up institutions that nudge the Romans away from ceaseless war toward a lifestyle of mingled cultural activities: religious observance, commerce, and the games. The next two kings, Tullus and Ancius Marcius, return to war-making after legalizing aggression through a new practice of sacral justification, the fetial laws; with these laws in hand they reconstitute the state as a multiethnic body of Romans and conquered Latins. Servius Tullius establishes the political and economic classes and centuries that (Scipio claims) are the foundation of the republican electoral and legislative order (2.39). As if in response to the powerful consolidating effect of this legislation, the next king is a tyrant, which leads to Brutus' expulsion of the kings and the establishment of republican government, where the cycle of antagonism between senate and people begins afresh.

Roman foundation is not a story about consent or consensuality. As the cycle rolls on, the senate never finally consolidates its power and the people never finally consent to it or any other power. They continually acknowl-edge the authority of the senatorial order, institutions, and the law, but their acknowledgement always occurs as a result of conflict, and the act of ac-knowledging itself tends to alter the balance of power, sometimes radically.

At the least, one side's acknowledgement of a given institution or practice tends to engender a supplemental that channels and reinforces the adversarial relation. As Franz Wieacker has noted, we should avoid "interpreting Roman politics as a 'permanent status quo or stable framework' of institutions and formal procedures, rules, and regulations, as it were, at a standstill. Rather we should learn to conceive it as a 'function of a continual political process.'"[37]

What of the consensus praised by Cicero in *Republic* 2.69? We are accustomed to viewing the formation of consensus as emerging in political discourse as a marriage of values or ideology and the assessment of the conditions of politics. Consensus may be formed around marriage equality, for instance, by the development over time of ways of thinking and talking about the issue that bring together ideas about equality, human rights, and sexual mores with factual data about the social and economic benefits of more people marrying. In republican Rome, as the work of Robert Morstein-Marx, Egon Flaig, Harriet Flower, and others suggests, consensus did not take the modern form of agreement about values and facts. Consensus involved agreements among members of the senatorial order and between that order and the *populus Romanus* about the rules of the political game, from elections to the public speeches called *contiones*. Collective consent regarding the rules of these constitutive competitions was "an indispensable precondition of competition as a pacified (and continually pacifying and stabilizing) mode of contending for a valuable resource: during the actual competition, the consensus about its norms and rules had to remain undisputed between all parties."[38]

This is the context in which to explain Cicero's opening argument in the dedication against the Epicureans' withdrawal from public life, where he agrees with the Epicureans' contemptuous dismissal of political life: "they say most politicians are worthless, that it is demeaning to be classified with them, and it's disagreeable and dangerous to come into conflict with them, especially when they have stirred up the mob ... nor does it befit a free man

---

37   Cited and discussed in Hölkeskamp, *Reconstructing the Roman Republic*, 17. See further his account of senatorial politics: "It was the very 'divisibility' of interests and 'fissility' of politics and policies ... [that] necessarily led to to a continuous shifting of coalitions, constellations, and for that matter, lines of confrontation.... [T]he only common denominator ... was their being highly volatile and ephemeral" (39). Flower both usefully emphasizes the need to beware of over-essentializing and simplifying the categories of *nobiles* and plebs and presents a "scheme of multiple republics" that "inevitably present a picture of a much more dynamic and fluid early Roman society, whose history was marked by bold experiments ... and by revolutionary moments of reform," 53, 55.

38   Hölkeskamp, *Reconstructing the Roman Republic*, 105–6.

to struggle with corrupt and uncivilized opponents, lashed with foul abuse and submitting to outrages" (*Rep.* 1.9).[39] As Chantal Mouffe argues, in the field of collective identities, we are always dealing with the creation of a "we" which can exist only by the demarcation of a "they"—not necessarily Schmitt's friend/enemy binary, but a distinction that always holds within itself the possibility of antagonism.[40]

Scipio's concern to underscore the way conflict plays out on the level of social class and institutional formation as opposed to private competition is most prominent in his omission of some of the most melodramatic parts of the traditional foundation narrative: most prominently, the private fraternal feud of Romulus and Remus.[41] Meanwhile, the people's resistance unleashes forces that the senatorial order never entirely contains. After the expulsion of the kings, as republican forms are being founded, the popular hatred for monarchy grows so heated, recalling the widespread popular suspicion of the nobility after the death of Romulus, that the people banish even the innocent relations of the royal family, the Tarquins (2.53). One of the first elected magistrates responds to the agitation by ordering the *fasces*, the sign of magistricial authority, to be lowered when the people are gathered in assembly, and the right of appeal in cases of corporal and capital punishment is made into law (2.54–55).

It is at this point in Scipio's historical account that concord appears for the first time. In book 1, concord was first mentioned in the context of angry resistance; here the term describes the time and space between the moment the pressure of senatorial domination is applied and the radical

39   *Gloria* is one reward for the good man's venturing into such dangerous territory: so says Dana Villa, in his Arendtian theory of "agonistic subjectivity"; also Honig's account of the self's "agonal passion for distinction" in *Political Theory and the Displacement of Politics*. The passage in full: iam illa, perfugia quae sumunt sibi ad excusationem quo facilius otio perfruantur, certe minime sunt audienda, cum ita dicunt accedere ad rem publicam plerumque homines nulla re bona dignos, cum quibus comparari sordidum, confligere autem multitudine praesertim incitata miserum et periculosum sit. quam ob rem neque sapientis esse accipere habenas cum insanos atque indomitos impetus volgi cohibere non possit, neque liberi cum inpuris atque inmanibus adversariis decertantem vel contumeliarum verbera subire, vel expectare sapienti non ferendas iniurias: proinde quasi bonis et fortibus et magno animo praeditis ulla sit ad rem publicam adeundi causa iustior, quam ne pareant inprobis, neve ab isdem lacerari rem publicam patiantur, cum ipsi auxilium ferre si cupiant non queant.

40   Mouffe, *On the Political*, 15–16.

41   Compare Vergil's representation of rivals in the underworld (6.756ff.). Though he mentions the rape of the Sabines, Scipio does not dwell on the serial rapes of women so prominent in Livy's foundation account. Scipio also says nothing of the fratricidal murder of Remus by Romulus: it not only represents morally repulsive behavior but recalls the highly personal rivalry between the generalissimos of the first century BCE that is irrelevant to Scipio's narrative. He remains tightly focused on class.

rupture of popular violence. Two consuls are said to "wisely" favor popular legislation for the sake of concord (*concordiae causa*, 2.54), but the nobility meanwhile retains its right to ratify all legislation passed by the people, and in general "all the important matters were being governed by the leading men with overall authority, with the people yielding" (*omnia summa cum auctoritate a principibus cedente populo tenebantur*, 2.56). Again—and Scipio's language stresses the inevitability—this concord does not last long. A little later (*non longo intervallo*), "that which the nature of things compels to happen" comes about, and "the people demanded a greater share in the law" (*id quod fieri natura rerum ipsa cogebat ut plusculum sibi iuris populus adscisceret*, 2.57). If concord is where hearts beat together, as its etymology suggests, it is a violent rhythm.

It is worth noting at this point that *concordia* was a violently contested term in Cicero's own day—a battle-cry in a generations'-long propaganda war, as one historian comments: "from a plebeian perspective, its very name seems ironic on an almost Orwellian scale, since the traditions surrounding it spoke volumes about the tense relations between the plebs and the senate over the centuries."[42] The goddess Concordia was the first abstraction to be honored as a deity with a temple in Rome; a small flood of temples and shrines in honor of Libertas and Rome herself soon followed. Ovid associates the earliest temple with the plebeian secession. In better-attested accounts, a plebeian, the son of a freedman and "defiant toward the nobles," is elected aedile in 304 and vows to build a temple to Concord after publishing notices that reveal the legal and religious arcana of the law and the calendar. This knowledge had previously been kept closely guarded by the nobility, and its availability greatly assists the plebs in negotiating legal cases. The angry senatorial nobility does its best to block his temple's construction, and the Pontifex Maximus agrees to dedicate the temple only under heavy "popular consensus" (*coactus consensu populi*, Livy 9.46).[43]

The temple to Concord that dominated the urban landscape in Cicero's lifetime was built on the ridge of the Capitoline Hill by the consul Lucius Opimius shortly after 121 BCE, after Opimius fought the popular tribune Gaius Gracchus in a pitched battle on the streets of Rome, not only defeating and killing Gracchus but later presiding over the capital trials of hundreds of Gracchan supporters (Sallust, *Jug.* 16.2; Vell. Pat. 2.7.3, Plutarch,

---

42   Morstein-Marx, *Popular Oratory*, 101.

43   "From that time forward," Livy continues, "the citizens were divided into two parties ... until for the sake of concord (*concordiae causa*)" Fabius reformed the electoral assembly. See also Pliny *NH* 33.19.

G. Gracchus 17.5). Opimius was later accused of the illegal murder of citizens, but acquitted on his argument that the killings were legitimate (Cicero, *Sest.* 140). The temple was viewed as an aggressive declaration of the power of the traditional senatorial elite: Julius Caesar planned to tear it down and replace it with a theater, along with the old prison (the Carcer, where Cicero, like Opimius, had executed conspirators on legally shaky grounds) and perhaps the Porcian Basilica, emblem of the ancestral power of the senatorial champion Cato.[44] So much for the symbolic meanings summoned by the goddess herself.

The final stage of the constitution's evolution is the "permanent revolution" described by Theodor Mommsen.[45] The plebeians engineer a secession of the people and establish the tribunate *per seditionem*, "through insurrection" (2.59). Once more the senatorial nobility gradually seizes power "with the patience and obedience of the people" (2.61), leading to aristocratic over-reach and a coup (2.62) that is met by a second secession, a "massive revolution and change of the whole republic" (*maxima perturbatio et totius commutatio rei publicae*, 2.63). Scipio defends this period later in the dialogue as a period when the people rose up in revolt to reclaim their property (3.44), recalling Cicero's celebration of the plebeians' "restoration of their ancient laws and liberties" in the *pro Cornelio* of 65.[46]

According to Peter Brunt, Cicero conceded to the people in the second book of his *Republic* "only a sufficient appearance of liberty to keep them content, not a share in real power (2.50)."[47] But Brunt's selective quotation destroys Cicero's point, which is rather the opposite. By giving the people a "little bit of liberty, as Lycurgus and Romulus did," Cicero says, "you will not satiate them with it, but you will set them on fire with desire for liberty, when you have given them only a limited capacity of tasting it; and meanwhile, that fear will always hang heavily over them, that an unjust king will arrive on the scene—as very often happens" (*inperti etiam populo potestatis aliquid, ut et Lycurgus et Romulus: non satiaris eum libertate, sed incenderis cupiditate libertatis, cum tantum modo potestatem gustandi feceris; ille quidem semper inpendebit timor, ne rex, quod plerumque evenit, exsistat iniustus*, 2.50). This passage does not prescribe deceit; it describes the historical and psy-

---

44 On Caesar's plans for the temple, *CAH* IX. 407.

45 Mommsen, *Staatsrecht* vol. ii.1.281.

46 Cicero, *pro Cornelio* fr. 48 Crawford (quoted in Asconius 76C): *leges sacratas ipsi sibi restituerunt*. Wiseman points out that Cicero's wording may be a homage to a speech delivered by the radically populist tribune (and possibly historian) Licinius Macer, as "recorded" by Sallust.

47 Brunt, "The fall of the Roman republic," 55.

chological motivation of the Roman people at a particular moment in history, when their limited experience of freedom sharpens their fear of oppression.

Several points may now be made about Cicero's representation of republican politics in *Republic* 2. First, class antagonism is the very condition of Rome's existence, with the exercise of power occurring only in the context of a periodic and repeated contest.[48] It cannot be understood as something to be brushed aside (a consistent strategy in today's obscurantist political discourse). By highlighting the theme, though, I do not mean to imply that class antagonism is an important issue, a problem that effective political deliberation can and should solve. My purpose is rather to consider how this changes our understanding of where, for Cicero, politics begins and where it ends. No defender of republican politics (as he idiosyncratically understands it), Jacques Rancière illuminates *Republic* 2 when he argues that

> the setting-up of politics is identical to the institution of the class struggle. The class struggle is not the secret motor of politics or the hidden truth behind appearances. It is politics itself.... This is not to say that politics exists because social groups have entered into battle over their divergent interests. The torsion or twist that causes politics to occur is also what establishes each class as being different from itself.[49]

This is how the republic is always both unified (as a political collective) and divided—because it is a political collective. The *res* that is *publica* is both an object of ownership by the people, as Scipio comments in a well-known passage, and an agreement or a partnership (*consensus ac societas coetus*, *Rep.* 3.43).

Cyclical in nature, the antagonism of Roman politics is never resolved. The power-sharing arrangement is never stable and consensus is never finally authorized. The second point, then, is that *concordia* comes into existence as a "temporary result of a provisional hegemony," and it always generates some remainder that returns to haunt and overturn the arrangement from within.[50] It is a translation of the Greek *homonoia*, like-mindedness, a bond that exists between senate and people that mandates treatment of the

---

48 Lefort, *Democracy and Political Theory*, 225.
49 Rancière, *Disagreement*, 18.
50 Mouffe, *The Democratic Paradox*, 104.

antagonist as legitimate adversaries. This is not necessarily a rational relation: indeed Cicero acknowledges that the people's demands are legitimate
despite the fact that he views their increase in intensity as irrational (*tamen
vincit ipsa rerum publicarum natura saepe rationem, Rep.* 2.57).

Concord is thus well suited for the temporality of republican electoral
politics, that is, as a momentary goal in a liquid narrative of power shifts and
flows, rather than a static condition. The temporal element is significant.
Book 2 opens with Scipio's declaration that Rome is multiply constituted
over time rather than in a single moment of constitution making (2.2). According to the elder Cato (an authoritative figure of the past), this makes the
Roman *civitas* superior to others, including Sparta's and Athens', because
"our republic was constituted not from the genius of a single man, but
many, nor in a single human lifetime, but over the course of many centuries
and ages" (2.2). Cicero objects to the Athenian identification of sovereignty
and autonomy with presence and immediacy, suggesting that Rome is
stronger because its very foundation (as well as its ongoing practices) is extended, repeated, and repeatable, not an instantaneous process.[51] Stretched-
out time and repeated cycles in time, important thematic elements in his
history, soften elements of urgency and violence in the narrative. We start to
glimpse a different notion of sovereignty in play at Rome: not simply a legitimating or authorizing will that exercises itself in elections or (in the case
of the legally binding *plebiscita*) yes/no votes on legislation; but as a con-
tinuum of power repeatedly reauthorized in multiple sites of conflict and
judgment (including in contexts not authorized by the elite).[52]

Third, and importantly for a theorist often taken to be a defender of elite
privilege, Cicero's framing of Roman history as serial conflict suggests that
political authority is a product of communal recognition in an antagonistic
context. He takes the people's power to be irreducible, and *Republic* 2 presents political legitimacy as authorized by the people's will. Yielding to the
people's power "wisely," as Cicero says, does not mean the nobility admit
defeat or are converted to the people's position through argument. They
yield in order to transform "antagonism into agonism," as Mouffe puts it, to
defuse the potential for violence and agree on a temporary compromise
that allows for disagreement to re-establish itself on agonistic grounds.[53]
Here, though I am departing from Cicero's text and venturing into political

---

51   Ibid, 34.
52   Urbinati, *Democratic Representation*, 20. On *circuli*, see Peter O'Neill, "Going around
in circles: popular speech in ancient Rome."
53   Mouffe, *The Democratic Paradox*, 104; also *On the Political*, 20–21.

psychology, it is tempting to view slaves and foreigners on the borders of the empire as groups ready-made to be the recognizable others against which the citizen community might aggressively define itself, temporarily containing internal antagonism.

Let me return to the notion of resistibility I raised in my discussion of Pettit's republicanism and Michael Fried's reaction to minimalist art. If legitimate authority must be subject to contest, it must be resistible. This explains why, in *Laws*, which locates the ultimate source of legitimacy in divine natural law, Cicero nonetheless defends the principle of resistibility in worldly law. In *Laws*, Cicero says that the origin of law is the *vis deorum immortalium*, "the power of the immortal gods" (*Leg.* 1.21; "the law is eternal," *Leg.* 2.8), but his articulation of the relation between the divine and the action of worldly political authority tellingly turns on a metaphor of speech: *vereque dici potest magistratum legem esse loquentem, legem autem mutum magistratum*, "One can say truly that the magistrate is a speaking law, and the law a mute magistrate" (*Leg.* 2.2). The commands of the magistrates must be just and they must be obeyed, and the magistrates may punish disobedience "unless the people prohibit it" (3.6); trials must be held before the people, especially when the death penalty is involved (3.11). In Cicero's version of Roman foundation, the legitimacy of authority finds its source in the realms of appearance and absolutes; it is both performative and constative. Even his appeals to the constative and eternal are laid out in the context of resistibility: his choice of a dialogue form for his work on politics means that his characters can testify to the resistibility of the constative anchor of "the law."

Indeed the definition of "power" in theory and practice is itself a matter of contestation in Cicero's writing and in Roman politics. Aristotle's *Politics* famously devotes its first book to articulating multiple forms of household rule (husband over wife, father over children, master over slaves) that form the pattern for his understanding of power. By contrast, Cicero works with many conceptions of power; there is no single Latin word for it, but a host of terms: *potestas, auctoritas, imperium, potentia, dominatio, vis*. Each of these is normative, but each is also constantly contested within a highly particularized set of political, social, religious, familial, and economic conditions.

Fourth, Ciceronian concord is a resolution to conflict whose cyclical form does not destroy but renews and strengthens the political association. By the same token, the senate and people do not view one another merely as rivals who may be reconciled through negotiation or deliberation. Cicero acknowledges the permanence of the antagonistic dimension of the conflict between senate and people, while also seeking the temporary possibility of its non-violent channeling.

How to channel antagonism while preserving resistibility? An ensemble of institutions, practices, and dispositions gradually takes shape that channels violence into less destabilizing forms of engagement, but these do not depoliticize antagonism nor do they resolve its cause. Instead advocacy, adversarial and often aggressive in nature, emerges as a crucial political strategy for both senate and people, but especially the people. Scipio's history of Rome suggests that the solution to the question rests in the figure of the advocate, institutionalized in the office of the tribunate. This solution is defended in the *Republic*'s partner treatise, *Laws*, and developed further in Cicero's rhetorical work, which presents the orator-advocate as the ideal citizen. It is to advocacy that I will turn briefly at the end of this chapter, and again in chapter 4.

MAKING THE REPUBLIC SENSIBLE

First, though, there is more to say about Scipio's story. I want to return to a key point in his account of pre-republican history, where the king Servius Tullius divides the populace into classes.

> ...eighteen of the greatest wealth. Then, after choosing a large number of *equites* out of all the people, Servius distributed the rest of the citizens into five classes, and divided the older from the younger. He made this division in such a way that the greatest number of votes belonged not to the multitude but to those in possession of rich resources, and he took care—which ought always to be maintained in the republic—lest the greatest number have the most power. If his set-up were not already known to you, I would explain it; but you see that the system is such that the centuries of *equites* with their six votes, and the first class, with the addition of the century of carpenters which adds the greatest utility to the city, add up to 89 centuries; and out of a total of 104 centuries, for that is the number left, should only eight centuries add to the 89, the whole power of the people would come together, and the remaining multitude of 96 centuries, which contain by far the most men, would neither be shut out from the vote, for that would be over-reach, nor be too powerful, lest that be dangerous. In this Servius took special care even with titles and names, for he called the rich 'money-givers,' because they paid the expenses of the state, and named those who had less than 1500 denarii or nothing at all except their own heads, 'child-givers,' to give the im-

pression that offspring, that is to say, the children of the *civitas*, were expected of them. A number of individuals which was almost larger than that contained in the whole first class was placed in every one of the 96 centuries of the proletarian class. Thus while no one was deprived of the vote, the most power in the vote was in the hands of those to whom it was most important that the *civitas* be in the best condition.

... duodeviginti censu maximo. deinde equitum magno numero ex omni populi summa separato, relicuum populum distribuit in quinque classis, senioresque a iunioribus divisit, easque ita disparavit ut suffragia non in multitudinis sed in locupletium potestate essent, curavitque, quod semper in re publica tenendum est, ne plurimum valeant plurimi. quae discriptio si esset ignota vobis, explicaretur a me; nunc rationem videtis esse talem, ut equitum centuriae cum sex suffragiis et prima classis, addita centuria quae ad summum usum urbis fabris tignariis est data, LXXXVIIII centurias habeat; quibus e centum quattuor centuriis—tot enim reliquae sunt—octo solae si accesserunt, confecta est vis populi universa, reliquaque multo maior multitudo sex et nonaginta centuriarum neque excluderetur suffragiis, ne superbum esset, nec valeret nimis, ne esset periculosum. (40) in quo etiam verbis ac nominibus ipsis fuit diligens; qui cum locupletis assiduos appellasset ab asse dando, eos qui aut non plus mille quingentos aeris aut omnino nihil in suum censum praeter caput attulissent, proletarios nominavit, ut ex iis quasi proles, id est quasi progenies civitatis, expectari videretur. illarum autem sex et nonaginta centuriarum in una centuria tum quidem plures censebantur quam paene in prima classe tota. ita nec prohibebatur quisquam iure suffragii, et is valebat in suffragio plurimum, cuius plurimum intererat esse in optimo statu civitatem ... (2.39)

This passage defends the wealthiest classes' domination of politics: their votes will always outweigh those of the poor. It also presents a key step in the formation of the republic in the form of a detailed image: the image of the republic as an ordered system. As it happens, Servius Tullius himself is not the product of political order: he came to power when the elder Tarquinius was assassinated, he deceived the people for a period of time about Tarquinius' death, and he began to rule not by formal command of the people, as earlier kings had done, but by their informal wish and consent (*regnare coepissent non iussu, sed voluntate atque concessu civium*, 2.28). Yet Servius' division of the republic persisted and, *mutatis mutandis*, shaped electoral and legislative practice until Cicero's lifetime and beyond.

So this image of a divided unity is one element that connects monarchical to republican politics: it is something the community has in common throughout the period of change. It represents, Rancière would say, a common, shared partition of the sensible: it is an image that becomes *common sense*. Political roles (including the values of these roles) are distributed according to the dividing lines of economic standing—a partition of sense that determines whether and how people literally become recognizable as citizens. This distribution is aesthetic, in so far as it involves creating an ideal image of the republic that comes to make political sense of the material conditions of life.

As the republic matures, the conflict between the senators and the people is repeatedly marked by scenes that draw attention to the function of appearances in the re-establishment of order after conflict. Publius Valerius orders the fasces to be lowered when he speaks to the people and avoids building a house at the top of the hill where King Tullius had lived (2.53). Publicola orders the axes to be removed from the fasces and modifies the employment of the lictors when an older man is elected as his co-consul (55). These men are "models" (*exempla*, 55) to which the rest of his narrative, Scipio says, must conform.

I lay great emphasis on these moments in *Republic* 2 because they suggest the deep link in Cicero's thinking between appearance—what one appears to be in front of others, or how a certain instrument like the fasces appears in the public eye—and the preservation of political order. This suits the tenor of Roman life as he represents it, from the speeches given in the senate and the Forum and the importance of the audience's reaction (in Cicero's rhetorical dialogues and his own speeches), to the requirement that citizens be physically present in the city in order to vote, to the variety of social interactions described in lyric and satire wherein (as we shall see in chapter 3) visible presence is deeply valued and attention is lavished on the appearance of men to one another. This link goes beyond the basic insight that "appearance matters." It suggests that political thinking involves the senses, or more precisely, dividing the body and its organs of perception and sensation, and assigning them roles in the making of political sense.

It is important that we see the biases at work in Cicero's hierarchy of the senses. In his orations, the good men or *boni* use vision and hearing to inform their prudential judgments, judgments they communicate to one another in common, in public and sometimes in private, using the privilege they have to speak. This process of sensing, judging, and communicating takes place in the context of plenitude. The people, subsisting in a context of deprivation, may feel hunger or other needs that there is no way to voice, as these needs have no part in the partition of the sensible that accompanies and corresponds with the partition of property. When Cicero asks the Roman people in his speech on the Manilian law to authorize the granting of emergency powers to Pompey, he asks them to look at Pompey, to hear Cicero's rehearsals of his virtues. When Cicero warns the people against the tribune Rullus' agrarian reforms, he asks them to remember past occasions on which noble factions seized power without limit or accountability; he asks them to feel the loss of their liberty, a pseudo-sensation which, tellingly, Cicero does not locate anywhere in the body. What he does not ask them to feel is their material want. Feeling hunger, for Cicero, is not a political sensation.[54]

In her work on the relationship between literary experiment and ideals of national community, Jacqueline Rose explores the significance of fantasy in political life and action, particularly in the traumatized cases of post-Holocaust Israel/Palestine and postcolonial Africa. She acutely describes the "fierce blockading protectiveness" that "walls up all around our inner and outer, psychic and historical, selves" and transforms blindness toward oppressed groups into hatred and disdain for them. In my reading of Cicero as a theorist of antagonism, I do not intend to conceal how antagonism functions in his own writings and speeches as an oppressive force. Antagonism is not in itself a virtue.[55]

ADVOCACY AND FREEDOM

Politics exists because those who have no right to be counted as speaking beings make themselves of some account, setting up a community by the fact of placing in common a wrong that is nothing

---

54   Consider how Terry Eagleton rejects sensation as a viable part of class politics in recent work in which he claims that when it comes to class, culture is "an optional extra." "Value, speech, image, experience and identity," he says in *After Theory*, "are ... the very language of political struggle ... in all ethnic or sexual politics. Ways of feeling and forms of representation are in the long run quite as crucial as childcare provision or equal pay.... [*This is not*] *quite so true of traditional class politics*." But Cicero's *Republic* suggests that ways of feeling and forms of representation are precisely what is important in understanding where politics begins, and what its central struggle will always be.

55   Andreas Kalyvas explores Arendt's response to revolution, and in particular the threat of violence (which destroys politics) in *Democracy and the Politics of the Extraordinary*, 235–47.

more than this very confrontation, the contradiction of two worlds in a single world: the world where they are and the world where they are not, the world where there is something "between" them and those who do not acknowledge them as speaking beings who count and the world where there is nothing.[56]

As we might guess by now, after tracing the cyclical violence in Scipio's early history of the republic, the partition of the citizenry by Servius does not guarantee liberty. Far from it. His distribution of the sensible by rein-scribing economic difference as political parts of the body politic creates a legitimate order that contains the people even as it counts them. The *populus Romanus* becomes vulnerable to the interplay of senatorial machinations and combinations of energies and interests beyond their control. The constitution risks becoming, and in the case of the decemvirs (*Rep.* 2.63) actually becomes, an institution of injustice. The solution is the tribunate (2.59).

"It does not escape me how great are the resources of the nobility which I, solitary, powerless, in the empty shell of a magistracy [the tribunate], I will try to expel from power (*dominatione*)." So says Macer in Sallust's *Histories* (3.48.3).[57] To Cicero, too, the tribunate exists to counter attempts by the senatorial order to dominate the people, but the tribunes also resist the extremes to which the people might go (*Leg.* 3.23–24). According to Sallust, Cicero, and other historians, the tribunate originates in the course of the first secession of the plebs (traditionally dated to 494 bce), when the plebeians elected spokesmen, named them "tribunes" (probably in imitation of a military title), and swore an oath to protect them from senatorial violence.[58] Tribunes enjoyed official "sacrosanctity," meaning that violence against them met with severe reprisals, a status they exploited when they interfered aggressively with senatorial proceedings, and even in public, for example, when they exercised their powers of arrest (Vell. 2.24.2, Cicero *Leg. Agr.* 2.101). "The physical element in the use of sacrosanctity to effect obstruc-

---

56   Rancière, *Disagreement*, 27.

57   On class conflict, see Sallust, *Jugurtha* 5.1–2, 31.9–10, 41.7, 85.19–22; *Catiline* 12.2, 20.9.

58   Livy 2.23–33, Sallust, *Hist.* 1.11; Dionysius *AR* 5.63ff. On the number of tribunes, their family and class origins, and their changing status vis-à-vis the senate over time, see Lintott, *The Constitution of the Roman Republic*, 32–33, 121–22, with further references. Collective memory of the secession provided compelling material even for conservative pro-senatorial politicians, such as the consul Catulus, who called his supporters to leave the city for a nearby hilltop (Plutarch, *Pompey*, 30.4).

tion was patent."[59] Their duties were formalized acts of resistance to the potentially tyrannical actions of the senate: their veto could prevent the senate from meeting and obstruct the outcome of any debate in the *curia* (Polybius 6.16.4). The *intercessio* was an aggressive method of resisting other magistrates or providing protection to a citizen who complained of magistricial interference. The citizen's appeal (*provocatio*) for the tribune's help (*auxilium*) sometimes led to collective consultation, and if this occurred in the public eye, as many early examples of tribunician assistance appear in Roman historiography, the people's opinion might sway the tribunes' action (e.g., Livy 8.32–35).

Cicero views the tribunate as an essential element in the Roman constitution because it is a guardian of liberty (*Leg. Agr.* 2.15) and because it figures resistance on multiple fronts.[60] In *Laws*, Cicero defends the virtuous role of the tribunate in protecting popular interests as a key element in sustaining senatorial legitimacy. His brother Quintus, arguing that the office of the tribunate foments sedition among the people (3.19), declares that the dictator Sulla was right to take away the tribunes' power (3.22). "There were the two Gracchi!" Cicero imagines his brother crying out, referring to the two brothers who served as tribunes in 133 and 123 BCE, and whose agrarian and judicial measures on behalf of the people led to their deaths at the hands of a group of senators and their followers. "Yes," Cicero tells Quintus, "and many more than the Gracchi," but the evil they represent is also a good (*sed bonum ... sine isto malo non haberemus*, 3.23; cf. 25).[61] He hopes that the tribunes will channel the will of the people according to the authority of the leading men, or that the latter will serve in the tribunate in a relation of antagonism buffering the people's rash will (3.26).

Cicero's guarded defense of the tribunate's responsibilities in voicing and channeling popular will in *Laws* takes a stronger form in his many comments on the speeches delivered in the non-voting public meetings called *contiones*. Such a meeting could be summoned by elected magistrates; ordinary citizens could legally neither summon a *contio* nor speak at one unless invited to do so by the presiding magistrate (contrast the civic right

---

59   Lintott, *Constitution*, 125.

60   On the potential for a renewed form of the tribunate to play a role in contemporary democratic politics, see McCormick, *Machiavellian Democracy*, 171–88.

61   In *de Oratore* 1, one interlocutor argues that eloquence causes evil as well as good, and his proof is the Gracchi, eloquent evil-doers (1.38). Tellingly, the main speaker Crassus never responds to Scaevola, but reduces his objections to a single point about the scope of the orator's knowledge—suggesting with an approving reference to the orator's capacity to rouse emotion (1.60) that the Gracchi are knowledgeable citizens.

of *isegoria* or free speech in Athens). Tribunes commonly addressed the people in *contiones* held in the Forum, usually standing on the steps of the temple of Castor and Pollux or on the Rostra, a high (at least three meters) and heavily decorated curved stone platform placed in front of the *curia* overlooking the Forum. Embodying the senate/people conflict in stone, on the Rostra stood numerous statues commemorating elite achievement alongside a statue of Marsyas unchained, a symbol of the legislation that early in Rome's history made debt-slavery illegal.[62]

Cicero equates the force (*vis*) of the people with the *contio* (*Q. fr.* 1.22.7; *pro Flacc.* 16).[63] In his own *contiones* and speeches defending men accused in cases that brought them before the popular assembly serving as jury, he describes it as the site where tribunes "defend your cause" (*qui vestram causam defenderent, Man. Leg.* 2; cf. *Verr.* 1.45) and celebrates the dynamism the *contio* injects into Roman politics.[64] Delivering speeches before the people helps to restrain "the powerful few" who wage extraordinary influence over policy and law, protecting popular liberty (*Leg. Agr.* 2.6–7). His provocative comparison between the *contio* and the theater and the games draws out the significant role played by emotion and spectacle in legitimating and channeling conflict (*scaena, de Orat.* 2.338; cf. *Amic.* 95–97). He privileges these areas of contest and resistibility—hyperbole, melodrama, gossip, comedy, spectacle—as the partners of the forum and the law court: all sites of reconstituting the republic through the temporary resolution of antagonism.

Defense of popular liberty is not only the task of the tribune. Cicero casts himself as that defender in his own *contiones* and law court speeches. In his analysis of these texts, Robert Morstein-Marx criticizes Cicero for avoiding the pros and cons of the legislative or juridical questions at hand: instead, he says, Cicero presents himself tendentiously as deserving credibility as a devoted guardian of the people's interests. He praises the Gracchi, poses as the defender of the people against the machinations of the rich nobility, and "mouths the central 'popular' slogans and catchwords" including *libertas*—a word used twenty-two times in a single speech before the people (*Leg. Agr.* 2).[65] Morstein-Marx concludes that there is no ideological competition in the *contio* and that authentic advocacy on the part of popu-

---

62   Coarelli, *Il foro romano*, 97–100.

63   Morstein-Marx, *Popular Oratory*, is the authoritative discussion. On the *contio*'s role in expressing popular will, see Eralda Noè, "Per la formazione del consenso nella Roma del 1 sec. a.C." Mouritsen calls the *contio* "the effective symbolic manifestation of the sovereignty of the people over the senate" in *Plebs and Politics*, 13–14.

64   On this trope: Sallust *Cat.* 38.3.

65   Morstein-Marx, *Popular Oratory*, 215–27.

lar interests was thus severely limited. What the people got were "paternal-
istic ideals of solicitude for the People and their interests on which all ostensibly agreed."[66]

Critics like Morstein-Marx are correct to point out that in practice, Cicero and other senators sought to exploit the antagonistic system he describes in his theoretical work by claiming (dubiously) that their motives
and those of the people were synonymous. My point is that there is a consistent thread in Cicero's claims in his speeches: that contional oratory
made the social and economic divide between senate and people a political
issue, and it drew to the fore the need for the people to defend themselves
against the manipulations of the rich. That everyone used this rhetoric (true
popularis or not) speaks *for* its centrality to the republican conception of
liberty and its essential vulnerability, and the need for antagonism between
senate and people to check the manipulations of the rich. While Roman
politics is never a matter of representation in the modern sense of authority
vested in elected representatives, we should see Cicero's preoccupation with
the contest of politics as an account of politics as contested representation:
the contested representation of terms, laws, characters, and peoples. Who
speaks? Who is given the opportunity to resist?

This explains Cicero's choice, in his rhetorical treatises, of the advocate-
orator as the model for the ideal citizen. The contest in the Forum and the
law court, the historical refuge of those suffering injustice, also mandates
the orator's moral responsibility. As Cicero explains most passionately in his
midcareer law court speeches, such as the orations against Verres, and his
consular speeches, especially *Catilinarians*, political action involves a willingness to make oneself vulnerable, to risk the sacrifice that brings glory in
perpetuity. The real challenge is to bring the struggles through which the
republic is in turn weakened and strengthened into institutions—especially
the law court, and to a lesser degree the public assembly, both of which Cicero sees as incubators of inevitable public strife (intra-elite in the case of
the courts; between elite and mass in the case of the assemblies). But the law
court and assembly are more than pressure valves for civic strife. By the
forceful logic of Cicero's view of politics as antagonism, and his association
of the temporary resolution of conflict with reconstitution, the republic is
repeatedly renewed through the channeled violence of forensic and deliberative argument.[67]

66   Ibid., 207.
67   I explore this further in my discussion of "law enforcement through language" in
The State of Speech, 70–71.

This is not to deny the obvious point that this account of oratory is self-serving.[68] But for a claim to be self-serving does not mean it is not intended to unlock potential—in this case, the ability of the orator to articulate resistance. Moreover, there is a more provocative point at stake. Importantly, and relevantly for us today, for Cicero the violence of forensic argument has the power to unsettle institutions. This is treated as a matter of moral prescription in Cicero's Verrine orations, written for his prosecution of the rapacious governor Verres for maladministration of his province, Sicily. In these speeches, Cicero presents himself as the model litigious citizen and the litigious citizen as the model for republican citizenship in general. The thrust of Cicero's argument in the *Verrines* is that the institutionalization of senatorial power has done almost irreparable harm to its legitimacy (1.7–9, 1.16–32, 2.4). Having removed themselves by law from the oversight once guaranteed through the participation of non-senators in the jury, the senators no longer police their own, and "it is openly and straightforwardly said that today the law courts are nothing" (*aperte iam ac perspicue nulla esse iudicia*, 1.20). If they are to avoid further popular unrest and deliver themselves from "hatred, resentment, dishonor, and disgrace" they must be subjected to litigious violence (1.43; cf. 2.22–23). The people demand advocates and their demand is justified (1.44).

Cicero's prosecution of the tyrannical governor is a procedure that disrupts the institutionalization of law, insisting on the need for dynamic action in its addressing of a wrong. The *Verrines* go beyond mere adversarial politics. Cicero constructs himself and the court as members of a litigious community in which the citizen properly takes the part of those who have no part—to pick up on a key exhortation in Jacques Rancière's redefinition of the political.[69] Nira Yuval-Davis describes the practices of Bolognese feminists who invite people together who live in difficult places such as Palestine to cultivate *taking* part, participating in what they have no part in, speaking where they are not meant to.[70] Similarly, Cicero's strategy in the *Verrines* was to introduce evidence from Verres' victims—giving provincial victims their day in a Roman court. He secures a crowd of witnesses and testimony (2.16) and instead of following the regular procedure by which

68   See now Hölkeskamp, "Self-serving sermons: oratory and the self-construction of the Roman aristocrat," in *Praise and Blame in Roman Republican Rhetoric*, 17–34.
69   Note that here, speaking on behalf of others is able to trump the immediate solidarity of political class: Cicero defends a collection of well-off and middling Sicilians against the rich Verres and his powerful senatorial friends on the jury—to Cicero's political advantage, to be sure (he gained great notoriety with this case).
70   Yuval-Davis, "Human/women's rights and feminist transversal politics," 280–82.

the advocates deliver long set speeches, he emphasizes the agonistic element, bringing in witnesses to testify, allowing for questioning and response (2.24–26).

The *Verrines* develop a key insight of the *Republic*, that consensus—whether it is elite or popular, the former being the most relevant issue in Roman politics—comes with risks that, unchecked, create injustice and overbalance the state. In the post-Sullan years, when the senators have aggregated juridical powers to themselves, they assume that all parties to the dispute are known "in a world in which everything is on show, in which parties are counted with none left over."[71] As the post-Sullan court collects authority and legitimacy in a single site, the jury, it drains public resistibility until the domain of the public threatens to erupt in revolt. This is a version of consensual post-politics that resembles our own today, where parties are assumed to count and stand for nearly all the citizenry and those left over are pure excess with no part in politics, and hence not worth the citizenry's thought. My point is not to compare the wronged well-off Sicilians with the disenfranchised citizens of today. It is rather to draw out the republican habit of flagging and resisting the tendency of selective participatory institutions or organizations gradually to lean toward policing over politics, even while they imply "a common purpose, joint action, a framework of shared values, continuous interaction and the wish to achieve collective benefits."[72]

ENVISIONING THE REPUBLIC

In a recent critique of Cambridge School republicanism, John McCormick asks: "Does elite control require class conflict in addition to general elections?"[73] He suggests via Machiavelli and Ian Shapiro that socioeconomic and political conflict may forge stronger allegiances than the pursuit of consensus.[74] I have argued here that Cicero's account of consensus in his *Republic* and of advocacy in the *Laws* and his rhetorical and oratorical works supports an answer in the affirmative.

---

71   Rancière, *Disagreement*, 102.

72   For further discussion of Rancière's thinking and a constructive response, see Erik Swyngedouw, "Where is the political?," especially 15–16, quoted here.

73   McCormick, "Machiavellian democracy: controlling elites with ferocious populism," 310.

74   On the strength created by conflict: Machiavelli, *Disc.* 1.6; on dissensus over consensus, Shapiro, *Democracy's Place*, 14–15.

I began with Michael Fried's critique of minimalist art, which illuminates an essential aspect of Roman politics in practice and theory: resistibility. Late republican and imperial accounts of the early legendary history
of Rome are filled with figures that turn themselves away or transpose
themselves between: sometimes in the act of creating revolution (the secession of the plebs), more often in the process of blocking or obstructing in
order to create conditions for political change. In the art gallery as in the
Forum, the resistible unfolds itself in the realm of the symbolic: it creates
the grounds on which common convictions are transformed, values are re-
oriented, and new political identities and allegiances are constructed. To say
that politics is eternally and inevitably an agonistic process implies that resistibility is a necessary element of freedom.[75]

I have argued that in Cicero's framing of political history as antagonism
punctuated by temporary compromises he represents political action as advocacy and accountability: the making of demands, the scrutiny and checking of institutions and institutionalization.[76] This politics is contestatory,
resistant, and dynamic; it is not reducible to a theory of community, dialogue, consensus; but nor it is reducible to a theory grounded in violence
and oppression. Cicero theorizes political authority as part of a broader conception of political action that privileges the virtuosic display of a speaker
whose authority must be resistible and whose legitimacy is subject to public consensus. His speech channels antagonism into institutions whose nature is essentially contestatory, far different from the kind of institutions
that provide a comfortable lap for the settling of authority. The action of
speech is never isolated; it is always part of a community; and one element
of necessary disruption arises from the welcome that speech can provide to
non-traditional members of the community, even "the uninitiated" (*de Orat.*
1.12). The legitimacy, indeed the inevitability of resistance is thus built into
Cicero's understanding of republican authority and order.

Where does conflict end? As the rivalry between Pompey and Caesar
through the 50s gave rise to increasingly violent conflicts in the streets of

75   Resistibility offers resources for thinking about freedom and about a sort of political change that is not the radical change of utopia, dictatorship, or mass revolutionary rupture,
in the terms laid out by Andreas Kalyvas in *The Politics of the Extraordinary*. For Kalyvas, extraordinary politics are tentatively construed as involving "high levels of collective mobilization,
extensive popular support for some fundamental changes; the emergence of irregular and informal public spaces; the formation of extra-institutional and antistatist movements directly
challenge the established balance of forces, the prevailing politicosocial status quo, the state
legality, and the dominant value system" (11–12).

76   Also in Cicero, and problematic: the willingness to risk oneself in exchange for the
future.

Rome and ultimately a bloody civil war, ending with Caesar's seizure of autocratic power after Pompey's death in 48, Cicero grew increasingly pre-occupied with the tendency of conflict to explode into violence. His *pro Marcello*, a speech I will discuss in chapter 5, powerfully articulates his view that speech, even under repressive conditions, preserves the space of resist-ibility to repression and violence. A quasi-panegyric to Caesar for granting clemency to an adherent of Pompey, the speech opens with what is now a familiar Ciceronian account of internal division. In 44 BCE, when this speech was delivered, Cicero had only reluctantly decided to break his long civil war silence. Ultimately, Cicero's defense of Marcellus is an apologia for oratory, an advocate's argument for the perpetuation of the field of political action over and against violence.

Now there are two objections against my argument here that deserve consideration. First, Cicero used language to incite rage, hatred, and vio-lence against his enemies. In speeches I have not mentioned—the *Catilinar-ians*, precursors to Cicero's decision to execute citizens without trial; the *pro Caelio*, where he viciously attacks Clodia, sister of his political enemy Clo-dius; the *Philippics*, famously vitriolic outpourings against Mark Antony; and others—he exploits his skills to turn audiences against his targets. These texts are more than important signs of the difference between theory and practice, or even the space between fantasy and theory. They put before us the lived danger of a republic in its end times, by showing us a writer whose efforts to secure his state were failing. And they remind us of the limits of normative theorizing. There is no way to ignore how Cicero exploits vio-lence for his own ends; were we to erase the moments when we glimpse those excesses and failures, we would make Cicero's republican life vacuous, a blanked-out canvas.[77]

I have so far emphasized the normative aspects of Cicero's thinking, which (like the articulation of most political and moral ideals) have the flavor of fantasy. I have described his work in terms of channeling violence, suturing ruptures. But it is also necessary to consider Cicero's *Republic* and philosophical treatises in light of their historical context, as a desperate ef-fort to heal breaches he himself had opened wide. I have argued that perma-nent concord makes no sense as a meaningful goal in Cicero's thinking; but if we see his philosophical work as part of his effort late in life to stabilize

---

77   I am reminded of Jacques Lezra's warning against the "blanked out, emptied, vacu-ous" expressions of solidarity with New Yorkers and with Americans that the international media reported after 9/11—expressions that by erasing and ignoring tensions, ultimately wors-ened them (*Wild Materialism*, 60).

an intense conflict that was out of control, it may remind us of the need to create our own stabilizers in intellectual and political work.

Perhaps even more potentially devastating to my argument here is the fact of the foundational place of slavery and xenophobia in the Roman republic. Turn for a moment to the American context. Consider what kind of country Alexis de Tocqueville saw: sprawling, aggressively egalitarian, diverse, inventive, competitive, patriotic, commerce-obsessed, materialistic, friendly, complacent, religious, both proudly xenophilic—welcoming outsiders when "they" make "us" better[78]—and intensely xenophobic, when "their" outsider values threaten "us." White men dominated all levels of government, and the higher the office the richer they were. Much has *not* changed since Tocqueville came to visit us in the 1830s. In that era, as we saw, genuine conflicts of interest were aired through hot debate where accusations of anti-Americanism abounded. Since then, the nature of the body politic has grown more inclusive. But this means that real conflicts of interest between rich and poor, urban and rural, white and non-white, have been transformed into psychologically and culturally laden anxieties over national identity: the culture wars. On the left and the right, the boundaries of permissible political disagreement have narrowed: it has become harder to see and debate issues clearly.[79]

To have a democratic politics where a plurality of views can circulate and be taken seriously, but where agreement on action must be reached, everyone has to accustom themselves to losing every once in a while (and perhaps often). Clearly, Pettit concluded, we need norms in place for political opinions and judgments: they must be based not on whim or sentiment, but reasoned deliberation undertaken in a civil mood. "In the general run, of course," he says in a sentence I quoted above, "people will be civil out of the sheer habit of civility."[80] Now in many, perhaps most, aspects of American life, basic civility reigns. My neighbors in New York might be prejudiced against my southern-accented cousins in Florida; my cousins might be suspicious of the pretensions of my urban and urbane friends. But as far as these things go, friends and cousins are likely to be civil toward one an-

---

78   Honig, *Boston Review*: http://www.bostonreview.net/BR27.6/honig.html.

79   "Both the postwar Soviet Union and the radical labor movement of [the 1910s] posed genuine threats to dominant interests in American society. . . . There were also real conflicts of interest between white Americans and peoples of color. But the countersubversive response transformed interest conflicts into psychologically based anxieties over national security and American identity. Exaggerated responses . . . narrowed the bounds of permissible political disagreement and generated a national-security state." (Michael Rogin, *Ronald Reagan, the Movie: and Other Episodes in American Political Demonology*, 68)

80   Pettit, *Republicanism*, 254.

other if they meet, say, at a party in my apartment. But what if they met across the lines in angry demonstrations where racist signs are waved or where talk is dominated by a vision of a state split in two, like Tubero's two suns?

How can we reconcile these images with the neo-republicanists' sparkling vision of the citizen as an engaged participant in civil debate? Pettit's answer is rather deflating: "we know little or nothing about how to generate widespread civility where it has more or less ceased to exist."[81] I think here of Thomas Jefferson and John Adams, who wrote sadly of their fear that the new republic might break up into factions, and who by the end of their lives were bitterly saddened at the rise of commercial competition and the accompanying decline (as they saw it) of civic virtue. We have the modern descendants of Jefferson and Adams in the recent wave of books and documentaries about "two Americas," red and blue, coast and center.

Which is the real republic—the cohesive community praised by Michael Sandel and Philip Pettit, or the nation divided we see on the news each day? And what kinds of citizen habits are appropriate for each? John Dewey, as we saw, a great worrier about collective identity, argued that the image of the polity we citizens hold in our minds exerts a profound effect on our views of politics and civic duties. It's important to get our political imagery right, Dewey argues, because it fires our imaginations, our intuitions about the horizons of the possible, and it guides our judgments. So it's an important question: is the natural end or best condition of the republic the unified, cohesive community, or it is something else?

In fact, as this chapter has sought to argue, we don't have to choose: choice is impossible. We have to do something harder: we have to live with both. Perhaps the single most interesting thing about the history of the idea of the republic in western political thought is that at any given time the republic is always a double signifier. Just as Rome has always symbolized both heroic self-sacrifice and thrift (the heroic Cincinnatus / George Washington) as well as self-indulgence (Nero / King George), so its ideal condition has been understood on the one hand as unity, consensus, and homogeneity, and on the other, as intense and relentless internal conflict.

We see evidence of this doubling in Machiavelli, Montesquieu, and the American founders, but it finds its roots in ancient texts. In the histories of Sallust and Tacitus, the virtuous Rome is a traditional Rome, and tradition meant unity: a single language, a shared history, communal civic worship, an empire gained under the united leadership of a strong senatorial order

81   Ibid., 253.

that assimilated everything foreign and alien. By contrast, the autocrat-ruled empire was a motley province, where rivers of foreign speech flow like sewers into Roman streets and arbitrary emperors toss positions of power to immigrant freedmen with no Latin.

In this narrative, eighteenth and nineteenth century American thinkers like John Adams and Thomas Jefferson found an exemplary fiction of cultural homogeneity and the terrors of its loss. Faced with the challenge of establishing a nation out of a large, diverse population, they praised the instillation of a common culture as the best strategy for the consolidation of identity. This was America as Rome as assimilation success story, where all the citizens spoke English as the Romans had spoken Latin (and where elites enjoyed the class-specific bond of also knowing French, as elite Romans had also known Greek). This was an American in which citizens farmed the land, worshipped the same god, and voted together in assemblies.

But while John Quincy Adams was at Harvard teaching young elites the virtues of this story, different Americans were latching onto the other story of Rome preserved in ancient sources. In the 1830s, New York City radical Levi Slamm named his paper *The Plebeian*. Labor activists, alluding to two murdered heroes of Roman popular politics, the brothers Gracchi, started signing the name "Gracchus" to columns in working mens' newspapers. An editorial in the mainstream paper the *New Orleans Bee* in August 1834 insisted that the faction of the American Senate had engineered "the prostration of republican liberties," countered by Gaius Gracchus, who "though old, full of holy zeal, stalks the forum and watches over the household gods of freedom." Mike Walsh, a tough Irish-American who ran a gang of Bowery radicals as well as a paper known as *The Subterranean* before he was elected to the New York State Assembly, praised a speech by the late republican general Gaius Marius in the histories of Sallust, in which Marius abused the effeminate nobility and proudly embraced his plain Italian upbringing and rough character: "Let every true Sub carefully read [this speech]. It is as applicable to the present day as it was to the times during which it was delivered. . . . If Gaius Marius were alive today he would be a Sub."[82] According to this narrative, the virtuous Rome is a conflicted Rome, because internal conflict means freedom and strength. As the title of chapter 4 of book 1 of Machiavelli's *Discorsi* puts it: "That the disunion of the Plebs and the Roman Senate made the republic free and powerful." This republicanism is defined by the collective advocacy of interests by both haves and have-nots.

82   All American evidence in Malamud, *Ancient Rome and Modern America*, 53–54, 68.

So it goes in the medieval and early modern period. On the one hand, readers like the Florentine Guicciardini understood aristocrats as the leaders of republican government: he believed that "the few needed the many to save them from corruption, and that when the many accepted the few as their natural leaders they did not cease to display critical judgment or active citizenship."[83] On the other hand, "for Machiavelli, equilibrium, properly understood, is intense socioeconomic antagonism between classes that stops just short of one or the other party's recourse" to violence.[84]

This latter view, putting conflict and class at the center, is the republican tradition that has gone largely unnoticed in the contemporary republicanist revival, the revival that John McCormick rightly calls "Guicciardinian." But my purpose here is not to trawl through history finding more examples. I want, rather, to explore how an image of the ideal republic that has conflict at its heart bears on the interesting question of the habits we, as citizens of a republic, ought to adopt in our civic practice.

Slavoj Žižek says that the goal of social-ideological fantasy is to construct a vision of society that does not exist as such, which is not split by an antagonistic division, in which the relation between its parts is organic, complementary. It is true that in stories like that of Livy's Menenius Agrippa such a vision is presented: a corporatist society as an organic whole, a social body, what Žižek calls "the fundamental ideological fantasy," a "fetish simultaneously denying and embodying the structural impossibility of 'society.'"[85] But we should not make the mistake of identifying Menenius' parable with Livy's vision, and still less with Roman self-understanding. Cicero's writing suggests rather that Rome is a society with antagonism built into it, an antagonism born partly from the extreme contradiction with which Romans live: a dual commitment to freedom and to the hierarchies and inequalities that threaten it. This is the myth of Remus and Romulus, the conflict of the orders.

In her wise book on *American Citizenship*, Judith Shklar reminds us that slavery and the conflict over the role of black Americans as citizens rests at the core of the American experience of citizenship—emphasizing that we are in critical need of habits of thinking that help us deal with deep-seated conflict. She suggests that we must think as citizens from and within "the stress of inherited inequalities," especially arising from race and racial rela-

83   J. G. A. Pocock, *The Machiavellian Moment*, 485.

84   McCormick, "Machiavelli against republicanism: on the Cambridge School's 'Guicciardinian moments,'" 628.

85   Žižek, *The Sublime Object of Ideology*, 126.

tions.[86] And the political theorist Ian Shapiro says, "The reality of dissensus in social life should play a central role in our thinking about ordering social practices justly."[87] I have tried to argue here that Cicero's normative theorizing about the republic and his opportunistic oratory should direct citizens of modern republics to grasp the fundamental role of antagonism in the republic, the importance of the aesthetic in perceiving and imagining the republic, the urgent need to create and preserve the condition of resistibility, and the danger of settled institutions. Many questions remain, not least the dangerous potential slip from disruption to violence, that fall outside my scope. With this, however, I have at least cleared the ground for the following chapters.

86   Shklar, *American Citizenship*, 21–23, 101 (source of the quoted phrase).
87   Shapiro, *Democratic Justice*, 15.

2

JUSTICE IN THE WORLD

THE EXECUTION OF *JUGURTHA*

MAKING JUDGMENTS

LIFE REQUIRES US to make judgments. John Dewey calls those choices to act that affect others "public" judgments.[1] How can we evaluate such public judgments? We are free to use the scale of bad, good, better, best—but this language seems more suited to judgments of exclusively personal interest, where benefits and disadvantages are simpler to weigh. For public matters a scale based on "just" suits better than one based on "good," for justice connotes the distribution of good(s) across the commonwealth. I have in mind here not only judgments made in juries and the voting box but in our daily lives, where our choices of what we eat, how cool or warm we keep our houses, the jobs we take, how we transport ourselves, how we spend our leisure time, and the aspirations we develop, to varying degrees, all bear implications for the community at large. In making these choices, how do we judge what is just? On what basis do we make judgments about how to live with one another in common?

For Hannah Arendt the horrors of the twentieth century made the question of judgment as intensely urgent as it is difficult to contemplate. In an essay that she wrote in the aftermath of the publication of *Eichmann in Jerusalem*, when she was harshly attacked for drawing attention to the role of Jewish councils in the Nazis' transportation of Jews into ghettoes, she reflected on a claim she heard repeated by both Eichmann and, unsettlingly, her own critics. "I was told that judging itself is wrong: no one can judge who had not been there."[2] Whether they sought to defend Jewish leaders or willing "cogs" in the Nazi machine, she concluded, those who resisted passing judgment in these extreme terms were driven by a deep if unacknowledged suspicion that our moral agency is not fully our own.

---

1   Dewey, *The Public and Its Problems*, 15–16, 26–27.
2   Arendt, "Personal responsibility under dictatorship," 18.

Facing the fact that humans are not creatures of God living under his law or beings possessing full and perfect autonomy, Arendt's critics were left doubting altogether both the possibility and the rightness of passing judgment. This represented the supreme danger, she insisted, for the atrophy of the faculty of judgment was precisely what had made the Nazis' crimes possible in the first place.[3]

Such doubt, Arendt decided, could not be succumbed to. "Denken ohne Geländer," "thinking without a banister," is how she described the fearsome yet exhilarating modern condition where we can no longer rely on divinity, nature, or any other metaphysical foundation for our judgments—yet we must make them nonetheless. The evolution of secular and scientific thinking through the nineteenth century, followed by the West's awakening to the horrors of its own colonial oppression, two World Wars, and genocide revealed that the dominant standards for belief and behavior, which for centuries had been unshakeably hooked to divine will or natural law, are in fact no more than the word from which "morality" derives: *mores*, customs, manners. "The few rules and standards according to which men used to tell right from wrong, and which were invoked to judge or justify others and themselves, and whose validity were supposed to be self-evident to every sane person either as a part of divine or of natural law ... all this collapsed overnight."[4]

The problem as Arendt saw it was not that Eichmann and the thousands of people like him had turned their faces away from the immutable commandments of God or from natural law. On the contrary, many who were aware of the extermination camps but chose to cooperate or to do nothing were members of respectable society educated in Christian principles and moral philosophy. Eichmann himself quoted Kant's categorical imperative in the Jerusalem court and insisted he had always tried to live by it. As an example he cited his refusal to give special treatment to Jews with money or

3   Hans Jonas, in *Hannah Arendt: The Recovery of a Public World*, cited in Beiner, "Interpretive essay," 116. In a panel discussion of Arendt's work in 1972, Hans Jonas concluded, "I share with Hannah Arendt the position that we are not in the possession of any ultimates, either by knowledge or by commitment or faith.... However, a part of wisdom is knowledge of ignorance. The Socratic attitude is to know that one does not know. And this realization of our ignorance can be of great practical importance in the exercise of the power of judgment, which is above all related to action in the political sphere.... Our enterprises have an eschatological tendency in them—a built-in utopianism, namely, to move towards ultimate situations. Lacking the knowledge of ultimate values ... we should at least abstain from allowing eschatological situations to come about. This alone is a very practical injunction that we can draw."

4   Arendt, "Some questions of moral philosophy," 50.

influential friends: he had always done his "duty," even when it went against his personal desires.

Arendt concluded that Eichmann's obedience to rules and standards was a key to the problem. The Nazis succeeded partly because their "'new order' was exactly what it said it was—not only gruesomely novel, but, and above all, an *order*."[5] People who habitually appeal to fixed rules are likely to adhere to whatever rules happen to be on offer. And this habit of thoughtless adherence displaces the habit Arendt believed crucial to judgment: conversation with the self, by which she had in mind not a solipsistic form of internal dialogue, but a subjective conversation oriented toward the world in common. This ongoing conversation, like a constant buzz in the active mind, serves to anchor a human existence now unmoored from absolutes.

To elaborate this view, she turned to Kant's *Critique of Judgment*. For Kant, human reason is capable of knowing truth and "the moral law within," but pure and practical reasoning cannot account for judgments of beauty. On this basis he distinguished taste as a separate faculty. We all know the experience of finding something beautiful, say a painting by Cézanne, then turning to a friend and recognizing that she judges differently. In such situations, Kant observes, we intuitively understand that there are no general rules girding our judgments of taste that are demonstrably true: we cannot argue that our judgment is true or right and our friend's wrong.[6] Yet we nonetheless persist in what Kant believed to be the reasonable hope that she—in fact, everyone who might embark on judging the painting with us—will agree with us and find the Cézanne beautiful.

How can we both accept and not accept a judgment of taste that differs from our own? Kant concluded that the faculty of taste involves a distinctive type of "reflective" judging that is not wholly subjective or autonomous. When we gaze at the painting by Cézanne, we consider it as it appears not only to us but to others in the gallery and in the world in general. That is, our judgment that it is beautiful silently takes others' judgments into account. This "enlarged mentality," to use Kant's phrase (2.40), depends on what Arendt calls "representative thinking": as I contemplate the painting, I talk with myself, I listen to myself internally, I represent my views to myself, I represent others' views to myself, I weigh them against one an-

---

5   Arendt, "Personal responsibility under dictatorship," 41.
6   Kant, *Critique of Judgment* 1.6, 8, 22. I choose the example of a Cézanne painting because it is the topic of an essay on phenomenology by Merleau-Ponty, whose thinking influences parts of this chapter.

other. What results is still my own judgment—but at the same time, it is not wholly my own.[7]

Arendt appealed to Kant's account in her thinking about judgment on two grounds. First, she viewed plurality as the fundamental element of the human condition.[8] I am not you, you are not me, I am not the person down the hallway. At the same time, we coexist, and in our coexistence, as different selves, we perceive the world differently. In the intersubjective and communal aspects of Kantian judgments of taste, Arendt saw an exemplary procedure for ascertaining agreement in the public realm while preserving the differences among people. Second, she believed that when we make judgments we work not with concepts or ideals but with appearances. That humans live in the world as it presents itself to us, the world of appearances, is a consistent theme in Arendt's thinking. It allowed her to claim that the phenomena we confront as we make political judgments have the same nature as aesthetic objects.[9]

When Arendt used the controversial phrase "the banality of evil" to describe Adolf Eichmann, she had in mind his total disconnection from the practice of judging in this Kantian sense. In doing his job as chief of transportation infrastructure, including the trains that brought hundreds of thousands of people to their deaths, Arendt argued, Eichmann was not insane, or even especially anti-Semitic; rather, he had forgotten how to think, and therefore how to judge. She called this "thoughtlessness." "The longer one listened to him," she noted in the book that emerged from her reporting on his trial in 1961, "the more obvious it became that his inability to speak was closely connected with his inability to *think*, namely, to think from the standpoint of somebody else."[10] To speak of thinking from the standpoint of somebody else may suggest that Arendt has in mind pure feeling or empathy, but there is a crucial difference. She is trying to describe a form of *thinking*: representative thinking, "being and thinking in my own identity where I am not."[11]

7   More on this in chapter 3, in my discussion of Horace's *Satires* book 1.
8   "Men, not Man, live on the earth and inhabit the world. While all aspects of the human condition are somehow related to politics, this plurality is specifically the condition—not only the *conditio sine qua non* but the *conditio per quam*—of all political life" (*The Human Condition*, 7).
9   Arendt, "Some questions," 138.
10   Arendt, *Eichmann in Jerusalem*, 49. Compare Kant's description in *Critique of Judgment* (2.40) of the man of "enlarged mind," who "detaches himself from the subjective personal conditions of his judgment, which cramp the minds of so many others, and reflects upon his own judgment from a universal standpoint (which he can only determine by shifting his ground to the standpoint of others)."
11   Arendt, "Truth and politics," *Between Past and Future*, 241.

Some critics have argued that this conception rests on a problematic idealization of noise-free dialogue that erases difference. How am I able to represent the views of others to myself in cases where I cannot recognize them as interlocutors—when I am rich and they are poor, I am a woman and they are male, and so forth? Linda Zerilli persuasively counters this criticism by emphasizing that Arendt's picture holds Kantian *imagination* at the center. Because Kant viewed imagination as mental free play, the kind of understanding made possible by exercising imagination does not direct pure or practical (moral) reasoning. Remembering that representative thinking is a sort of free play helps explain why taking another's standpoint, in Arendt's sense, is not equivalent to or subsumed under assuming an identity or particular local perspective. It does not involve "walking a mile in another's shoes," as the old saying goes. Imagination enables us to see objects and events afresh, "outside the economy of use" and standard narratives of cause and effect. Zerilli also underscores Kant's original insistence that imagination does not work toward an end. It is by definition not normative. It cannot, then, help create or stand in for the moral rules or laws of which Arendt was so skeptical. On the contrary, the practice of imagination "expands our sense of what is real" and what we can communicate to one another.[12]

Imagination also distinguishes Arendt's thinking about character from Alasdair MacIntyre's influential work on virtue. Arendt saw a deep connection between a person's manner of judging and his character. By his judging, a person "discloses to an extent also himself, what kind of person he is."[13] MacIntyre, too, is interested in character. But where his thinking rests on the claim that the "highest concept" for moral life is "the concept of a rule," Arendt tenaciously insists on the pitfalls of rule-making and the advantages of novelty and imagination in representative thinking.[14] Elusive as her thinking can be, it compels us to reconsider our habit of regarding political judgment as a process bounded by rules, institutions, familiar attitudes, concepts, or values. In minds crowded with mental furniture composed of concepts and rules, she enjoins us to make space for imagination and for worldly experience of "the things themselves" that compose the world. "For at the center of our politics lies concern, not for man, but for the world."[15]

All the elements of Arendt's moral and political thinking I have mentioned so far everywhere entail the necessity of turning outward, of engag-

12   Zerilli, "'We feel our freedom,'" 178.
13   Arendt, "The crisis in culture," in *Between Past and Future*, 223.
14   MacIntyre, *After Virtue*, 112.
15   Arendt, "Introduction *into* Politics," *The Promise of Politics*, 106.

ing with the world. Her remarks on what she called Eichmann's "thoughtlessness" continue: "No communication was possible with him, not because he lied but because he was surrounded by the most reliable of all safeguards against the words and the presence of others, and hence against reality as such."[16] His thoughtlessness did not cause him to fail to care about others or to sympathize with their plights; for he believed and repeatedly insisted that he had cared, that he had felt sympathy; and he described several moments when he had acted on those feelings. His thoughtlessness was the loss of the habit of thinking of himself as a person in the world. This led to two important consequences. First, Eichmann forgot the fundamental human condition of plurality, a loss that allowed him to believe that others experienced the world the same way he did: Arendt cites as an example his expressions of disbelief that his Israeli judges would not permit him to "find peace with his former enemies."[17] Second, he lost the ability to see himself at a distance from the world, "to occupy a standpoint from which to live together with himself explicitly—the standpoint of the 'intercourse with oneself ... which ... we usually call thinking.'"[18]

When she speaks of the urgent need to have concern for the world, Arendt is thinking anti-Romantically, against empathy and the modern belief in the power of empathy to make people better. George Kateb argues that Arendt considered the inner life in general to suffer from an "existential inadequacy." Of her arguments about the world, he concludes: "to spend a life in watching oneself, refining one's self-perception, trying to catch the feeling or the motive as it leads its evanescent existence, trying to be fulfilled in one's own inner process, is to misspend one's life. There is no freedom or worldliness here."[19] Nor is she interested in pursuing politics in the terms of what Socrates would have called a "craft," an artful form of policy-making. For Arendt as for Jacques Rancière, this turn is a turn against politics, because politics has no identifiable end, as crafts have, and because real politics escapes ordinary measurements and values.[20]

To maintain a sense of the constantly changing common world in which we live, and to sharpen our awareness of the others with whom we are con-

---

16   Arendt, *Eichmann in Jerusalem*, 49.

17   Ibid., 52–53.

18   Pauer-Studer and Velleman, "Distortions of normativity," 12, quoting Arendt, "Personal responsibility under dictatorship," 45.

19   Kateb, "Freedom and worldliness," 146.

20   This understanding of politics is central to Rancière's thinking: see, e.g., *Disagreement*, 15, 29. For critiques of Arendt's view, consult Pitkin, *The Attack of the Blob*, and Dietz, "'The slow boring of hard boards': methodical thinking and the work of politics."

stantly creating the world afresh, we need to stay acutely alive to our senses and judgments. This attention embeds us in the world more effectively than rules based on abstract notions of justice, which tend to prove either insufficient or dangerous. As Arendt argues at the end of "The concept of history," in *Between Past and Future*, it is terribly easy for us to fall into a condition of world-alienation—the sense of loss that occurs when we retreat into our own heads, or when the world as we have come to know it changes irremediably in times of crisis or war, when tradition and authority collapse, leaving no obvious replacements in sight.

THE VIVIDLY REAL WORLD

"One is at once amazed and affected with the mournful account Sallust gives us of the Romans in his time," remarked the radical Whig who called himself "Cato" in the *London Journal* of April 1721: "We see what a market these men made of power, and what a degree of degeneracy they introduced."[21] Sallust's major surviving works *Catilina* and *Jugurtha*, highly focused accounts of episodes from the previous half-century of Roman history, were written in the chaotic aftermath of the assassination of Julius Caesar. Praised by Martial as "foremost" of the Roman historians (*primus*, 14.191), Sallust supported Caesar and served under him as a provincial governor.[22] His lively and swift-paced histories influenced late medieval and early modern thinkers seeking alternatives to monarchical rule and a new rhetoric of commonwealth government.[23]

Modern interpretations of Sallust's political thought begin in earnest with Theodor Mommsen, who treated him as a political propagandist fighting for Caesar. In the 1920s and 1930s, attention turned to the presence of Stoic themes in Sallust and the possible influence of thinkers like Posidonius. A few decades later, the Marxist classicist Antonio La Penna saw Sallust as an Italian bourgeois whose class-based criticism of the corruption of the old Roman families fueled his Caesarian partisanship. Meanwhile, D. C. Earl, in an approach constrained by conventional assumptions about the static and conservative nature of Roman political culture and thought, took Sallust's main concerns to be archaic Roman *gloria* and *virtus* and

21   "Cato" was the pseudonym of Thomas Gordon and John Trenchard; the quotation is drawn from *Cato's Letters* No. 27, written by Gordon (200–201).

22   On his career as a *novus homo*, his inglorious service as a general, and his reputation as a rapacious governor (largely based on Cassius Dio 43.9.2), see Syme, *Sallust*, 29–42.

23   Osmond, "Sallust in Renaissance political thought," provides a clear and learned overview (and quotes Martial, 129).

their decay. In the wake of post-structuralist theory and narratology, critics have concentrated on what we might call the "anti-conceptual" aspects of Sallust's writing: specifically, his habit of constructing and then undermining oppositions like vice and virtue.[24] He has emerged as a complex thinker whose allusions to and borrowings from Greek and Latin epic, drama, and lyric complicate what might at first seem to be simplistic claims about virtue.[25]

In a searching reading of the anti-closural elements in Sallust's longer and more ambitious narrative, *Jugurtha*, David Levene notes how readerly attention is repeatedly directed beyond the boundaries of the text: in the end, he concludes, the effect is "to place the emphasis away from what we have seen within the work, and onto what is to come outside it."[26] Following Arendt's turn to the external world as it is seen, shared, and created intersubjectively, Richard Rorty argues that the questions we should devote ourselves to are not "What shall I be? What can I become? What have I been?" but "What sorts of things, about what sorts of people, do I need to notice?"[27] Like Rorty, Sallust directs his readers to things and people rather than concepts or identities. His histories do not only look beyond themselves in terms of past and future; they look outward to the world as it is lived.

They begin with the human body, its presence in space and movements in the world, and its inescapable influence on the subject's viewpoints, values, and choices. The body is ever-present in the Sallustian text, and the body in extremity, whether at the height of its powers or in the face of death, plays a central role in the political struggles represented in the histories. Catiline's and Jugurtha's physical beauty, strength, and courage are key to their experience of the world and their ability to manipulate the people around them (*Cat. 5, Jug. 6*). Bodily experience motivates action—indirectly in the case of Catiline, who is encouraged in his ambition by poverty and the atmosphere of dissipation and avarice (*luxuria atque avaritia*, 5.8), and directly for Jugurtha, who plans his first steps toward usurping the rule of Numidia when Hiempsal, the younger of his two cousins who are the legitimate rulers, contemptuously refuses to allow him to seat himself on a level

---

24   Some of the most effective of these readings, because they are willing to leave the text open-ended, are Batstone, "The syncrisis in Sallust," and Levene, "Sallust's 'Catiline' and Cato the Censor." Wiedemann, "Sallust's *Jugurtha*: concord, discord, and the digressions," less persuasively insists on a coherent pattern in the text where parallels among the major digressions map Sallust's interest in political concord.

25   See further Due, "Tragic history and barbarian speech in Sallust's *Jugurtha*."

26   Levene, "Sallust's *Jugurtha*: an historical fragment," 55.

27   Richard Rorty, *Contingency, Irony, Solidarity*, Kindle location 1932 of 3206.

equal with himself and his brother (11). The ambitious older man immediately plots his revenge. After he discovers that Hiempsal is living temporarily in a house belonging to a "dear and beloved" servant of his own, Jugurtha

> ...loaded with promises the servant who had been put in his way by chance, and compelled him to go to his house as if to check up on it, and to have false keys made for the gates; for the real ones were brought to Hiempsal [each night]. Meanwhile, Jugurtha promised to come himself with a large force when the time was right. The Numidian swiftly carried out his orders, and as he had been directed, let in Jugurtha's soldiers by night. After they rushed into the house, they scattered seeking the king, slaughtered some people in their sleep and others as they fought back, explored all the hiding-places, bashed down doors, and turned the whole place upside-down with shouting and bedlam, and meanwhile, Hiempsal was found hiding in a cleaning woman's shack, where he had fled at the start, terrified and unfamiliar with the place. The Numidians, as they had been commanded, brought Jugurtha his head.

> ...casu ministrum oblatum promissis onerat impellitque uti tamquam suam visens domum eat, portarum clauis adulterinas paret—nam verae ad Hiempsalem referebantur—ceterum, ubi res postularet, se ipsum cum magna manu venturum. Numida mandata brevi conficit atque, uti doctus erat, noctu Iugurthae milites introducit. Qui postquam in aedis irrupere, diuersi regem quaerere, dormientis alios, alios occursantis interficere, scrutari loca abdita, clausa effringere, strepitu et tumultu omnia miscere, cum interim Hiempsal reperitur occultans se tugurio mulieris ancillae, quo initio pauidus et ignarus loci perfugerat. Numidae caput eius, uti iussi erant, ad Iugurtham referunt. (12)

From the false set of keys to Hiempsal's hiding place in the compound, from the detailed descriptions of the soldiers' nighttime raid to the reasons for the young prince's disorientation, Sallust provides many more details than we need to grasp the event.

Rhetoricians call this effect "vivid description," or *enargeia*. With the rhetorical background in mind, critics usually read Sallustian *enargeia* against other examples of the general ancient interest in persuasion, in terms of both truth-value and morality. Ann Vasaly, Graham Zanker, and Ruth Webb argue that Roman writers seek to exploit what they assume to be a natural connection between the reader's vivid imagination of a scene and her conviction of its truth, invoking Stoic views on the nature of the "images" that strike the mind, *phantasiai*.[28] Andrew Feldherr notes a trend in modern interpretations of Livy, which take that historian's powerful imagery to be advancing the historian's ethical project. *Enargeia* highlights moral and political themes and imparts them to the reader with the greatest possible power.[29]

Quintilian's definition of *enargeia* suggests something rather different. "As for *evidentia*," he says, using Cicero's term for *enargeia*, "it is in my belief undoubtedly an important virtue of narrative, when a truth requires not only to be told but in a sense to be exhibited (*ostendendum*).... *Enargeia*, which Cicero calls *illustratio* and *evidentia*, makes us seem not so much to be talking about something as exhibiting it (*ostendere*). Emotions will ensue just as if we were present at the event itself" (4.2.64, 6.2.32).[30] Quintilian suggests that vivid details appeal to sensory experience, which in turn summons up emotion in the reader, who reacts "as though present at the event," i.e., experiencing the same emotions as those felt by people at the scene. Quintilian's formulation suggests that we need to understand *enargeia* as more than witnessing a spectacle and experiencing certain emotions or apprehending certain truths as a result. *Enargeia* actively engages the reader in the scene. It places us in the space of appearance, attuning us to the look and feel of bodies and things in action in the world.

The short but intense spotlight Sallust shines on Hiempsal's desperate attempt to conceal himself is typical of other passages that feature human bodies in extremity. Later in the text, after the Romans have launched their war in Numidia, Sallust describes the attempt by the citizens of Lepcis to get help from the Roman commander Metellus. Sallust's report of the town emphasizes its associations with political and natural violence: founded by Sidonians escaping from civil war, it lies in a bay famous for its terrific sea-swells (78.2–3). Prompted by the sheer fact of physical association, or so he says in two different ways (*quoniam in eas regiones per Lepcitanorum negotia venimus ... eam rem nos locus admonuit*, 79.1), Sallust tells a strange story. In the days of Carthaginian domination of North Africa, Carthage and the

28   Vasaly, *Representations*, 98–99; Webb, "Imagination and the arousal of the emotions," in Braund and Gill, *The Passions in Roman Literature and Thought*, as well as *Ekphrasis, Imagination, and Persuasion in Ancient Rhetorical Theory and Practice*, especially 87–106; also Zanker, "*Enargeia* in the ancient criticism of poetry," 297–311.

29   Feldherr, citing Burck 1935=1967, 143.

30   Insequentur enargeia, quae a Cicerone inlustratio et evidentia nominatur, quae non tam dicere videtur quam ostendere, et adfectus non aliter quam si rebus ipsis intersimus sequentur (6.2.32).

Greek city of Cyrene disagreed over their common boundary. After a long cycle of wars, anticipating in miniature the struggle between Rome and Numidia, the two cities finally agree to settle the dispute by sending out parties from the edges of the disputed territory. The border is to be set wherever the parties meet. Two Carthaginians (the Philaeni brothers) and two Cyrenians are chosen; the Carthaginians make good time, but the Cyrenians are delayed. When they finally meet, the Cyrenians accuse their rivals of cheating and suggest a new agreement: either the border will be set on the spot the two Carthaginians have reached, but they will be buried alive there; or the Carthaginians will allow the Cyrenians to advance the line as far as they wish, with the same capital condition applying to them. The brothers accept the terms and are buried alive, and altars are constructed in their memory both on the spot and at home (79.2–10).

Like the story of Jugurtha's attack on Hiempsal, the story of the Carthaginian sacrifice directs attention to the fleshy experience of bodies facing death, as if their dramatic extremity grants the reader an embodied knowing of the world. Further, and rather mysteriously, Sallust's descriptions of the perceiving, moving, intentional, living-then-dead body show that far from being a passive instrument of the agent's will or an inert surface on which power inscribes itself, the body helps compose its environment. In the cases of Hiempsal (whose death is matched by his older brother not long afterward) and the Philaeni brothers, this act of composition is literal, because the ends of the living bodies change political life. They create space for new rule, rewriting the map. As the tender vulnerability and rash risk-taking of the flesh is revealed as the stuff of power relations, we readers are alerted to the importance of bodily actions rather than abstractions or universal principles in the field of politics. Here the sensations of confusion and curiosity that the Philaeni brothers' tale elicits—on what basis did the Cyrenians make their charge, and why did it convince the brothers?—directs attention more urgently to the meaning of their bodies as just that, bodies. We learn of no arguments, no rational judgments. As for Jugurtha, we know that he wants power, but what Sallust's narrative of the murder of Hiempsal underscores is the sheer cruelty of that will to power, its brutal impact on the world. *Enargeia* substitutes the *sensations* of feelings, bodies, and objects for the rational knowledge of abstract entities like "courage" or "virtue" or "injustice."

In an earlier book, *The State of Speech*, I argued that in Cicero's view, the measure of a good man is his capacity to speak, which involves active understanding and control of his body and the extent to which it shapes his relation to the world. The citizen who can arouse his fellow citizens' passions and engage with their capacity for rational thought, who has "sought into, listened, read, debated, handled, and experienced the material" of human life, is the only citizen who can stage that knowledge in a meaningful way in the public sphere (1.61–3, 3.54). The ideal speaker is judged as such not by abstract standards of virtue, but by the traditions, sensibilities, and passions of his community. Cicero's ideal speaker abjures the plain style of speaking praised by the Stoics because it bespeaks a way of life that is disembodied—even, not fully human, in that it sets aside human emotion and sensation. To Cicero, the state is made up of citizens linked by their embodied experience of living in the world in common. Sallustian *enargeia* takes on new and richer significance as an instrument of awakening readers to the significance of mortal flesh in the political experience. This is, however, just the first step.

In a recent, deeply thoughtful book that considers Arendt alongside Cicero, Machiavelli with Livy, Montesquieu with Tacitus, and Foucault with Seneca, the political theorist Dean Hammer reflects on the prominence of decay and decline in late republican and imperial Roman political thought. He diagnoses this preoccupation as a response to the terrible loss of bearings the ruling class suffered during the turbulent century-long transition from republican to autocratic rule.[31] Romans writing about politics, he argues, are less interested in rational arguments about concepts or utopian experiments than in recovering themselves and their audience by concentrating on the summoning up of "felt meanings," meanings that matter. Cicero turns in the *Tusculan Disputations* from abstract Platonic ideas to a notion of the eternal that is nourished in the sensual particularity of things we come to treasure through experience and memory. In his exemplar-studded history of Rome Livy exploits the essential relation between his readers' images of the past and their ability to imagine how best to live together. Livy's interest in moments when politics becomes visible—when private greed is revealed and corrected by the public rendering of justice—and invisible— when the citizenry is blinded by haste, fear, or false hope—speaks to his view of the motivating power of *exempla* for imagining in*sight* into new possibilities for politics. Tacitus, too, is committed to clearsightedness, teaching readers how to recognize, and to a degree correct for, the psychological trauma created by the clouding effect of autocratic power on individual moral judgment. Imperial writers live in an unpredictable world where the historian's project of re-animating exemplary images seems hopelessly out

---

31   I discuss Hammer's *Roman Political Thought and the Modern Theoretical Imagination* in more detail in *Political Theory* (Connolly 2012).

of reach. For Seneca, then, the self must be envisioned anew through rigorous exercises of self-analysis undertaken in the company of others (thus recovering the self from the moral isolation imposed by the despot) and refined in the sensual act of writing, which ignites both writer's and reader's powers of creative self-making. Through these Roman writings, Hammer exhorts us to regain the deep and rich "feel for the world" that results from self-conscious, invested engagement with worldly things, relations, and sensations.

In *The Life of the Mind* and her essays in *Between Past and Future*, Arendt suggests that the Romans wanted to make philosophy useful, a road that first leads one out of this world and then back to it. Hammer concludes that her notion of "the cultivation of the soul thus directs us back to, and instills a particular attitude toward, the tangibility of the world."[32] Hammer appeals to Arendt's thinking about culture and aesthetics to fortify his claim that the cultivation of affective associations through felt meanings helps redeem politics, or at least improve the conditions under which political action takes place. He is particularly interested in those aspects of Arendt's thinking that promise to connect us to the world by helping us to see it for what it is—not in deceptively "realist" terms, but seeing with all the imaginative, plural, and affective capacities involved in political judgment.

Take, for example, Cicero's exhortation to cultivate the soul with a view to perceiving the "true nature" of things (*Tusc.* 1.20.47) and his nostalgic representation of the republic in *de Republica* 5, where he compares the republic to a marvelous painting. Because recent generations have failed to renew (*renovare*) the original colors and outlines, now fading with age, the republic is falling into decay (5.1.2).[33] If *Tusculans* is not recognizable as a work of political theory to us today, Hammer insists nonetheless that as a "deepened reflection" on the habits and attitudes required for "the recovery of durable markers by which we orient ourselves in the political world"; it teaches us how to reason, and no less important, how to care for the things that matter in the world, the world we have in common. This is the world captured so effectively in Cicero's own "work of art"—both the particular passage that paints the republic in words in *de Republica* 5 and the dialogue as a whole.

Hammer's is a phenomenological reading of Roman writing. In his *Phenomenology of Perception*, Merleau-Ponty sought to study the essence of things, human and worldly "facticity," which emerges from the body's inter-

32   Hammer, *Roman Political Thought*, 42.
33   Ibid., with discussion continuing, 42, 76–77.

action with the world. All his efforts "are concentrated upon re-achieving a direct and primitive contact with the world."[34] Hammer sees how Roman texts describe lived meaning over time, its unceasing determination to bring us face to face with familiar signs, to embed us in an affective, corporeal world; their efforts to think from within existence, including the oscillation of past and present, rather than from outside existence. This mode of thinking promises to rethink the world, as one scholar of the political possibilities in Merleau-Ponty puts it, in terms of our "embodied directedness toward the world."[35] So, to Hammer, the experiences of reading the account of the republic as a faded painting, imagining it in the mind's eye, and experiencing inspiration or mourning or hope transcend mere spectatorial theater. Texts like *Tusculans* and *de Republica* are important for thinking politically because their dense fabrics of associations and emotions constitute an affective and reflective engagement with appearances, prompting and enriching our sensual appreciation of, and affection for, the republic. In Hammer's reading, affection leads to reflection, and further. Close attention to phenomena is, if not exactly a guarantee of right action (a claim he does not make), at least a meaningful turn for the better—in his terms, a restoration of "sensitivity," a stirring of "the impulses so that 'a tumultuous and badly ordered' body can be animated to act for the good of the community," a quickening of our "ties of mutual recognition and collective action."[36]

It will be clear from my discussion of Sallust so far that I think Hammer is right to understand the close attention Roman texts give to the phenomenal, the sensual, and the material as a serious, meaningful contribution to political thought. What I cannot follow—despite my devout wish that this were an easy argument to make—is his assumption about the political efficacy of our recognition of our affective attachments to the world. What prevents deeply felt meanings from falling prey to fantasy, from cultivating destructive passions in us, or from becoming a form of pleasurable spectatorship? Consider *Law and Order*, an enormously popular television show (and one of the most financially successful in history) whose dramatizations of the workings of the American justice system arouse intense emotions, and even have been documented to shape beliefs about crime and the law. Each episode places viewers face to face with the sometimes shaky opera-

34   Merleau-Ponty, *Phenomenology of Perception*, vii, quoted and discussed by Coole, *Merleau-Ponty and Modern Politics*, 101.

35   Coole, *Merleau-Ponty and Modern Politics*, 104.

36   Hammer, *Roman Political Thought*, 77, 131 (quoting Machiavelli, *Discourses* 3.14), 226–27. Hubert Dreyfus and Sean Dorrance Kelly recently made a similar argument, and encountered similar criticism to mine below, in their popular book *All Things Shining*.

tions of justice, encouraging them to value the district attorney's attempts to render justice in a consistent, fair way, and to feel sympathy for characters the show portrays as victims, including the (usually ill-educated, poor, and marginalized) perpetrators. But the show appears to foster spectators' desire to see criminals punished even at the same time that they feel sympathy for them: in fact the effective cultivation of sympathy for and even limited identification with the criminal seems to increase the emotional reward experienced by watching his or her punishment.[37]

This simple example suggests the difficulty of explaining how sensual immersion in a morally and socially complex world and love of that world—even keenly attuned awareness of others and intense affective associations with political institutions—might lead us to act at all, let alone to act in a just and right way. Little in Hammer's thought-provoking argument speaks to the problem of judgment, that is, the problems that ensue when our passions heat up destructive impulses, for instance, blood-and-soil patriotism. Is it possible to bridge the gap?

EMBEDDED KNOWING

When queried in an interview about the phenomenology of the critic, Paul Ricoeur replied: "You did very well to ask . . . , because up to the present we have chiefly had a theory of the literary object, and the [critic's] activities on the literary object. But, what are the activities on the subject of the critic?"[38] Sallust invites this question (and scholars have tended to try to answer it) by offering an account of himself in the first paragraphs of both *Catiline* and *Jugurtha*. His explanation of his decision to write history as a fitting response to fleeing the chaos of civil war politics is embedded in a series of highly generalized comments about the benefits of virtue and the life of the mind and the dangers of bodily desire. "Dishonest political and personal apologia wrapped in scrapbook commonplaces," as Ernst Badian complained, the prefaces are usually understood as Sallust's apology for Caesarian partisanship or for taking up the non-active and perhaps not fully "Roman" or "free" career of writing, all in the context of establishing his conventional moral authority—if only to call it into question later (*Cat.* 3.5–4.2, *Jug.* 4.1–9).[39]

---

37   Kimberlianne Podlas, "Please adjust your signal: how television's syndicated courtrooms bias our juror citizenry," and Elayne Rapping, *Law and Justice as Seen on TV*.

38   Ricoeur, "Phenomenology and theory," 1089.

39   Badian, review of La Penna, 103. Batstone argues in "The antithesis of virtue" that Sallust sets up virtue and moral authority as themes only to revise them or pit them against one

As a self-identifying move, the prefaces' self-accountings also position Sallust as an interpreter of the world who scrupulously locates himself at once inside and outside politics, and who consequently implicates himself in the very problems he diagnoses. The prefaces both situate him and represent him as engaged in situational thinking, thinking in contact with his and others' lived experience.

To think phenomenologically, according to Edmund Husserl, is to begin by taking one's surrounding environs as one's explicit starting point. That is, a thinker properly attentive to phenomena must first clarify her relations with the world, so that she and the reader understand how the surrounding world emerges from out of the thinker's own history. "There is a push and pull between consciousness and things present in the world," one Husserlian theorist observes. The subject thinking phenomenologically "proceeds from his own ego, and this purely as the performer of all his validities, of which he becomes the purely theoretical spectator," and his ego "is then no longer an isolated thing alongside other such things in the pre-given world," but something for the reader to know and take into account as the account of the world unfolds.[40] Once we are alive to the particular position Sallust has adopted in the world, including and inflected by his personal history, we are primed to approach the action he describes in a this-worldly sense of meaning. This is an approach to historical and political inquiry in which the play between particulars and generalities (like the philosopher-manqué language at the opening) draws attention to the activity of the world.[41]

A phenomenological sensitivity to the human condition provides the moral framework in which Sallust grounds his historical account and his appeal to his readers. He opens both his histories with expressions of what he represents as irrefutable universalistic truths: that individuals and peoples decline, that virtue is corrupted by wealth, that the mind "matters" more than the body. But the text's swift move to specifics—first his career, and very soon thereafter, the physical and mental qualities of his histories' main characters—suggests that we can only understand virtue and greed, strength and decline, through a dialectic of the universalistic and the specific, the general and the particular, the intellectual and the corporeal.

At the same time, the significance of Sallust's explanation of why he chose to write about these particular topics, Catiline's conspiracy and the

---

another; Sklenar sees this tactic as helping to create a stasis in the text that "destroys traditional systems of signification" ("La République des signes," 218).

40   Gyllenhammer, "Phenomenology as an ascetic practice," 317.
41   Frederick Dolan, review in *Theory and Event* of Villa's *Arendt and Heidegger*.

Numidian war, becomes clearer, and we move closer to bridging the gaps between attention, reflection, and political judgment. Sallust chose to write about Catiline after abandoning his own "evil ambition" (*ambitio mala*), his desire to succeed in political life after that life had lost all virtue (4.2). Catiline too suffered from ambition and greed. What remains unspoken in *Catiline*'s preface—but which Sallust articulates in Catiline's first speech and again explicitly in the prologue to *Jugurtha*—is the particular structural element in the this-world of Roman politics that created the conditions for Catiline's and Jugurtha's (and Sallust's) downfall: the struggle between mass and elite, which ends in an overthrow on a scale that encompasses not just Rome, but Italy, indeed virtually the entire cosmic order.

> I will write about the war which the Roman people fought with Jugurtha the king of the Numidians, first because it was long and savage, and victory was uncertain, and second because at that moment, for the first time, there was a push back against the arrogance of the nobility. This struggle threw everything divine and human into disarray and reached such a point of frenzy that in these civil struggles war and devastation made an end of Italy.

> Bellum scripturus sum quod populus Romanus cum Iugurtha rege Numidarum gessit, primum quia magnum et atrox variaque victoria fuit, dehinc quia tunc primum superbiae nobilitatis obviam itum est. Quae contentio divina et humana cuncta permiscuit eoque vecordiae processit, ut studiis civilibus bellum atque vastitas Italiae finem faceret. (*Jug.* 5.1)

The wreck of Sallust's career and the crimes of Catiline and Jugurtha all arise from the violence of republican politics, familiar from chapter 1: the senatorial order's grab for power, driven by blind greed, and the resulting defensive paranoia among the people.

These passages show that the common world we share, the this-world, comprises both mental and corporeal activities, more closely intertwined than we might like to admit, where the desire for immortality slides into destructive greed. In this world, politics is a field of structural antagonism. Sallust himself is a product of this violence: he has lived it, and now his written histories will examine it. Beyond attuning readerly sensibilities to the lived grain of republican institutions and affections, *Catiline* and *Jugurtha* embed the reader in the sensual knowledge of the structural forces of class, as well as a force that to a degree escapes structure: sheer contingency.

From the prefaces, we see how materiality and ideality, matter and meaning, mind and body are irreducibly interwoven at *every* level, from the corporeal to the philosophical. Sallust's histories suggest that the virtuosity particular to politics is grounded in "an ontology of the between, intercorporeality and intersubjectivity, wherein agonistic capacities emerge."[42] We should understand the criticism of bodily desire in both prefaces not as oppositional but as dialectical, bidirectional, representing the reflexivity of the relations of the mind with the body and the body with the world.

When Roman texts like Sallust's histories spur the imagination, take close notice of sensual experiences, insist on the significance of the particular, and attend to how experience composes political judgment, they attune readers to the corporeal and material elements that empower and constrain political life. This is a world where rules have lost their purchase, and by that logic it is also clear that contemporary corruption and malice make appeals to the past otiose. We had better not understand his text in terms of moral outcomes or even ambiguous ones. What is being offered here is a model of noticing specific bodies and objects in the world and making judgments about them; that is, a model for recognizing the particulars of the republican situation.

Sallust does not simply bring his readers face to face with the body in all its vicissitudes. The corporeal vice that drives all others, as he and several speakers argue in *Jugurtha* and *Catiline*, is greed. As the histories attune us to sensual experience of the world, they also teach us how to recognize the structural violence of class politics, the crucial importance of recognition, the danger of focusing on ends, and the significance of process. The text clarifies an important truth—that politics cannot be limited to *internal, personal* morality or evil. "Once politics is reduced to the morality of the inner self, structural violence remains uncontested."[43] After considering how Sallust weaves attentiveness to process into his historical narration, I will turn to his treatment of justice and recognition.

POLITICS AS PROCESS

The purpose of bribery, of course, is the distortion of civic process, and *Jugurtha* dramatizes the distortion by unmooring actions from motivation and consequences from actions. Bribery makes the plot begin over and over again. The undermining of intentionality and the privileging of fortune it

---

42   Coole, *Merleau-Ponty and Modern Politics*, 163.
43   Ibid., 52.

causes lead to the breakdown of civic judgment. When the senator Calpurnius Bestia leads an army to Africa (111 BCE), Jugurtha bribes him and agrees to surrender in exchange for keeping his throne. This act ripples onward as war is deferred to the following year. Caecilius Metellus is placed in charge, and the action is again extended when Jugurtha recommits himself to the war (*rursus*, 62.8) and begins the war anew (*ab integro bellum sumit*, 62.9–10; *bellum incipit*, 66.1). Metellus is accused by his rival Marius of prolonging the war because of his greed for power (64.6), but Marius himself soon restarts the war again (*rursus tamquam ad integrum bellum cuncta parat*, 73.1), and in a series of repetitions of what has become a key word, Marius and Sulla begin negotiations with Bocchus, the Mauritanian king whose support will win the war for Rome (*rursus*, 83.3). After Jugurtha bribes Bocchus to rejoin his forces (*rursus*, 97.2), in a final tortuous series of events, Bocchus pretends to deal with Sulla, decides to betray him under pressure from Jugurtha, but again, and finally, agrees to betray Jugurtha (*rursus*, 103.2).

In short, both *Jugurtha* and Jugurtha are masters of strategic diversion, confounding movement forward with movements of repetition and reversal. The central action of the text is triggered by waywardness: the prince Mastanabal's turn to a woman not his wife, who gives birth to Jugurtha (*ortus ex concubina*, 5.7).[44] Having been sent as a young man to train with the Roman army—a stalling tactic devised by the Numidian King Micipsa, who is unsure how to handle the potential rival to his sons (6.3–7.2)—Jugurtha is well placed to exploit the army's weaknesses when it arrives in Numidia. His main tactic is delay, which compels the two Roman leaders (the consul Metellus and his legate Marius) to perform their own act of divergence, by splitting the army into two separate forces. Jugurtha inhabits a middle ground of action, never fully following up on apparent intentions, always shifting his targets: "he showed himself now to Metellus, at other times to Marius; he attacked those at the end of the line (*postremos in agmine*) and immediately retreated into the hills; again (*rursus*) he threatened other men, and later others, neither giving them battle nor allowing them rest, but only hindering the enemy from its purpose (*ab incepto retinere*)" (55.8). As a description of the structural logic of *Jugurtha*, this passage works very well. The initial encounter between Jugurtha and Metellus' forces anticipates the

---

44   Kraus argues that Jugurtha is a figure for absence and deviance, on the grounds that the primary marker of textual presence, his speech, is muted and alien (only eight words of direct speech, by contrast to Catiline's two speeches and a quoted letter), and that he is associated with the perverting power of money ("Jugurthine disorder," 221–22).

movement of the narrative, forward and backward, but above all, beginning again (*rursus*).

In the preface, Sallust explains his selection of topic as a choice to investigate beginnings: the Jugurthine War offers not only the typical stuff of history—greatness, savagery, and shifting fortunes—but the beginning (*tunc primum*) of popular resistance to the arrogance of the nobles (5.1). We will see later on the series of Roman commissions sent to supervise the government of Numidia: the senior legates arrive "against Jugurtha's hopes" (*inceptum*, a word that also means "beginning," 25.6). The repetition, delay, and restart of the war's beginnings recalls the analysand's need to repeat, rather than simply remember, the past, as described in Freud's essay "Remembering, repeating, and working through."[45] On the one hand, the repetition uneasily acknowledges Rome's violent, conflicted nature as a state engaged in permanent war. But Sallust has also put his finger on the problem of exemplarity, the characteristic Roman habit of admiring and imitating the past. In *Jugurtha*, by contrast, going back and starting over again is an option only for the reader of history, who looks back, revisits, and experiences the past through Sallust's writing. Surely, however, the reader is intended to translate the experience of reading backward into the habit of thinking forward.

According to the anonymous author of the rhetorical treatise *Ad Herennium*, a jury properly judging a case must understand the orator's *narratio* of events, especially its movements from action to effect. When many indications and signs that are in mutual agreement concur, the orator speaking in the law court must present a clear case, not a muddy one (*rem conspicuam, non suspiciosam, Rhet. Her.* 2.7.11). Once the jury probes the likely motivations and intentions of the accused, they become capable of choosing what consequences the accused will endure. *Jugurtha*, an indictment of the wayward crimes of the nobility, models in its own narrative structure the impossibility of judgment in a corrupt system. Various characters repeatedly conceal their motives as they "plot" the plot; and as the text progresses even intended action leads to empty consequences. During Metellus' campaign against Jugurtha, for instance, after making a heroic dash to the city of Thala, Metellus attacks it even though he seems to know that Jugurtha has fled. A terrible forty-day siege ends in mass suicide and destruction, so nothing is left for the Roman conquerors (76).

This is also the explanation for Sallust's recurrent emphasis on chance and *fortuna* at key moments in the plot: it problematizes the intentionality

45   Brooks, *Reading for the Plot*, 98.

of agents in the text.[46] Rather than simply holding off or randomizing the action, delay and chance ripple unsettlingly within the text—and within history, Sallust suggests—to undermine the processes of judgment and reaction. Hence his stuttering use of ellipsis in the text. Elliptical language creates the very gaps in understanding that Sallust asks us to understand.

Twice in the course of narrating *Jugurtha*, Sallust explicitly refuses to judge the root causes of the republic's ills—first in the preface, and later, in a passage that seems at first to finish the story the preface begins. The preface delves into the conditions of injustice that currently reign in Rome, with the powerful few (*potentiae paucorum*) enslaving the many, noble men seeking wealth instead of glory, and corrupt men winning office (3.3, 4.7, 4.8). "But I've gone on too freely and in too much depth, feeling shame and pain at the morals of the country: I must return to the beginning," Sallust says (*nunc ad inceptum redeo*), and changes the subject (4.9). Later, when Sallust returns to the history of struggles in Rome between rich and poor that engendered the first wave of injustice and violence in republican politics, he runs out of time (*tempus quam res maturius me deseret*) and announces his return to the plot with the same phrase, *ad inceptum redeo* (41.5).[47]

These moments of self-silencing could be taken as evidence of the disorder ruling Sallust's text, or of an effort to undermine his own moral authority as a historian. But it is important to see that Sallust's refusal to conduct extended analytic criticism of the republic's decline does not mean that his text conveys only uncertainty or ambivalence. A few valuable points emerge from these moments of self-imposed silence. First, they present the narrative as one where analysis of the past is not "therapeutic"; returning to the past offers no obvious solutions for present problems.[48] Second, the silences prod the reader's attention toward the plot and characters, to whose actions Sallust now returns. These, suggestively, are meant to matter most. Third, by leaving the matter hanging, they prompt the reader himself or herself to answer the question on the evidence that is presented in the text. It is made clear from the start that *Jugurtha* is a story about the obligations and miscarriages of justice, a response to the human tendency to lament mortality and the fall of chance when, Sallust says, men should see that the truly good life has no need of good luck (1.1–3). What the good life requires is concern for

---

46   The words used are *fortuna* or *fors*, not *fatum*, which occurs only once in *Catiline* (*Cat.* 47.2): so Syme, *Sallust*, 246. The consul Philippus notes that "fortune favors the better men" (*fortuna meliores sequitur*, *Hist.* 1.77.21).

47   In an interesting parallel, the senior legates who summon Jugurtha to Rome for his failed trial arrive in Africa *contra inceptum suum venisse*, "against his [Jugurtha's] project" (25.6).

48   Levene, "Cato the censor," traces Sallust's problematization of the Catonian past.

honorable things instead of depraved ones—a matter of good judgment that, we recall, the text implicitly promises to teach when Sallust explains his choice to write history as a replacement for the political career he has abandoned (1.4–5; cf. 3.1, 4.4).

Finally, though, the text resists reduction to a particular message or end. In *Jugurtha*, Sallust repeatedly undermines the notion of ending. This is a text that recounts many deaths, but it stops short of describing the one that brings the story to what we might think of as its natural end: the death, by legal execution, of its protagonist, the bastard prince Jugurtha, whose seizure of the kingship and murder of his legitimate cousins pulls Rome into war in Numidia. All Sallust says at the end is this:

> After it was announced that the war in Numidia was finished and Jugurtha was being brought to Rome in chains, Marius was elected consul in absentia and the province of Gaul was assigned to him, and on the Kalends of January, with great glory, the consul celebrated a triumph. And at that time the hope and resources of the state rested in him.

> Sed postquam bellum in Numidia confectum et Iugurtham Romam uinctum adduci nuntiatum est, Marius consul factus est et ei decreta prouincia Gallia, isque Kalendis Ianuariis magna gloria consul triumphauit. Et ea tempestate spes atque opes ciuitatis in illo sitae. (*Jug.* 114-3–4)

Other Greek and Roman writers report the details of Jugurtha's last journey to Rome, his degradation and death, but not Sallust.[49] As his text hastens to its conclusion, leaving our knowledge of Jugurtha's life incomplete, the meaning of his history is also left suspended in uncertainty. The space in the prison where Jugurtha is killed is the space of final judgment that Sallust does not represent.

In fact, though the concluding clauses first pretend to be about an ending, they describe a beginning. Once the cessation of hostilities is formally declared with the closural gesture of *nuntiatum est*, "it was announced," the sentence turns to Marius' assignment to save Rome from its next threat, the invasion of Italy by the northern European tribes of the Teutones and the Cimbri. As every Roman of Sallust's era (and every reader of *Jugurtha*) al-

---

49   Sources for Jugurtha's imprisonment and execution: Livy, *Per.* 67; Plutarch, *Marius* 12.4–5. On the end, see further Levene, "Sallust's *Jugurtha*," 54–56.

ready knows, the triumphant consul's thirst for *gloria* will initiate a cycle of violence in which a civil war between Marius and Sulla (another figure appearing in the history) presages the civil wars of the next generation—between Pompey and Caesar, between Caesar's assassins and the alliance led by Antony and Octavian, and the final war Sallust no doubt anticipated but did not live to see, between Antony and Octavian.[50]

The significance of the end of *Jugurtha* is most fully grasped by reading it against the closing pages of Sallust's earlier work, *Catiline*. The last scene set at Rome occurs in the senate, where Cato and Caesar debate the just punishment for Catiline's captured co-conspirators: imprisonment or death. Cato's arguments in defense of the latter persuade the senators, and the captives are swiftly executed in a scene Sallust describes in detail:

> In the prison, where you climb a little to the left, is the place called the Tullianum, roughly twelve feet below ground. Walls enclose it on all sides, and above is a room with a vaulted stone roof: but it is repulsive and horrifying in aspect, filthy, dark, and fetid. There, when Lentulus had been sent down, the executioners of capital crimes, following orders, strangled him with a noose. In this way a patrician from the famous *gens* of the Cornelii, who had held consular authority in Rome, met a death worthy of his character and actions. Cethegus, Statilius, Gabinius, Caeparius were punished in the same way.

> est carcere locus, quod Tullianum appellatur, ubi paululum ascenderis ad laevam, circiter duodecim pedes humi depressus. Eum muniunt undique parietes atque insuper camera lapideis fornicibus iuncta: sed incultu, tenebris, odore foeda atque terribilis eius facies est. In eum locum postquam demissus est Lentulus, vindices rerum capitalium, quibus praeceptum erat, laqueo gulam fregere. Ita ille patricius ex gente clarissuma Corneliorum, qui consulare imperium Romae habuerat, dignum moribus factisque suis exitium vitae invenit. De Cethego, Statilio, Gabinio, Caepario eodem modo supplicium sumptum est. (*Cat.* 55.3–6)

Carefully describing the sight, smell, and feel of the prison, the text makes a point of lingering in the place where the most extreme act of justice, the

---

50   According to Jerome, Sallust died in 35 BCE; Earl, *Political Thought of Sallust*, surveys his career and chronology. On the tense balance of power between Antony and Octavian after Philippi, see Syme, *Roman Revolution*, 202–93; on the earlier period, Rawson, "The aftermath of the Ides," 468–90.

ending of a life, is carried out—the very scene *Jugurtha* omits. As *Catiline*'s concluding chapters move away from the city, the core of Roman justice, they remain absorbed with the process of rendering just judgment. They describe the last battle, where Catiline and all his free citizen supporters are said to have been killed. In the strong closural movement of the final chapter, which begins by gazing backward ("once the battle was over," *confecto proelio*, 59.1), the reader is left with the impression that all accounts have been balanced:

> Nor had the Roman army achieved a joyful and bloodless victory; for all the toughest fighters had either died in battle or left the field badly wounded. Also, many men who had come out from the camp to look around or loot, when they turned over the corpses of the enemy, found friends, men whom they had once welcomed as guests, or who had welcomed them, and relatives; there were also those who recognized personal enemies. And so, throughout the whole army, happiness, sorrow, grief, and rejoicing were variously felt.

> Neque tamen exercitus populi Romani laetam aut incruentam victoriam adeptus erat: nam strenuissumus quisque aut occiderat in proelio aut spoliandi gratia processerant, volventes hostilia cadavera, amicum alii, pars hospitem aut cognatum reperiebant; fuere item qui inimicos suos cognoscerent. Ita varie per omnem exercitum laetitia, maeror, luctus atque gaudia agitabantur. (*Cat.* 59.7–9)

This closure is multivocal, but it still speaks in terms of harmonious wholes and balances, with *neque . . . nam, aut . . . aut* (repeated three times) and the chiasmus of the nouns in the last sentence. The orderly testament to the array of reactions to the battle puts the closing touch on Catiline's conspiracy and its suppression.

By emphasizing the closural aspects of *Catiline*'s ending, I do not mean to simplify the deaths of Lentulus, the others in the Tullianum, or of Catiline. The executions were in fact highly controversial, and quickly became political fodder, as Sallust knew: Cicero paid for them with a sentence of exile in 59 BCE. Sallust's decision to render Catiline's death on the battlefield in heroic terms is the last of many steps in the text's systematic thwarting of its own distinctions between virtue and vice, which emerges first in his initial description of Catiline, which mingles corrupt and admirable attributes (*Cat.* 5), and reaches a climax in Catiline's rousing celebration of justice and virtue in a speech to his supporters (*Cat.* 20).[51] But Catiline does meet an end that is congruent with his own vision, expressed in his furious promise in the senate when his plot is unmasked: "Since I am surrounded, driven headlong by my enemies, I will douse my own fire with devastation" (*quoniam quidem circumventus, inquit, ab inimicis praeceps agor, incendium meum ruina restinguam*, 31.9).

In his influential study of plot, Peter Brooks argues that ambition constitutes the readability of the novelistic text, by providing it with an instantly recognizable logic of narrative progression. The ambitious hero, as he aggressively moves forward in the effort to encompass more and more, to make the world obey his commands, figures the reader's efforts to encompass the meaning of the text, to construct meanings that order the world.[52] Brooks is inspired in part by the connection Walter Benjamin draws between closure and moral authority in his account of narrative in the essay "The Storyteller," from which the epigraph to this section is drawn. Beginning from Solon's advice in Herodotus to call no man happy until he is dead, since no one knows the value of a life until the life is over, Benjamin argues that death is the source of narrative's power.[53] The death in question may simply be the narrative's—the end of the story, whose nature helps clarify what has come before—but the better model, according to Benjamin, is an equal exchange: the death of the character who has earlier given the narrative life. Though *Catiline*'s closing scenes cannot be said to offer a definitive moral or political answer to every question the text has previously raised, the ends of Catiline's ambition are achieved and clarified through his destruction. In the unfolding of Catiline/*Catiline*'s plot, the reader discovers a line of intention that holds the promise of progress toward meaning, toward the desired moment of rendering judgment on the action and the characters.[54]

Jugurtha, though its protagonist exhibits Catiline-like ambition, articulates no such vision and achieves no comparable clarification. It is worth recalling that during the years Sallust composed his historical works, justice

---

51   Batstone, "The antithesis of virtue: Sallust's synkrisis and the crisis of the late republic," concentrates on disclosing the resonances between characters and between character and author in *Catiline* (28). On the revelation of the paradoxical and fragmentary nature of virtue revealed by the text's deployment of historical *exempla* (e.g., the elder Cato), see Levene, "Sallust's 'Catiline' and Cato the Censor," 182.
52   Brooks, *Reading for the Plot*, 39.
53   Herodotus, *Hist.* 1.32.
54   Brooks, xiii.

was thrown into disarray by the assassination of Julius Caesar, when the progression of events raised urgent, increasingly baffling questions about justice and the closure it brings. According to Velleius Paterculus, writing half a century after events,

> The senate was convened [on March 17, just two days after the Ides], and since Dolabella, whom Caesar had designated as his replacement in the consulship, had seized the fasces and insignia of the consul, as the author of peace, he sent his own children as hostages to the Capitol and granted Caesar's murderers safe conduct down from there. Then the *exemplum* of the famous decree of the Athenians, proposed by Cicero, of amnesty for past history, was approved by the decree of the senate. (2.58.3–4)

The word Velleius uses for "amnesty" is *oblivio*, modelled on the Greek for "forgetfulness, lack of memory": it refers to the amnesty passed by the Athenians after the tyranny of the oligarchic regime known as the Thirty had been overthrown.[55] Almost immediately, however, the amnesty was itself intentionally forgotten, as Marc Antony first abolished the office of dictator forever, but then found himself on the political defensive, his own laws and acts annulled (Appian, *Civil Wars* 2.121, 142–45; 3.2). In 42 BCE, the lead conspirators Brutus and Cassius were killed at Philippi, but the civil war continued through the terrible siege of Perusia in 41, and fighting in the Mediterranean with Sextus Pompeius over the next two years. By Sallust's death, around 35, the empire seemed to be splitting in two, between Marc Antony in the east and Caesar's heir Octavian in the west. Throughout this period, the closure that the execution of justice can provide was in short supply.

Many critics have been drawn to *Jugurtha*'s failure to execute Jugurtha. It has been interpreted as evidence of the way the historian's subject "infects" his text, the final demonstration of disorder's triumph in late republican Rome, and as a hint to the reader to look beyond the limits of what is an essentially fragmentary work to see the pattern of Roman decline extending in cycles as far as the inner eye can see.[56] This line of reading broadly follows John Henderson's work on Lucan in examining the way texts about civil war follow their subject matter, fragmenting and turning against themselves. An example of Sallustian *brevitas* and *velocitas*, the ending may also

---

55   Cf. Plutarch, *Life of Cicero*, 60.
56   On the silence as proof of the text's "infection," see Kraus, "Jugurthine disorder," 245.

be taken as a deliberate overturning of narrative balance and harmony, indicating the author's eschewal of traditional aristocratic (and Ciceronian) *gravitas*.[57] The sentences convey Sallust's love of country, muting the North African margins in favor of celebrating events in the city, the imperial core, which will triumph over the peripheral Gauls in the coming war.

The final reference to the people's trust in a single man, Marius, recalls earlier warnings by the popular tribune Memmius against the threat of tyrannical domination—an uncomfortable note on which to end a history that began with the claim that the significance of the Jugurthine War derived from its role in fostering the people's resistance to the nobles' arrogance (*superbiae nobilitatis*, 5.1). Marius is not a member of the *nobilitas*, and his speech to the people on the occasion of his election as consul repeatedly attacks *superbia* (85.38, 45, 47). But his longing for glory and furious resentment when it is initially withheld (*cupidine atque ira*, 54.5) hint ominously at his blind belief in the inevitability of his own authority, a belief stoked by a Utican soothsayer (63.1–2), which leads him to make a bloody bid for tyrannical power in the last years of his life. As the last pages withhold the scene of justice rendered and gaze ahead to the domination of Marius, *Jugurtha* feels emptied of the moral authority Roman history normally claims for itself. Robert Sklenar concludes that Sallust confronts a world warped by civil strife, whose moral vocabulary is "so riven by ambiguities and contradictions" that even villains like Catiline or Marius find ways to appeal to virtue.[58] Faced with this horror, all Sallust can do is try to suture the fractured signs of moral discourse.

Still, in the "end," conclusions are not conclusions. "At that time the hopes and the resources of the city were placed in that man" (*et ea tempestate spes atque opes civitatis in illo sitae*, 114.4). This is a man, Gaius Marius, whose over-reaching will lead Rome straight into civil war. *Sitae* means "placed" or "situated": and with this new situation, *Jugurtha* "ends."[59] In fact, as we have already seen, the text has *situated* its readers with great and detailed care. The ending must be understood in light of the fact that the text's failure to execute Jugurtha is the last of a series of moments when Roman justice is withheld, deferred, or executed incompletely. The repeated deferrals and delays alert the reader to the characters' embedment in time and space, not in the abstract, but in the particular structure of Roman politics, where, it

---

57   This is Syme's interpretation of Sallustian style in *Sallust*, 265; see Woodman's persuasive development of this view, "Style and attitude: Sallust and Livy," 120–28.
58   Sklenar, "La République des Signes," 219.
59   Observed in Levene, "Sallust's *Jugurtha*," 55.

turns out, time and space are warped by a fundamental social and political imbalance. So far we have grasped the pattern of the narrative and the role of individual players in its drama: now it is time to examine Sallust's attention to the structural violence of Roman politics.

THE SIGNIFICANCE OF CORRUPTION

Pierre Rosanvallon argues that in the case of politics, we need to resist the temptation "to deny and dissimulate the contradictions of the world through the illusory coherence of doctrine." Some of this work can be done, he believes, through literature. Artful prose and poetry "open us up to the presence of the world by the devices of language. . . . [Literature] surveys the ambiguity and clears the silence of language; it remains open to the contradictions of the world and never allows concepts to exhaust the density of the real."[60] This holds true for Sallust. To see how greed matters in his text, and precisely what readers may learn about the dense real of the structural violence in republican politics, we must carefully, patiently follow the text's unfolding. There are few unambiguous concepts; there are no clear ends.[61]

At the start of *Jugurtha*, as we have seen, Sallust offers two reasons for his choice to write about this particular war. Like many an ancient historian before him, he explains that it was a great and violent conflict whose outcome was uncertain; moreover, "it was the first time there was resistance to the arrogance of the nobility" (*superbiae nobilitatis*, 5.1–2). Sallust has prefaced the passage with a bitter comparison between archaic virtue and industry and contemporary corruption (4.7–9), but this is more than moralist commentary or an acknowledgment of recent historical events: the effect is to cast bribery as class violence, and to place that violence in a cosmic context. The following sentence describes the consequences of resistance as a struggle that threw "everything divine and human" into disarray, ending in civil war and the devastation of Italy (5.2–3). The proper order of things has been overthrown.

It suits the broader historical context of Sallust's literary production, then, that the protagonist of *Jugurtha* personifies the overthrow of justice. Even before his usurpation of the Numidian throne, Jugurtha—born outside the law, illegitimate—marks himself as a force that overturns law. The

---

60   Rosanvallon, *Democracy Past and Future*, 49–50.
61   Batstone speaks of Sallust's alertness to "a division in Roman society, at the level of concepts and words and actions, so deep that it was intellectually insoluble, even in leisure afterward" ("The antithesis of virtue," 29).

first thing he does after the old king Micipsa's death is recommend to his cousins that all the "judgments and decrees" the king made over the previous five years be cancelled (*consulta et decreta*, 11.5). From his birth to his death, his career encompasses an extended cycle of events and episodes in which justice is withheld, deferred, or executed incompletely: his off-stage execution is only the final turn of the narrative wheel. Some of these are minor incidents, designed to illustrate the broader consequences for law and order when Jugurtha shows bad judgment and loss of self-control. Others are pivotal in the text's development of plot and character. In the pattern that gradually emerges, we begin to see how Sallust draws on the narrative resources offered by plot and character that the forms normally adopted in philosophical discourse cannot.

Impossible to miss, the repetitive representation of the withholding of justice suggests that much more is at stake than Jugurtha's character and career. Roman *iustitia* in all its connotations—law, rights, and equity—is at stake. The moment where this is clarified occurs in the senate, a space adjacent to the seat of justice, the lawcourt, where Adherbal, the son of the dead king Micipsa and now the lawful prince of Numidia, pleads his case against his cousin Jugurtha. His speech is about judgment—specifically, his judgment of the republic's moral obligation to himself and his family, using language that pointedly recalls Roman values of reputation, equity, and moral obligation, and the Romans' responsibility to judge the world and act on those judgments. He "used to judge" the Romans to be honorable allies, he says (*existumabam*, 14.12), on the grounds of past obligation: Numidia had supported Rome in the wars against Carthage. Even if the relationship no longer holds, he argues, justice is the responsibility (*cura*) of Rome: "on account of the magnitude of your dominion, every aspect of justice and injustice is rightly your concern" (*quibus pro magnitudine imperi ius et iniurias omnis curae esse decet*, 14.16–17, see also 21). Adherbal's argument recalls Catiline's accusation in Sallust's earlier work that Rome has failed to maintain itself as a just empire (*iustum imperium, Cat.* 52.21). In their rebuttal of Adherbal's charges, Jugurtha's envoys invert Adherbal's appeal to Roman justice. They claim that he, not Jugurtha, is the true criminal (15.1).

Ironically, both sides' oratorical efforts are in vain, since the case is ultimately decided by the corrupting power of money. Jugurtha bribes a number of senators, under whose influence the senate dismisses Adherbal's claim and establishes a commission that will divide Numidia into two kingdoms for the cousins to rule separately (16.1–2). A kind of justice is thus rendered, but it is incomplete and destructive. The commission fails almost immediately (21.4), since it is swayed by the arguments Jugurtha's envoys had earlier made before the Roman senate: Jugurtha is the victim of the crime of attempted murder, and Rome would be acting "neither honorably nor justly" if it prevented him from acting in accordance with the law (22.4). Clearly they make a bad jury. Jugurtha makes a promise to them, never fulfilled, to send legates to Rome to explain his actions at a later date (*postremo*), and they depart, having failed to seek out Adherbal's version of events (22.5). When Adherbal sends a final desperate appeal to the senate from the town of Cirta, where Jugurtha is besieging him, the cycle of delay begins again. A new commission travels to the Roman part of Africa and summons Jugurtha to explain himself, but their diplomatic efforts are frustrated, and they return to Rome like the junior commission before them (*multa tamen oratione consumpta legati frustra discessere*, 25.11). Immediately, Jugurtha storms Cirta and has Adherbal brutally tortured and murdered.

Suggestively, in his speech to the senate, Adherbal had exhorted himself in a melodramatic apostrophe to avenge the *iniuria* against his brother or die (14.23): like Catiline, he accurately predicts the future conditions of his life and acts in such a way as to bring them about. While his death is an unjust act of murder on Jugurtha's part, then, it also makes Adherbal a sign—unusual in this text—of transparent intentionality and closure. Sallust also notes that a number of Italian merchants are slaughtered along with Adherbal. The reputed size of the massacre may be the product of his habitual anti-aristocratic hyperbole, but the passage also underscores the consequences of the Roman failure to render justice on the part of the lawful antagonist, a decision that rebounds directly onto Rome's citizens abroad (26.3).[62]

The plot-structuring dynamic of justice deferred takes on momentum in two closely interrelated scenes set at Rome, where Jugurtha finally arrives to testify at the people's investigation into his acts of bribery. As popular anger in Rome about the events in Cirta grows, the senators whom Jugurtha had earlier bribed delay the senate once more with interruptions and other time-wasting measures (*interpellando . . . trahundo tempus*, 27.1). When the senate finally agrees to dispatch an army to Numidia—the first of three to be sent there—the avarice of key senators, notably the consul and serving general Bestia, perverts their intentions. Bestia's mind is easily turned from his official purpose, diseased as it is by greed (*animus aeger avaritia facile convorsus est*, 29.1).

---

62   Morstein-Marx argues that this passage reflects *popularis* propaganda rather than historical events, "The alleged massacre at Cirta and its consequences (Sall. *BJ* 26–27)."

The popular tribune Memmius, known for his hatred of the senatorial nobility, convinces the people to bring the matter to the attention of the courts on the grounds that the crime of bribery must not go unpunished (*ne tantum scelus inpunitum omittatis*, 31.25). But Jugurtha travels to testify at the trial under the official sign of justice deferred—the protection of the secret pledge of the praetor L. Cassius that he will come to no harm (*privatim praeterea fidem suam*, 32.5). To make doubly certain of his safety, Jugurtha bribes another Roman official, this time a tribune, Gaius Baebius, and when he is summoned to speak before the people's assembly, Baebius interposes his tribunician veto before he can utter a word (34.1). Here Sallust makes the abrogation of justice explicit: though the people tried to persuade the tribune to change his veto with shouts and gestures, Jugurtha's "shamelessness conquered" (*vicit tamen impudentia*, 34.2). Soon after, in the second scene, when an associate of Jugurtha's is arrested for a politically motivated murder, the prince smuggles him out of Rome—and here justice is doubly perverted, Sallust notes, since both Jugurtha's act and the henchman's trial were illegal on technical grounds of Roman law (35.7). The situation is the same outside the city. When the political newcomer Gaius Marius grows angry with his commander and rival Metellus, he loosens military discipline in order to gain popularity among the troops (*laxiore imperio quam antea*, 54.5).

With the perspective gained by this extended analysis, *Jugurtha* is revealed as an extended textual *epideixis* of political disorientation, where the withholding of justice initiated by bribery kicks off the terrible violence of civil war and even the overturning of the cosmic order. Sallust's closural strategy caps a narrative pattern of silence and deferral in the text, a pattern that bespeaks a fundamental dislocation in the republic of the relation between being and doing, intention and action—the very things that make civic judgment and the rendering of justice possible. This dislocation also marks the representation of the other main characters in the work. Each carefully balanced between virtue and vice, they personify the hard-to-calculate distance between appearance and action—Metellus the intelligent, self-disciplined, and arrogant noble, Marius the plain-spoken and passionately ambitious "new man," and Sulla the successful, pleasure-loving schemer.[63]

What is the significance of this for understanding Sallust's political thought? If the text's withholding of justice constructs the thematic frame

---

63   Levene, in "Sallust's Jugurtha," explains his (quite similar) view of the characters in detail (60–64).

for *Jugurtha*, marking the birth, life, and death of its protagonist, then bribery, as the principal cause of justice's withholding, is the multivalent point from which Sallust's political thinking splits into three interrelated directions. We have already seen how bribery distorts the senators' execution of civic and military prudence, leading them to treat Jugurtha favorably, to delay battle with his forces, and so on. Bribery also spotlights the disparity of wealth between the impoverished mass and the senatorial elite, raising questions about economic and political equity. And bribery breaks down the trust between senate and people, drawing attention to the governing order's psychologically destructive disregard of the citizen populace.

Bribery is the key factor in the political breakdown to which Sallust directs our attention, the initial cause of the withholding of justice within the world of the text, and the spark of popular resistance. Jugurtha's successful bribery of the greedy senators is memorialized in the history's most notorious quotation: "There is a city ready to be sold, and ripe for destruction, if only it can find a buyer" (35.10). Sallust signals the importance of bribery early on, in an ironic account of the Roman general Scipio Aemilianus warning the youthful Jugurtha to be on guard against it (8.2). The senators' eager receipt of bribes is the clearest sign of the moral decay of the Roman *nobilitas*, first fired up by the plundering of rich nations abroad. This is a story Sallust tells at great length in *Catiline* (7.6–13.5), and before going further, it is worth glancing at that text once more, since it reveals how Sallust views the relationship of fully empowered civic identity and justice to the just distribution of wealth.

Catiline fits the characteristically Roman pattern of "reforming" nobles whose ambition drives them to seek support among the people, especially debtors and the poor. Through his own self-indulgence, Catiline himself is heavily in debt (*Cat.* 5.7), and he focuses his efforts to enroll supporters in his conspiracy on men much worse off, whether from debt or spending on luxuries (14.3, 28.4). Catiline's appeal to the poor (or men whom he constructs as poor, which for the purposes of my argument amounts to the same thing) reiterates themes Sallust has laid out earlier in the narrative: the corrupting power of luxury and avarice is ruining the republic (5.8); desire for money, in tandem with ambition, forces elite and mass to separate as the leading men become greedy for money instead of fame (7.6). Focusing his efforts to enroll supporters in his conspiracy on financial losers in this environment, he justifies his conspiracy on the grounds that the governing order has abandoned its responsibility along with its moderation, leaving the circumstances of survival uncertain (*condicio vitae*, 20.7; cf. 10–11).

This run of complaints, not unfamiliar, draws a clear link between poverty and political disempowerment articulated by Sallust himself. This is his famous account of Rome's early decline:

> So good morals were cultivated at home and in war abroad, and there was the greatest concord, the least greed, and justice and the good were dominant among them, not by means of laws more than by nature.... By these two arts—bravery in war, and when peace came, by equality—they looked after themselves and the republic.

> igitur domi militiaeque boni mores colebantur, concordia maxuma, minuma avaritia erat, ius bonumque apud eos non legibus magis quam natura valebat.... duabus his artibus, audacia in bello, ubi pax evenerat aequitate seque remque publicam curabant. (*Cat.* 9.1, 3)

Here Sallust's criticism transcends the form of the moralistic diatribe against the softening effect of foreign conquest. While the ancestral Romans' virtuous nature originally bore the lion's share of sustaining concord and justice, he says, reliance on virtue alone was and is insufficient for the good of the republic. Once the citizenry was no longer devoted full-time to making war, the nurturing of *aequitas* was necessary to keep the state on an even keel. Desirable under other conditions, leisure and riches became a source of misery in the republic (*otium, divitiae optanda alias, oneri miseriaeque fuere*, 10.2) because they destroyed its equality and justice, *aequitas* and *iustitia*. Quickly, Sallust explains that *aequitas* makes laws that restrain or punish those who take what does not belong to them. His pointedly chosen examples are young nobles who run wild with desire for wealth (12.2) and private men who undertake unnatural expenditures on lavish versions of simple necessities (*privatis*) such as food and housing (13.1).

The link between material deprivation and political disempowerment is also the touchstone for the popular tribune Memmius (*Jug.* 31.9) and Memmius' successor in the tribunate, Mamilius Limetanus, who eventually carries Memmius' proposal to investigate Jugurtha's bribery in the senate (40.1–3). His action, which meets with mixed success, introduces Sallust's meditation on the divisions that wealth creates between senate and people. There he endorses the Gracchi brothers' efforts "to rescue popular liberty and expose the crimes of the nobility" (42.1), and portrays current politics as a zero-sum game, where the nobles' quest for wealth and power serves themselves while oppressing the people with heavy military service and poverty (*populus militia atque inopia urgebatur*, 41.7).

Finally, in the *Histories*, the tribune Macer remonstrates with the people, pointing out that bribery dehumanizes them: it is the one of the signs of a lawless system that transforms citizens into cattle:

> All the others elected to guard your rights have turned all their power and authority against you, driven by personal interest, hope, or bribes, and they judge it better to commit crimes for hire than to do right for free. And so everything has yielded to the tyranny of the few, who on the excuse of war have pillaged the treasury, the army, client kingdoms, and the provinces, and who have built themselves a castle out of booty that belongs to you, while you, a crowd, like cattle, give yourselves over to be owned and exploited by individual masters.

> quamquam omnes alii creati pro iure uostro uim cunctam et imperia sua gratia aut spe aut praemiis in uos conuortere, meliusque habent mercede delinquere quam gratia recte facere. itaque omnes concessere iam in paucorum dominationem, qui per militare nomen aerarium exercitus regna provincias occupauere et arcem habent ex singulis habendos fruendosque praebetis. (*Hist.* 3.48.6)

Macer, Catiline, and the rest of Sallust's popular tribunes link the subservience of the life of poverty to the breakdown of justice and the end of political liberty. That is, they talk about poverty not only in what we now call economic terms (focusing on lowness of income or wealth) or utilitarian terms (focusing on low concentrations of satisfaction), but in terms of capability deprivation—here, the thing deprived being the capacity to function politically as fully free citizens.[64] The wars that the corrupted nobles take to be a quest for status and glory in truth engender massive economic inequalities that create a state of quasi-slavery, the deprivation of citizens' capability to behave or even view themselves as citizens, and manipulation from the top. Here Sallustian moralism ventures into the terrain of prescription, flagging economic parity as a civic priority, a matter of urgent concern to the citizen reader who wishes to learn how to avoid the decline Sallust so bitterly mourns.

Love of liberty, even more than the espousal of a politics of virtue or principles of participation and representation, is the distinctive mark of thinkers who compose the European and American tradition of thinking

---

64   Sen, *Development as Freedom*, 19.

we now call "republican."[65] By most accounts, though Roman liberty meant different things to different people, signifying one particular set of ideas in *popularis* speeches, another in Cicero's letters to his friends, in general the Romans understood liberty as the condition of not being a slave.[66] The Roman citizen's liberty includes both what modern theorists call "negative" and "positive" liberty, including both freedom from the arbitrary interference of magistrates and the freedom to participate in the political process. Before the evolution of rights theory, early modern writers followed Aristotle and Cicero in seeing personal liberty as the prerequisite for participating fully in the life proper to men, the life where the individual's capacity to govern himself translates into participation in the government of the community. Popular liberty was also a bulwark against the tyranny of nobles or kings, and commitment to it evolved alongside the notion that civic standing should be granted according to merit rather than birth. As the poet Ralph Knevet wrote in the 1620s:

And by his proper actions doth descrive;
A Gentleman: for Fortune can't inherit
(By right) those graces, which pertaine to merit:
 And wretched is that Gentrie, which is gotten
 From their deedes, that long since be dead and rotten.[67]

Precisely on what grounds civic merit should be awarded to the ungentle citizenry was a question debated centuries before Knevet's lifetime that remains unresolved today. The earliest and greatest challenge to the traditional governing order in early modern Europe arose in the form of the newly powerful commercial class: bankers, merchants, speculators, and entrepreneurs. The emergence of this class and its ethic of work corroded the ancient belief that the state is best governed by citizens enjoying the leisure to participate in politics by virtue of their possession of landed property. According to the new rules of the commercial world, merit rested on the accumulation of wealth—notably, alienable wealth whose protection and increase demanded constant supervision. Could men engaged in the toilsome work of commercial enterprise truly be said to be free, or were they

---

65 Skinner, *Liberty Before Liberalism*, sketches the history of republican thought about liberty as it applies to states (22–30) and to individuals (61–79).

66 Brunt, *"Libertas,"* 283.

67 From his *Stratiotikon: or a discourse of militarie discipline*, cited in Peltonen, *Classical Humanism and Republican Thought*, 274.

more properly considered the modern descendants of Aristotle's banausic laborers, whom he excluded from full citizenship (*Pol.* 3.5, 1287a8–14)? Like the elder Cato, the classical depictor of traditional rural life, some early modern republican thinkers argued that it was not possible for a good businessman to be a good citizen. Today, the American infatuation with politicians who identify themselves with the countryside—George W. Bush, for instance, who successfully rebranded his Texas estate as "the Crawford ranch"—is partly a fantasy in which the traditional values of simplicity and honesty attributed to rural community life are transported to Washington, and partly the product of an anxious desire to forget the urban world of business and commerce, the world that creates the wealth belonging to most American politicians. The deeply rooted republican suspicion of wealth clashes constantly with the knowledge that the rich hold high status and power even, perhaps especially, in republican government.

Underpinning this conflict is the deeper, more troublesome problem that Sallust so eloquently acknowledges: how the political and legal equality of a republican commonwealth is affected by conditions of economic inequality—in short, whether economic equality is necessary for a republic to sustain its citizens' liberty. If wealth corrupts the republic at the top, must not poverty and deprivation corrupt it everywhere else—especially deprivation so severe it leads to the diminishment of citizens' sense of themselves as such? W. E. B. Du Bois drew the line between citizenship and the economic autonomy granted by earning power by comparing poor workers favorably to slaves in the American South, whose "laboring force is voiceless in the public councils and powerless in its own defence."[68] It is no accident that Martin Luther King gave one of his most famous speeches at a mass meeting in Washington called "March for Jobs and Freedom."

The Romans define liberty as the opposite of slavery, that is, the condition of freedom from domination. At the core of our self-identification as free people is our capacity to provide for our own basic needs—food, water, housing, healthcare—without needing to look to another source of sustenance, a source that might be tyrannical or arbitrary. In short, our liberty derives from the independent ownership of the means to look after ourselves. As for those incapable of doing so, especially the impoverished, beginning with Thomas More's *Utopia*, and continuing with James Harrington's English Civil War–era advocacy of equal land ownership and Thomas Jefferson's proposals for agricultural allotments, republican thinkers have proposed programs of property redistribution that would resolve

68   *The Souls of Black Folk*, 198.

the freedom-destroying disparity of wealth in the state. Until the nineteenth century, many were able to defend their solutions by appealing to the republican infatuation with agrarian freeholding. But their visions of property redistribution have collided with the republican notion of liberty, one that represents republicanism's most important point of contact with classical liberalism: the defense of property rights. Then and now, republican thought incorporates a seemingly insoluble conflict between the philosophy of government as "pursuit of the common good," where the wealth of the citizenry is distributed fairly among all, and a theory of liberty that ties its notion of personal autonomy to the possession of property.

Sallust has nothing to contribute to the redistribution debate. However, his withholding of Jugurtha's execution caps a narrative pattern of deferral that bespeaks a fundamental dislocation of the relation, in the republic, between intention and action, between being and doing. It is caused, at almost every plot point, by the improper circulation of money. Bribery is the main problem, because to Sallust politics is a field of action, access to which depends on the ownership of wealth. The concern with wealth and its effects on senatorial bodies is reflected in the style and narrative strategy of the historian. We sense the importance of corporeal knowing, but that is not enough; it must be accompanied by aliveness to another kind of knowledge—knowledge that politics is structural violence. This is the turn to the collective that Sallust signaled at the beginning, with his explanation of why he chose this period to write about. This is what gives the work a political edge, moving it outside the bounds of the strictly moral.

There is an epistemological point to the story about bribery. Greed dislodges: it unmoors intention from action, reason from intention, observation from reason. Greed is not a corrupting force because of the general moral decay it causes, or because it distracts from the attainment of *gloria*. It corrupts because it contributes to structural inequities. And it blurs sight—not in a vague sense of disconnection or groping in a cloud. Specifically, greed and the resulting inequality makes it impossible for the rich to see the poor.

Bruno Latour has pointed out that if the "political" appeals etymologically to a discourse that roots itself in the Greek *polis*, what needs to be retrieved now is that politics is also a discourse that circulates around "things."[69] Etymologically, "public things," in the Latin form *res publica*, suggests that politics is not a sphere, a profession, or an occupation, but (Latour says) a concern for things that are brought to the attention of a public. Suggesting

69   Latour, *Making Things Public*, 15.

that political philosophy has "often been the victim of a strong object-avoidance tendency," he asks: "What would happen if politics was made to turn around things disputed in public?" By giving bribery a central role in thwarting the translation of public intention into action, Sallust makes politics turn around a disputed thing: unlawful possession of money, exchanged in secret, away from public sight and hearing.

We have seen Sallust articulate, in terms that draw attention to the grain of fleshly feeling, the antagonism of class. Bribery also spotlights the disparity of wealth between the impoverished mass and the senatorial elite. In doing so, it discloses the structural violence done in republican politics, where economic inequity undoes ideals of harmony and liberty. And as bribery breaks down the trust between senate and people, it reveals the governing order's destructive disregard of the citizen populace. Citizenship emerges as more than a legal status: it is a psychological state where, far from being simply free autonomous beings, it turns out that citizens rely on mutual regard to give them a sense of belonging in the civic body.

RECOGNITION

According to the conventional account of Roman thought, questions of equitable distribution and material goods are assumed to be irrelevant to politics. Neal Wood and Eric Nelson, in particular, dismiss Roman thinkers for ignoring questions of equity. But this does not accurately describe Sallust. In *Catiline*, when Sallust declares that he cannot distinguish between greed and political ambition (*avaritia, ambitio*, 11.1), his incapacity drives home the intimate relationship between economic and political wrongdoing. In *Jugurtha*, the senators' eager receipt of bribes is a clear sign of the moral decay of the Roman *nobilitas* not only because the money fuels the luxury-consumption that softens and effeminizes them—effects alleged but never illustrated in the text—but because inequitable distribution of wealth is the key to the *failure of recognition* that destroys civic identity. Sallust explores this issue throughout his corpus.

In a scene I mentioned briefly above, the tribune Memmius, whom Sallust introduces as a man intensely resentful of the power of the nobility (*Jug.* 27.2, 30, 3), summons the people to a *contio*, a formal public assembly where, attacking the senators' acceptance of bribes, he exhorts the people to resist senatorial domination. His speech links their wealth—the fruit of illegal plunder—with a particular notion of injustice that encompasses both economic and psychological effects:

In earlier times you silently fumed that the treasury was being pillaged, that kings and free peoples paid tribute to just a few nobles, and most of all, that those same men gained the highest glory and immense riches. But they were not content to have committed these awful crimes with impunity, and so as time went on the laws, your sovereignty, and everything divine and human were handed over to the enemy. Nor are those who did these things ashamed or sorry, but they walk abroad before your eyes, magnificent, some showing off their priesthoods and consulships, others, their triumphs, just as if they held them due to honor rather than robbery.

Superioribus annis taciti indignabamini aerarium expilari, reges et populos liberos paucis nobilibus vectigal pendere, penes eosdam et summam gloriam et maxumas divitias esse. Tamen haec talia facinora impune suscepisse parum habuere itaque postremo leges, maiestas vostra, divina et humana omnia hostibus tradita sunt. Neque eos, qui ea fecere, pudet aut paenitet, sed incedunt per ora vostra magnifici, sacerdotia et consulatus, pars triumphos suos ostentantes; proinde quasi ea honori non praedae habeant. (31.9–10)

He goes on to recall the series of significant turning points in accounts of the early history of the republic, the so-called secessions of the plebs. As Livy and other sources have it, large groups of plebeians withdrew from the city in 494 BCE, in what is often referred to as the "first secession." The next secession, occurring in 450/449 BCE, led to the passing of laws guaranteeing the right of appeal to the people, *provocatio ad populum*, against scourging or capital punishment by a magistrate, and the third secession in 287 finally terminated debt-slavery and gave legislative authority to the assembly of the plebs. Memmius blurs the condition of slavery with the condition of being poor by referring to slavery whenever he contrasts the citizens with the excessively wealthy nobles. In his picture of the contemporary republic, popular suffering is identical in level and cause to that which provoked the archaic secessions, except this time the people are being enslaved not by the legal debt-slavery called *nexum* but by a nobility themselves enslaved to unchecked greed.

The public action Memmius is trying to orchestrate is not secession but public approval of the legal investigation of Jugurtha's influence in the senate, and as we have seen, it fails when Jugurtha is saved by a tribune he bribed for the purpose. Sallust's description of the assembly's reaction tellingly stresses their resentful awareness of their status: they withdraw, seeing that they are being treated "like a joke" (*populus ludibrio habitus*, 34.2). The nobles' greed is more than an indictment of their moral fitness to lead or of the economic inequality that, inflaming the citizenry's anger, threatens the concord of the republic. Their receipt of bribes, as it publicly undermines the consensual values on which the nobles stake their claim to govern, reveals naked contempt for the people. Their shamelessness is a blatant refusal to recognize the opinions or values of the rest of the citizens (*neque eos qui ea fecere pudet et paenitet, 31.10*).

Later in *Jugurtha*, Marius develops Memmius' critique in the speech he delivers upon assuming the consulship, whose guiding theme is the contempt the established nobility exhibits toward him. His opponents accuse him of being rude and uncultivated, because he does not indulge in their vices of gourmet cookery and fancy literature: let them do so, he says, because he and the people know the truth—that "elegance is proper to women, hard work to men; it is better for good men to have more glory than riches, and that weapons, not furniture, are their glory" (85.39–40). His rhetoric of recognition, in addition to making gendered claims, valorizes the social and cultural experience of the non-wealthy, naming them as the custodians of Roman values and the prudent anchors of the political process.

In *Catiline*, Sallust claimed that leisure and riches, desirable under other conditions, had become a weight and a source of misery in the republic (*otium, divitiae optanda alias, oneri miseriaeque fuere, 10.2*) because they destroy its equality and justice, *aequitas* and *iustitia*. From an empire that was "most just and best" Rome grew "cruel and intolerable" (*imperium ex iustissumo atque optumo crudele intolerandumque factum, 10.6*). Catiline's speech to his fellow conspirators clarifies the connection linking justice, liberty, and political recognition. He begins by emphasizing his reliance on, and strong sense of common cause with, his supporters, who, he says, hold the same view of good and evil (20.3), the true hallmark of "strong friendship" (*firma amicitia, 20.4*). His own zeal for armed resistance grew from his contemplation of the powerful few's (*paucorum potentium*) abrogation of law (*ius*): slavery looms "if we ourselves do not stake a claim on our liberty" (*nisi nosmet ipsi vindicamus in libertatem, 20.7*).

> All the rest of us—hard-working, good men, both noble and common—we have been a mass without influence and without authority, subservient to those to whom, if the republic were truly strong, we should be a source of fear. And so all influence, power, honor, and wealth belong to them, or go wherever they wish: to us they leave danger, defeat, harassment by the law, and poverty. How long will you suffer these things, o bravest of men?

ceteri omnes, strenui boni, nobiles atque ignobiles, uolgus fuimus sine
gratia, sine auctoritate, iis obnoxii quibus, si res publica valeret, formi-
dini essemus. Itaque omnis gratia potentia honos diuitiae apud illos
sunt aut ubi illi uolunt: nobis reliquere pericula repulsas iudicia eges-
tatem. Quae quo usque tandem patiemini, o fortissumi uiri? (20.7–9)

Catiline's choice of the marked word *obnoxius*, "subservient" or "under obligation," to describe himself and his supporters, and his claim that "all the
rest of us, hard-working, good men, both noble and common" are citizens
as worthy of political consideration as the rich nobility, acknowledge the
mediating role of social institutions in creating identities, identities which
shape the terms in which individuals treat each other and understand
themselves.

More radically, Catiline claims that being a citizen of republican Rome
is a matter not only of law and political freedom, but economic standing.
The rich hold "influence, power, honor, and wealth"; "to us they leave danger, defeat, harassment by the law, and poverty." In the *Histories*, the consul
Lepidus equates the people's loss of *libertas* under the tyranny of Sulla to
the loss of their homes and property and expulsion from their lands (*Hist.*
1.55.4, 24). He too connects the people's political disempowerment to their
poverty and to the contempt in which they are now held by the wealthy:
"the Roman people, not long ago the master of nations, are now stripped of
power, glory, and rights; they lack the means of living (*agitandi inops*), and
are the object of haughty disdain (*despectus*); they possess not even the ra-
tions left over for slaves" (11). In these speeches, Sallust develops his critique
of economic inequality, showing how the republic is harmed when citizens
who perceive that they are dismissed—unrecognized—by others because of
their relatively low economic status also perceive themselves to be unrecognized as full citizens: we recall Macer's bitter comparison between the people and cattle (*Hist.* 3.48.6).

In the terms of contemporary political theory, Sallust sees the question
of economic standing as a matter of political recognition. The concept of
recognition occupies a central place in current work, especially on citizenship. A starting point was John Dewey's early twentieth century *The Public
and Its Problems*, which argued that the citizenry must recognize itself as
such (as a collective), and that citizens must recognize each other as such (as
equal and equally empowered members of the body politic). Charles Taylor's 1992 essay "The politics of recognition" proposed that humans share
an essential need to be recognized, each as the bearer of a distinctive identity, and that democratic movements must recognize the specificities of

these identities. Later work, building on Taylor's thesis, identified the most urgent distinctions of identity for liberal democracies in the West: race, gender, ethnic identity, religion, sexual orientation, mental or physical handicap, and so forth. What was missing, as Nancy Fraser began to argue in the 1990s, was consideration of the universally shared identity of economic status: class. Programmatically speaking, the politics of class, because it transcends gender, race, and other social differences, stands in tension with the effort to guarantee the recognition of social diversity. Though the two are closely interrelated, she concluded, recognition must be analyzed separately from redistribution; class is not status; culture is not political economy. In her most recent work, under the influence of critics such as Judith Butler and Iris Marion Young, Fraser has suggestively explored a new approach: the analysis of the patterns of exclusion and inclusion of people from politics, the "framing" of citizen concerns.[70]

Roman citizenship is normally understood to involve certain legal and political freedoms and protections, but like Fraser, Sallust sees that citizenship crucially invokes tangled notions of social and economic standing as well. In a certain sense, this may come as no surprise: after all, the Romans organized electoral practices around the census, dividing citizens into voting groups according to economic worth and then weighting the votes of the rich more heavily than those of the poor. My point is that Sallust's emphasis on equal standing broadens the definition of justice to include considerations of economic equity. The deeply rooted connection between poverty and the limits of recognition is the cause of revolution in *Catiline* and the spur to popular resistance against oppression in *Jugurtha*. These texts attune the reader to antagonisms traversing the political order that disempower some citizens, that exert heavy force on the collective understanding of what is properly political in the first place, and that hinder the execution of intention.

CONTINGENCY

In the preface to *The Golden Bowl*, Henry James observed that "The whole conduct of life consists of things done, which do other things in their turn." In *Jugurtha*, as the effects of Jugurtha's bribery make themselves felt, the

---

70   Fraser, "From redistribution to recognition? Dilemmas of justice in a 'post-socialist' age." Markell helpfully clarifies the debate in "Recognition and redistribution," 455–59 (esp. 458–59).

consequential relationship James has in mind breaks down. Evidence for this is the prominent role of luck in the plot, especially when bribery enters the picture, blurring the obligations of citizens and their capacity to predict the consequences of their actions. This is another kind of recognition the Sallustian text models: the necessity of living with contingency. Political life is messy. When Sallust recovers meaning from the corrupt and confused past, he puts it in an order that contaminates its own efforts at purity, constantly deferring the moments at which unity might be achieved. Sallust is under no illusions; despite the distinctions he draws between Rome and barbarian Others, he generally resists the desire to see Rome as a logic, as a "necessary, determined, predictable outcome of the premises about human interaction."[71]

Bodies are messy, unpredictable things, and embodied knowing also involves attention to the messiness and unpredictable aspects of political life. In an unusual, vividly described episode that anticipates the ending's silence regarding the execution of Jugurtha, Sallust shows the non-execution of another character who, by internal logic, also seems to deserve death. The action, whose swift, suspenseful narration plays out an Aristotelian drama of recognition and reversal, revolves around Jugurtha's chance discovery of a plot organized by his closest advisers. Nabdalsa, one of the conspirators, receives a letter from the leader, Bomilcar, but he happens to be exhausted from exercising, and falls asleep with the letter on his pillow (71.1). His secretary, finding him asleep, impulsively reads the letter, not suspecting its treasonous content. Immediately after he reports Nabdalsa to Jugurtha, the king orders that everyone involved in the conspiracy be executed—but he appears to spare Nabdalsa, for reasons that are not clear (72.1–2).[72] The arbitrary nature of the usurper's action symbolizes the disorder that has come to rule his life; he is soon nearly driven mad by terror and distrust (72.2).

Chance plays an important role in the plots of both *Catiline* and *Jugurtha*: characters act for arbitrary reasons and fortune guides events. In *Jugurtha*, the old Numidian king Micipsa, worried about the young Jugurtha's growing popularity, sends him to military service with the Romans fighting in Spain, on the chance that he will die there (*fortuna*, 7.1). But the roll of for-

---

71   I am inspired here by Dolan's observation about Puritan rhetoric, *Allegories of America*, 30–31 (quotation from 59).

72   Sallust says that Jugurtha soon stopped the executions in order to avoid widespread rebellion in Numidia, but he does not specify Nabdalsa's fate.

tune's dice leads instead to Jugurtha's corruption by ambitious young Romans. After Micipsa's death, the older prince Hiempsal stays with a friend in Thirmida by chance (*forte*, 12.3), and again by chance (*casu*, 12.3) Jugurtha successfully bribes the friend, his soldiers gain access to the house and murder Hiempsal. In Utica, by chance (*forte*, 63.1) Marius meets an omen-reader who predicts a great future for him. Marius' ambitious hopes for the consulship are unleashed; he asks his commanding general Metellus for permission to stand for election, but Metellus refuses, warning Marius "against setting his mind above his *fortuna*" (64.2). Marius rejects these terms in his consular oration, which rewrites his *fortuna* as his main advantage (85.15). Not long after, during a difficult siege of a mountain fortress near the river Molucca, Marius ponders whether he should persist in his efforts in the hope that *fortuna* will turn his way (93.1). And fortune is indeed on his side: there is by chance (*forte*, 92.7) a Ligurian soldier in the army who, on a search for water, discovers snails on the ground, which happen to be his favorite dish (*forte* again, 93.2); by chance an ilex tree is growing nearby that helps him climb up the mountainside, and he discovers a secret path up to the fortress which wins the battle (*forte*, 93.4). Chance (*forte*, 94.6) brings Marius the glory that sets him on the path to his future greatness—which we readers know leads to civil war.

From this overview, *Jugurtha* is revealed again as an extended *epideixis* of political disorientation. No one is as he seems; few deeds turn out as they are intended. Jugurtha's ambition and habits of bribery undo him; several times his failure to act is utterly mysterious. Meanwhile, Rome does not act either: on both sides the conventional structural logic of event and reaction is overturned. The question is not (as some critics have said): what is the use of virtue when the outcome of a battle depends on snails and the revelation of a plot hangs on the bad timing of a nap? The point is rather stated by Sulla, a notoriously lucky man who will become a tyrannical dictator, when he tells the Mauretanian king Bocchus that human affairs are governed by *fortuna* (102.9; cf. 95.4). The play of chance rests at the core of the human experience of politics. Sallust has an eye for the unpredictable plays of chance that shape the world, and his text awakens us to be similarly alert. Chance creates conditions for unexpected change, most notably in the case of Marius' and Catiline's careers; it is not moral in and of itself, but it allows people to make choices that make the world afresh. It opens up the possibility for novelty—for new movements, new types of civic recognition, and perhaps, new conflicts—what Andreas Kalyvas calls "the politics of the extraordinary."

CONCLUSIONS

As I close, then, I return to the problem of endings. Recognition is an ongoing challenge in contemporary politics: failure to recognize parts of the *populus* as sensible parts of the body politic, as we saw in chapter 1, tends to lead to violence. Another aspect of politics that emerged in that chapter is that recognition occurs not in a single moment but over time: it is a long process in the course of which obstacles (social standing, economic inequity) must be overcome or made irrelevant. The winding narrative and the ending of *Jugurtha*, or lack of an ending, also suggest that the end is not the end, that no single moment in the drama of the story deserves attention more than the *process* of corruption and civic breakdown.

Let me turn back briefly to the movement that opened this book, which at the time of this writing (late summer 2013) is quiescent: Occupy Wall Street. The question critics, sympathizers, and everyone in between asks about Occupy is "What are its goals?" "What do they want to achieve?" "What are their ends?" Participants in the movement tend to answer the question in three ways. First, for many of them, what matters most are words and beliefs: political discourse. These Occupiers want to change political discourse by raising popular consciousness, especially about class and the power of organized wealth. Consequently Occupy demonstrators in the fall of 2011 carried signs with memorable, timely slogans like "I'll believe corporations are people when Texas executes one," "The people are too big to fail," and "Too bad the war on poverty isn't a real war: we'd be putting money into it." Occupy activists created the highly publicized website "We are the 99%," which posted short handwritten accounts of people's struggles to make ends meet in a world where, as one poster put it, "In 3 days my CEO makes more than I do in a year!"

The second common answer is more ambitious. The Occupy protesters did not choose to meet together each day for an hour or more to chant and hold signs. They chose to sleep and eat together in public, to compel others to watch them living the lives of the homeless, the displaced, the dispossessed. In doing so they sought to bear witness and prompt moral reflection in themselves and those who watched them. In a world where, as Kimberley Curtis insightfully remarks, we live with a "new found fragility of our capacity to sense reality, to be present to 'what is,'" these people aimed to change the culture, to encourage passersby in New York and observers around the world to reconsider their life choices—spurred by witnessing the stripped-down lives that their fellow citizens were leading, some by choice, others by necessity.[73]

The third answer, whose spirit was effectively conveyed by the much-reproduced signs "Shit is fucked up and bullshit" and "I'm so angry I made a sign," expresses a radically different perspective. These Occupiers didn't have a goal, and by their own account, they didn't want one. They believed, and presumably still believe, that serious reckoning must be done before they pursue any end or encourage others to do so, let alone an end that corresponds with the standard operating procedure of established political habits. At least two different beliefs seem to ground this principle. One: the arc of intention and action in the formal political process has been decisively disrupted by multinational corporate influence. Two: the process of goal-setting itself runs the risk of shutting down new possibilities, specifically, new ways of thinking about and engaging in politics. Consciously or not, Occupy activists who took this stance were embracing Hannah Arendt's and Jacques Rancière's rejection of the definition of politics as policing and policy-making, as well as Arendt's peculiar commitment to the idea that natality, the property by which new things enter the world, is the mechanism that powers political action, and Rancière's view that politics begins from the partition of people into those who have a part in politics and those who do not.

One of the most notable markers of the Occupy movement was their use of the "human microphone" to enable public communication in the "general assembly" organizational meetings at Occupy sites after police banned the use of regular microphones. The human mic resembles the game of Telephone, but one in which the repetition serves to amplify, rather than dissipate, the signal. One person (having previously entered her or his name on the "stack" of those wishing to speak) speaks in blocks of words short enough for the crowd to repeat—sometimes, if the crowd were large enough to warrant it, in two or more waves moving outward from the center. In addition to carrying the speaker's words over large crowds, this practice gave everyone present at the meeting the opportunity to feel the sensations involved in speaking as a member of a pluralistic collective. As Occupiers repeatedly said, in these telephonic conversations the point was to focus on the *process* by which people take part in deliberation or action: the necessity of repeating each speaker's points meant that the entire dialogue was carefully, deliberately articulated by the entire assembly, each individual taking the time both to hear and to speak every point, those they agreed with and

73   Curtis, "Aesthetic foundations of democratic politics," 46.

those they disagreed with alike. The human mic also gave people with little or no experience speaking or acting in public the opportunity to gain confidence and know-how by first mimicking others' words; and special care was taken to discuss why some activists continued to feel excluded despite the measures devoted to welcoming their contributions. It was a slow and often maddening experience. But barring moments of crisis, when food was low, sodden clothing had to be laundered, or a response to eviction was required, the point of the general assemblies, the Occupiers said again and again, was neither to hasten toward ends—including the end of agreement or consensus—nor to agree on a set of guiding concepts. This was a mode of public discourse where people could experiment with and gain familiarity with the *processes* of politics.

To Occupy activists, citizens of democracies have been so caught up with outcomes, so tightly focused on ends, guiding concepts, and static institutions, that we have forgotten to remember beginnings, questions of access, process, bodies, and practice. As Bruno Latour suggests, "We live in rather discouraging times as far as political life is concerned. This is why it might be a good occasion to rethink what politics is about . . . our definition of politics itself is failing us."[74]

What does all this have to do with Sallust? According to the writers of the traditional histories of politics and political thought, nothing at all. According to their story, the political thinking done by republican Roman writers like Sallust concentrates precisely on well-defined ends: most importantly, the acquisition of military glory, the preservation of the republic and its institutions through the establishment of *concordia*, the sustaining of elite privilege, and the attainment of virtues, conditions, and capacities defined through *exempla*, including courage (*virtus*) and personal authority (*auctoritas*). As I noted in the Introduction, because many of these typically Roman ends strike us as unsavory in essence or in context, we might well hesitate to turn to elements of Roman thinking in our own political discourse.

But I hope I have shown so far that Sallust's political thinking does not end with ends. And it is worth noting the benefit of drawing distinctions between what we may call "Roman political thought" and "Roman ideology" and the "values" espoused by the governing class at Rome. It's tempting to mold the existing textual evidence into a neatly uniform set of dispositions, as A. A. Long does when he defines Roman ideology as "the system of values expressed by such terms as *virtus, dignitas, honestas, splendor, decus*, and

74   Latour, *Making Things Public*, 1.

above all, *laus* and *gloria*."[75] But such a view obscures the multiple, possibly contested, meanings of these words. To take an example from a previous chapter: if, in Cicero's philosophical works, liberty and senatorial status or *dignitas* are interdependent, it is also true that Cicero sees the emergence of popular *libertas* in economic terms, as a reaction against debt-bondage (*Rep.* 2.59)—this is not the conventional elite conception of *libertas*, but one that Cicero can utilize and exploit. The point is that tweaking the meanings of familiar values and concepts is not the best way to read Sallust's histories, or Roman texts in general. We need to recognize them on their own terms, which are literary and rhetorical rather than conceptual and philosophical.

Reading Sallust means, among other things, encountering a model for political thought marked by a strong sense of what phenomena deserve to be matters of concern for citizens: political access and process rather than ends, material inequity, embodied experience, awareness of the play of chance. This interpretation goes against the grain of scholarship on Sallust and on the nature of Roman historians' political thought more generally. It challenges, in particular, the conventional assumption that Roman historians are focused on static states, both states in the constitutional sense, that is, the nature of the *res publica*, and states of being, the state of being virtuous. It also challenges the claim made by Robert Goodin and others that republicans are totally indifferent to questions of material things, specifically the distribution of wealth and problems of inequity.

Jugurtha's reluctance to end its own story exhibits an interrogative, self-critical ethos. It offers a critique of politics that inverts the values of politics: "magistracies and commands are least to be desired" (*magistratus et imperia*, *Jug.* 3.1). Sallust himself digresses and silences himself (*Jug.* 4.9, 41.3), and recognizes in his prefaces that he is implicated in the problems he poses. In Sallust's attentiveness to decline, we catch what Stephen White, in his reflection on the history of Western political philosophy, calls the "common postulation that modern western social life, despite its many achievements, carries within itself a certain 'malignancy.'" It "identifies some logic embedded in that life that undermines, in a deep and systematic way, the prevailing authoritative values and institutions" of Western modernity.[76] Sallust's focus on the importance of resistibility to the forces of corrupting money and radical inequity stands against the claims of contemporary critics that republicans are indifferent to distributional questions. His attention to bodies—the phenomenological experience of politics—and to contingency

---

75   Long, "The politics of Cicero's *de Officiis*," 216, quoted above, p. 19.
76   White, "Continental political thought," 6.

awakens us to the limits of judgment, a theme that will be central in Horace's poetry, the subject of the next chapter.

What happens when we take the priorities of *Jugurtha* as a model for our own political thinking? We will attend to the structural violence of political life, where radical economic inequity limits access to politics and disrupts the arc of intention and action; we will investigate other material reasons for the gaps between being and doing; we will attend to the corporeal aspects of life that shape our sense of the world, and especially the sensations of collective experience; we will pay more attention to who speaks and who is silenced. We will work on the understanding that to undertake political action without considering what we don't know and what is subject to contingency is a dangerous failure of prudence.

Sallust's text warns us to be wary of the deferrals of justice we enact in our own political lives. His heroic, popular tribunes use slaves as the demonized opposites of free citizens in order to unify and energize their audiences. To whom do we fail to grant recognition? To what extent do our fantasies of civic identification rest on creating equivalents to Sallust's slaves—people who do not immediately count as part of the collective "we" we have in mind when we make political judgments as Arendt enjoins us to do?

3

NON-SOVEREIGN FREEDOM IN HORACE'S *SATIRES* 1

People often have no determinate beliefs at all about a variety of subjects; they often don't know what they want or why they did something; even when they know or claim to know what they want, they can often give no coherent account of why exactly they want what they claim to want; they often have no idea which portions of their systems of beliefs and desires—to the extent to which they have determinate beliefs and desire—are "ethical principles" and which are (mere) empirical "interests." This is not simply an epistemic failing, and also not something that one could in principle remedy, but a pervasive "inherent" feature in human life.... We are wrong to try to evade it.[1]

I N CHAPTER 1, I defended the claim that the republican conception of freedom is grounded in the understanding that politics is constituted in the fundamental antagonism between the haves and the have-nots. Chapter 2 turned to the the obstacles to justice as Sallust represents them: the vulnerability of the political process to greed and corruption; the dangerous failure of the senatorial order to recognize the poor and marginalized; and finally, the constraints on just judgment created by the irrepressible play of chance. I sought to point out, too, how Sallust exposes and works with the corporeal element in world-perception.

Each of these things—finitude, acknowledgment, self-sovereignty, antagonism, recognition, vulnerability, chance, and corporeality—come together in Horace's thinking about the nature of the free self. This is a theme Horace underlines with his repeated references to his freedman father—a delicate subject in the highly privileged milieu of his Roman audience, at whose core sits Horace's patron Maecenas. In the first part of his career, the unsettled decade after the Ides of March, Horace wrote satire,

---

1   Raymond Geuss, *Philosophy and Real Politics*, 2–3.

Rome's only unique literary invention: "it's all ours," wrote the rhetorician Quintilian (*satura tota nostra est*, 10.1.93). From Horace's lifetime, and perhaps largely due to his influence, satire is a genre about judgment, and in his hands, living a certain style of life, a free style, is closely bound up with judging others and oneself.

Horace is associated with the Epicureans, but his philosophical roots are broad and deep.[2] In the Greek philosophical tradition, how we think about the world around us is connected to who we are, so the quest to know and regulate the self—the core of the moral project—is a major preoccupation for thinkers interested in epistemology. In Plato's moral psychology, the self is perpetually engaged in the act of judging, insofar as the virtuous self governs itself, each part doing its part and not interfering with the others. Such a self is—a key point—free from the enslaving power of desires that interfere with judgment. For Aristotle, the self seeking *eudaimonia* cultivates a disposition according to which one judges appropriately. For the Stoics, the self selects goods for a life in accordance with nature, given the particular characteristics of the self; for Epicurus, those who live virtuously do so because they know how to judge their individual needs correctly.

As the philosopher John McDowell puts it, in ancient virtue theory "a conception of right conduct is grasped, as it were, from the inside out.... Occasion by occasion, one knows what to do, if one does, not by applying universal principles, but by being a certain kind of person: one who sees situations in a certain distinctive way," and makes certain types of judgments.[3] Being a person, which is to say living one life and not another or someone else's, involves choices that expose and reinforce what makes the self unique, like a train laying its own tracks. Further, as Socrates' example of dialogue undertaken in public suggests, the free self is characterized by his capacity to *account* for himself, that is, not only to engage in silent reasoning but to explain his reasoning and its results to others.

The mutually supportive relations of judgment, self-knowledge, self-sovereignty, self-accounting, and freedom in ancient ethical and political thought can be sketched in only bare detail here. But they are important and enduring. Whole modern political theories are grounded in the complex connections among them. Both contractarianism and voluntarist conceptions of the self anchor theories of sovereignty in a notion of the self that

2   On Horace's philosophical eclecticism, within certain bounds that generally exclude the Stoics (as we shall see), see David Armstrong, "Horace's *Epistles* 1 and Philodemus," 292–93.

3   McDowell, "Virtue and reason," 331.

knows itself, judges, and makes choices—whether in its consent to be governed or in its will to yield sovereignty or to vest authority in representatives. In modern democratic politics, civic freedom is bound up with acts of judgment: we make judgments when we vote for candidates, when we adopt political positions, and so forth.

What does it mean to judge freely? Hannah Arendt ties together freedom and judgment in unexpected ways. Reflecting on the limits of human action, she notes that we act never fully knowing what we are and what we do, never fully knowing or controlling the consequences of our acts, never fully understanding their meaning: this is the essence of what she calls the "simultaneous presence of freedom and non-sovereignty" in the human condition. Yet our very capacity to act harbors "certain potentialities which enable it to survive the disabilities of non-sovereignty."[4] Against Plato's belief that self-mastery is the foundation of freedom, Arendt argues that freedom resides in the self's "mastery" of "the darkness of human affairs" through forgiving and promising, two signally important potentialities (which she believed the Romans first incorporated into Western political life).[5] The judging involved in both demands the presence of others (for they are meaningless in isolation), the recognition of "the unpredictability of human affairs and the unreliability of men as they are," and the construction nonetheless of "guideposts of reliability." Forgiving literally frees another from the consequences of acts; promising judges the self capable of acting freely on behalf of another in an unknowable future. With these habits in common, people may hope to claim a "limited independence." We cannot fully rely upon ourselves, but we can and must act in that knowledge.[6]

Contemporary political philosophy has returned to the Platonic link between judgment, autonomous self-knowledge, and self-accounting, pressing hard on the notion that the judging capacity is closely bound up with the self's freedom. The political theorist Samuel Fleischacker recently published A Third Concept of Liberty, which he defined as the freedom to act on our capacity for judgment. Legal thinker Ronald Dworkin's book Justice for Hedgehogs argues that judgments of value lie at the heart of any determination of the good life, freely chosen and lived. The philosopher Philip Pettit, starting from the other direction, has argued that freedom should be defined as the fitness to be held responsible for one's actions. For him, too, the

4   Arendt, *The Human Condition*, 235–36.
5   Ibid., 236–48 and "Introduction *into* Politics," 174–79. On this much-debated argument, see Kateb, "Freedom and worldliness," 169–70.
6   Arendt, *The Human Condition*, 244–45.

capacity to account for oneself, to offer justifications for one's reasons and feelings, is centrally important. He takes fitness for responsibility to be theoretically constituted by "discursive control": that is, the self that may be held responsible has the capacity to engage in non-dominating discourse with others, a capacity that rests on prudential judgment.[7] For Pettit, the power of control over oneself mandates a sense of the self as something mastered and governable.

Isaiah Berlin had traced the roots of this view of the self in classical thought in his famous 1958 essay *Two Concepts of Liberty*. It derives, he pointed out, from the wish of the individual "to be his own master":

> I wish my life and decisions to depend on myself, not on external forces of whatever kind. I wish to be the instrument of my own, not of other men's, acts of will. I wish to be a subject, not an object; to be moved by reasons, by conscious purposes, which are my own, not by causes which affect me, as it were, from outside. I wish to be somebody, not nobody; a doer—deciding, not being decided for, self-directed and not acted upon by external nature or by other men as if I were a thing, or an animal, or a slave incapable of playing a human role, that is, of conceiving goals and policies of my own and realizing them.... I wish, above all, to be conscious of myself as a thinking, willing, active being, bearing responsibility for my choices and able to expain them by reference to my own ideas and purposes. I feel free to the degree that I believe this to be true, and enslaved to the degree that I am made to realize that it is not.... [It is not] the elimination of desires, but resistance to them, and control over them.... I am free because, and in so far as, I am autonomous.[8]

This is an empowering vision of a self enabled to govern itself by knowing itself in the consciousness of communal norms, where autonomy provides a literally self-fulfilling standard of judgment. But Berlin's purpose is not to

---

7   Pettit, *A Theory of Freedom*, 12, 75–79.

8   Berlin, "Two concepts of liberty," 131–32. I am not suggesting that Berlin's comments on positive freedom summarize Pettit's account of freedom. Pettit is a liberal thinker who believes that freedom from interference is a key issue—so much so that he designed his "republican" concept of freedom as freedom from domination as a strengthened version of the classic liberal non-interference formula (*Republicanism*, 21–27). Pettit also follows Nippel and Skinner in arguing that freedom in the Roman republican tradition has non-interference at its core (*Republicanism*, 27–31). But it is still fair to say that at the heart of Pettit's treatment is the notion that self-mastery is something desirable, something to be "achieved" (22).

praise what he calls "positive freedom" but to weigh its disadvantages against those of "negative freedom," freedom from interference.

His critique of positive freedom is twofold. The first objection is psychological. Berlin rejects the dual view of the self familar to readers of Plato, where we are "two selves," one made of reason, the other of impulse or desire. The problem is that the self primed to think of himself or herself as two selves feels the breach between them and unconsciously longs for it to be healed. All too often, Berlin points out, the healing factor is a dangerous valorization of reason and control that moves from the individual into the public psyche, and it becomes plausible and even attractive to coerce men in order to raise them to the "higher" level of free life sustained by reason.[9] His second objection touches on ontological, ethical, and political terrain. "The ends of men are many," he says, and "the necessity of choosing between absolute claims is then an inescapable characteristic of the human condition."[10] Any conception of freedom that demands all people to live according to a particular ethos, to adopt a particular ethic, to know and govern themselves in a particular way stands in contradiction to freedom as Berlin sees it. While acknowledging its discomforts and frustrations, Berlin settles on pragmatic advocacy for the basic human right of pluralistic self-determination.

As Berlin acknowledges, human pluralism exists in the context of a collective social life that has rules and norms by which we are "consciously or subconsciously guided."[11] This reference to the influence of external factors in determining the nature of the individual adds another wrinkle to the question of freedom now familiar from the work of Michel Foucault, Slavoj Žižek, and other post-structuralist, post-humanist thinkers. Judith Butler puts it this way: "There is no 'I' that can fully stand apart from the social conditions of its emergence, no 'I' that is not implicated in a set of conditioning moral norms, which, being norms, have a social character that exceeds a purely personal or idiosyncratic meaning." The "I" is always displaced to some degree by the social conditions in which it comes into existence.[12]

Butler is quick to stress that this displacement does not undermine our efforts at moral inquiry. On the contrary, it commits us to tackling the problem afresh and reorders our priorities. To understand the nature of freedom, we must discover how the self understands itself, which we can track by

9   Berlin, "Two concepts of Liberty," 132–34.

10   Ibid., 169.

11   Ibid.

12   Butler, *Giving an Account of Oneself*, 7–8 (quotation from 7).

examining examples of how it accounts for itself and judges itself. Because self-judgments are necessarily guided by social norms, this examination must also consider the self in relation to others—how the self judges others and sees itself being judged by others.

To readers of Michel Foucault this looks like familiar ground. In the second and third volumes of his *History of Sexuality*, Foucault argued that Hellenistic ethics sought to establish conditions under which a self could take itself to be an object of reflection and cultivation. In the course of this cultivation, the self internalizes external norms by elaborating them into a style of living. Norms of mastery that anchor the elite man's domination of others become parts of *ascesis*, self-discipline, a set of practices made visible in the man's look and walk as well as his internal habits of self-criticism; norms of sexual withholding at the heart of notions of ideal femininity become practices of modesty, beauty of soul, and manners. As a kind of making or *poiesis*, self-constitution as Foucault describes it takes on a creative aspect. It even becomes a potential site of critique and resistance, as the self's internal dialogue tests whether the terms by which it seeks to live a good life are being met by social conditions, and if not, how to remake those conditions. With this interpretation of self-mastery as creative self-stylization, Foucault sidestepped the constrained binary picture of an "I" constantly responding or in opposition to external norms, and suggested that the result of self-preoccupation is not necessarily narcissism but social change. As Butler says, there is no "I" apart from the conditions of its emergence: Foucault brings out the reflexive relations of self and social conditions over time.

In his last works, Foucault further refined his thinking about the self, focusing intently on the process by which the self comes to know itself by frank self-accounting in the presence of others. Reading Plato's dialogues and Seneca's treatises and letters, Foucault concluded that the interaction between selves is part of the creative process of self-formation. "So the question that arises [in connection to Seneca's letters] is this: What is this action of the other that is necessary for the constitution of the subject by himself? How will the other's action be inserted as an indispensable element in the care of the self? What is this helping hand, this 'eduction', which is not an education but something different or more than education?"[13] Crucially, he introduced the terms "forgiving" and "cost" into his discussion of self-constitution. Butler summarizes: "He will not say that there is a demise of reason here, but he is also taking his distance from a self-satisfied form of

13   Foucault, *Hermeneutics of the Subject*, 134.

constructivism. He is making clear that we are not simply the effects of discourses, but that any discourse, any regime of intelligibility, constitutes us *at a cost*.[14] The punitive feel of *ascesis*, which always stood in a certain tension with Foucault's claims about the creativity of self-formation, receded slightly, and some space opened up for Foucault to consider in more detail the intersubjective elements of self-constitution. His final lectures turn to scenes of teaching, conversation, and friendship.

But Foucault's new interest in the role of the other does not go so far as to allow the self to be displaced or disrupted by the other. Though dialogue, self-examination, or confession occur with or in front of another person, care and mastery of the self persists as the goal of these practices. In Plato's *Apology*, Epictetus' *Discourses*, Seneca's letters, and Dio Chrysostom's philosophical speeches, the confrontation with the other "leads [the interlocutor] to internalize this parrhesiastic struggle—to fight within himself against his own faults, and to be with himself in the same way that [the other] was with him."[15] Foucault's ancient self is still a sovereign self, or at least a self that strives for sovereignty, unfinalizable as that quest may be. Is Foucault correct to characterize the Roman vision of the free self in these terms? And what might these texts tell us about our own desired ways of being free?

ROMAN NOTIONS OF FREEDOM

It was once the case that the Greeks and the Romans were viewed as the theoreticians and practitioners of what Isaiah Berlin called positive freedom. Benjamin Constant argued that they had and desired "an entirely different liberty" from that enjoyed by "modern men":

> [Ancient liberty] consisted in exercising collectively, but directly, several parts of the complete sovereignty; in deliberating, in the public square, over war and peace; in forming alliances with foreign governments; in voting laws, in pronouncing judgments; in examining the accounts, the acts, the stewardship of the magistrates; in calling them to appear in front of the assembled people, in accusing, condemning or absolving them. But if this was what the ancients called liberty, they admitted as compatible with this collective freedom the complete subjection of the individual to the authority of the community.

14   Butler, *Giving an Account of Oneself*, 121 (her italics).
15   Foucault, *Fearless Speech*, 133, discussed in Butler, *Giving an Account of Oneself*, 127.

You find among them almost none of the enjoyments which we have just seen form part of the liberty of the moderns. All private actions were submitted to a severe surveillance.[16]

The picture has taken on more nuance in recent years, as we saw at the beginning of chapter 1, and political theorists are more likely to acknowledge the presence of what Berlin called "negative liberty" in Roman political practice—particularly in the people's efforts to protect themselves from the interference of the senatorial order.[17]

What persists is the assumption that Roman thinkers treated individual freedom in Plato's terms as they are commonly understood, as a state grounded in self-control, self-knowledge, integrity, and immutability. The Romans (if we can use the phrase) are notorious for treating freedom as the proper domain of one particular *exemplum* or model of selfhood—the "good man" (*vir bonus*), who possesses liberty, autonomy, authority, integrity, and masculinity. This nexus of attributes defines and empowers adult free men of property to be the judges of Roman society. Legally, only well-off free male citizens can judge others; women, slaves, and the poor—all those socially, economically, and legally dependent on others—are banned from the juries. The elder Cato is the exemplary moralist who brooks no dissent and whose deepest anxiety, according to the ancient biographical tradition, is the risk of vulnerability. He was famous for his biting comments about tyranny and his insistence that Rome defend itself from tyrannical encroachment. When the Greek king Eumenes visited Rome, the senate received him with great pomp, and the leading men of the city competed for his attention. "But Cato clearly looked upon him with suspicion and alarm. 'Surely,' someone said to him, 'he is an excellent man, and a friend of Rome.' 'Granted,' said Cato, 'but the animal known as king is by nature carnivorous'" (Plutarch, *Cato Maior* 8.7). Cato figures tyranny as a form of aggressive consumption.

Cato's horror of domination from without made itself felt with equal strength in the case of personal relations. A lover, he said disapprovingly, has

16   Constant, "Speech given at the Athénée Royal," 209.
17   "The very notion of liberty (whatever word be used to denote it in any language) is full of self-contradictions. There was, and could be, no single Roman and no single Greek idea of freedom": Brunt, "*Libertas*," 283. I discussed the assimilation of the idea that the Roman plebs valued negative freedom by Pettit and other contemporary theorists (and the problems with that assimilation) at the beginning of chapter 1. Pettit (*Republicanism*, 27) cites Hanna Pitkin: "The Roman plebs struggled not for democracy but for protection, not for public power but for private security. But *libertas*. . . was 'passive,' 'defensive,' 'predominantly negative.'" ("Are freedom and liberty twins?", 534–35).

a soul that "dwells in the body of another." Again according to Plutarch, he himself, in the course of his entire life, had repented of only three things: "once when he entrusted a secret to his wife; once when he paid ship's fare to a place instead of walking there; and once when he remained intestate the whole day" (9.6). Exposing himself to another person, relying on the strength of a power other than himself, and opening himself and his property up to the contingency of chance or the interference of others are repugnant to Cato. He must be purely himself and live purely on his own terms. Integrity, unchangeability, and certainty are linked in enabling freedom. His notorious criticism of Greek influence on Roman culture, especially the vulnerable Roman youth, reveals the extent to which he equates the purity of Roman social identity with Roman authority and autonomy. Cato appears unwilling to acknowledge the obvious presence of Greek culture in his "own" society.[18] He bases his stance on the claim that the Greeks speak words that are "born only on their lips, where those of the Romans are in their hearts": being able to argue both sides of the same case is unsettling if you are what you say (12.5). Cato never second-guesses himself. He faces no other whom he does not judge or master, and in most cases the two acts go together.

Horace's first book of *Satires*, the inaugural entry of an illustrious career, was composed in the 30s BCE, before Octavian (soon to take the name Augustus) consolidated his autocratic domination of the Roman *res publica*.[19] It counters the equation of judgment and self-sovereignty that characterizes Cato's and the Platonic view with another vision, one in which trust in the self-knowledge that supports judgment is a delicate and dangerous aspiration, and judgment is recognized as a potentially violent act that reinforces patterns of vice. Horace is also keenly sensitive to the intersubjective aspects of judging and being. The roughly chronological narrative of his first book of satires, which looks to the past, present, and future, consists of a set of carefully chosen episodes that illuminate how relationships with family and friends and material conditions leave an irreducible mark on the narrator's habits of judging, and bend and reshape his sense of himself.

Why examine a poet's exploration of self-constitution, sovereignty, freedom, and judgment? The case is best made by the argument itself. For now,

18   On the complexity of Cato's self-presentation see Erich Gruen, *Culture and National Identity in Republican Rome*, 52–83; and Enrica Sciarrino, "Putting Cato the Censor's *Origines* in its place."

19   I cannot address here the question of Horace's change of orientation as a poet and a citizen/subject over his whole career; for a rich account of his later Augustan concerns, see Lowrie, *Horace's Narrative Odes*, especially 317ff.

I will only make two observations. First, as we saw in chapter 2 when Pierre Rosanvallon discusses what he calls "the permanent crisis" of the language we use when we talk about politics, he skewers any attempt to deny the contradictions in the world "through the illusory coherence of doctrine." I share his view that fiction and poetry, by contrast, remain open to the contradictions of the world and never permit "concepts to exhaust the density of the real."[20] The density we will sense through Horace is a social and interpersonal density that makes itself felt through face-to-face relations. Second, as Arendt shows, judgment is a complex process with a long history of philosophical treatment in the aesthetic as well as the purely rational realm. Arendt follows a venerable tradition of philosophical thinkers as varied as Adam Smith and Heidegger in her tenacious refusal to accept cognition as the core task of political judgment. She insists that it also takes place in the non-conceptual realm of sentiment and taste. As we saw in chapter 2, she says that because it occurs in imagined communication with others, judging is dynamic, anti-automatic, essentially dialogic.

If we agree that free political judgments are bound up somehow with our aesthetic sensibility, we had best develop a critical language in which we can better grasp the sources of our spontaneous sensations and feelings, their consequences for our political commitments and judgments, and the possibilities of communicating or changing them. Satire's particular aesthetic illuminates the act of judgment in the world. It examines the sensations that enable or accompany our experience of thinking, and how they affect us. It exposes how we relate to the look and sound of people and ideas (because ideas do have looks and sounds)—and because, as we shall see, the aesthetic of ideas is an intersubjective phenomenon, it illuminates how those relations between self and other shape the formation of political belief. Most urgently, Horace's work prompts insights into how the socially and morally necessary act of judging vice and virtue around us relates to our existence as people, as individual selves. This is the role of a poet, an expert in the creation and manipulation of *aesthesis*: to influence and grant us insight into the sensorium.

One last word. If Roman satire strikes us as a moral or private rather than a political project, it is all-important to remember first that the *Satires* (like Vergil's *Eclogues*, another book of ten poems that appeared at roughly the same time as the *Satires*) carefully present themselves as attracting an audience full of men at the center of Roman public life. Just as importantly, we should recall how heavily the Romans invested themselves in defining the

20   Rosanvallon, *Democracy Past and Future*, 49–51.

res publica as a moral enterprise in which individual endeavor is difficult to distinguish meaningfully from collective undertakings. As David Levene puts it in his acute study of Livy's view of the purpose of writing history, the historian guides readers into an interpretation of Roman imperialism as operating successfully "in a context where morality was the paramount object of concern."[21] Though it was (as it is now) impossible for each individual citizen to be virtuous, individual citizen virtue was (and to a certain extent still is) nonetheless understood as the defining feature of the Roman Empire and its political order. There are no clear boundaries between public and private, prose and poetry, and the four categories cannot be mapped statically over or onto one another. Political theorists who seek to understand Roman political thought are urged to read a translation of Horace's *Satires* before continuing: they will find a diverse world introduced by a complex, fascinating voice.

THE INCOHERENT SELF

A surviving fragment of the second century satirist Lucilius hailed as emblematic of his poetic program runs:

> *Virtus* is knowing what is right, useful, and honorable for a man.
> Virtus scire homini rectum, utile, quid sit honestum. (fr. 1196–
> 1208W)

According to Horace, Lucilius taught his readers to know precisely what was right, useful, and honorable by describing their opposites: "he rubbed the city down in a lot of salt" (*sale multo / urbem defricuit, Sat.* 2.1.3). The old poet did not spare himself, but described his virtues and his faults with equal care in his books (2.1.31–32).

> And so it happens that the whole life of the old man lies open as
> though inscribed on a votive tablet.
>
> > Quo fit, ut omnis
> votiva pateat veluti descripta tabella
> vita senis. (2.1.32–35)

In the act of writing, his life becomes aestheticized, an object hung up on a wall for men's contemplative gaze.

---

21   Levene, "History, metahistory, and audience response in Livy 45," 106.

Horace's *Satires*, or to give the original Latin title of the first book, *Sermones*, is a two-book collection of poems punctuated by references to Lucilius and his forebears in Greek *iambos* and comedy. The work seems designed for continuous reading, like a novel. In fact the question of just how "poetic" the prosy verses are is raised explicitly more than once (most famously at 1.4.39–45). Some readers have argued that each book demands to be read all in one go, on the grounds that references in certain poems (notably the beginning of 1.4 and 1.10) assume that earlier phrases, themes, and unfinished questions are still fresh in the reader's mind.[22] Though the poems are hexameters, the meter of epic, the first-person narrator sets a personal, quotidian tone in his account of the world as he sees it. The world of the first book is composed of different milieus: the wealthy friends of Horace's patron Maecenas, a busy law court in Asia Minor, motley groups of men and women on the streets of Rome, a wind-blown burial ground for the poor where women cast spells at night.

Most scholars believe that Horace's contemporaries were ignorant of the genre we now call satire. Though his title *Sermones* or "Conversations" does not explicitly identify his topic—the word *satura* appears only in the second book—skimming the book confirms that judgment is the central theme: judgment of men and women in general and certain poets in particular, including Horace himself, whose status and reputation is a recurrent concern.[23] The first line of book 1 establishes the narrator as a critical observer of men and embeds him in dialogue with another, Maecenas, who turns out in the fourth and sixth satires to play a crucially important judging role for the poet, that of patron—the person who judges the poet worthy of money and a sort of friendship. The opening passage is a multiply reflexive scene of and about judgment wherein (with a view to judging them, as we will quickly see) the narrator contemplates with Maecenas the case of men who judge men who have judged it best to live a certain way:

22   Steven Oberhelman and David Armstrong, "Satire as poetry and the impossibility of metathesis in Horace's *Satires*," in *Philodemus and Poetry*: "the first 35 lines of Satire 4 summarize for the reader the previous three poems, which are assumed to be still fresh in the mind, and the opening of Satire 10 reopens a discussion which . . . Horace purposely left unfinished in 4 so that he could finish it here. . . . The only chronology of Book 1, in other words, is the reading of the scroll, of the words that strike the eye as the scroll is unrolled or that fall upon the ear when recited in the reading performance, of the thematic and verbal threads between what is being read and what has preceded and what will follow" (237). They demonstrate in persuasive detail the tendentiousness of Horace's claim to be a "prosy" poet and consider his careful style (especially his arrangements of words) in the context of Epicurean ideas about language and the unity of *ars* and *ingenium*.

23   Some, perhaps many, readers might have drawn a connection between the word *sermo* and the Greek Cynic-Stoic tradition of the self-examining, moralistic *diatribe*.

How does it happen, Maecenas, that no man lives content with the lot that either his reason has granted him or chance has thrown his way, but praises those who follow different ways?

Qui fit, Maecenas, ut nemo, quam sibi sortem
seu ratio dederit seu fors obiecerit, illa
contentus vivat, laudet diversa sequentis?

To judge others in a voice that others can hear is to make public and subject to others' judgment a process that first occurs internally and silently. In the single passage in the book when the narrator explicitly describes the experience of reflecting on himself and his own moral progress, he describes it as done "with lips closed tight" (*haec ego mecum compressis agito labris*); only after some time has passed does he "play around" with writing about it (*illudo*, 1.4.137–39). Making this internal process public is awkward, as the first poem soon shows. After giving examples of men who judge other men's lives to be better than their own, the narrator claims that even if Jupiter offered to grant them different lives, they would abruptly refuse (*nolint*, 19): though they are unhappy, they prefer to remain themselves. In a brief aside, the narrator sympathizes with Jupiter's frustration at mortal inconsistency: why don't these men act in accordance with their judgments and desires? As though punishing himself for taking a god's role, the narrator adopts a series of lightning-quick changes in attitude: he distances himself from a comic pose ("I don't want to rush over the topic grinning like someone who makes jokes," *ne sic ut qui iocularia ridens / percurram*, 23–24), contradictorily asks why he should not utter the truth while laughing (*ridentem dicere verum*, 24), and then sets aside games for "serious matters" (*amoto quaeremus seria ludo*, 27), a line that introduces a new set of exemplary anecdotes about greed and the need for self-control.

The lesson that follows is repetitive and familiar, even clichéd: take care of yourself and those closest to you; moderate your body and its pleasures and fears; live a life free from the slavery of obligation to other men or one's own desires. If, as the narrator had suggested back at line 24, it might be appropriate to laugh while speaking the truth, like the Lucretian teacher who gives his pupils sweet things to eat along with bitter lessons in grammar (25), after this rehearsal of platitudes we may wonder who's laughing.

How seriously we should take a speaker who can't even decide how to express himself is a question the poem raises again and again. Just before he describes Jupiter's offer to dissatisfied humans, the narrator declares that he does not want to delay his listener for long, unlike the garrulous Fabius (*ne te morer*, 14). Halfway through his repetitive list of moral examples, he again promises not to keep us: "It's not a long story" (*non est longa fabula*, 95). Twelve lines later he guarantees once more that the poem is nearly finished: "Now I return to where I began from" (107). The poem ends with an ambiguous statement of self-restraint that also sounds like an apology: "now that's enough: lest you think that I've pillaged the works of bleary-eyed Crispinus, I will add not one more word" (120–21).

Why should the narrator want to stop talking? Why should he place the idea in our minds, even as he disavows it, that he resembles blabbermouths and philosophical dogmatists like Fabius and Crispinus—and this in the first of a sequence of ten longish poems?

The end of the first book poses the question once more. The tenth satire circles back to the first, thematically: its subject is judging. It defends the narrator's style and his harsh judgments of earlier satirists as well as contemporary rivals, and it describes his ideal audience, a group that includes Maecenas, Vergil, and other men associated with the study of Epicurean philosophy in the bay of Naples. In the closing lines, the narrator hopes that his readers will find pleasure in his book, and he scornfully dismisses his rivals (84–91). He ends: "Go, boy, and quickly add these things to my little book" (*i, puer, atque meo citus haec subscribe libello*, 92).

Where the first satire raised questions about the consistency of the narrator's self-constitution and his confidence in the value of his work, or at least his ability to hold his readers' attention, the ending of the tenth satire takes the question of the constitution of the narrative voice in two different directions. On the one hand, the sharp quotidian imperative "go" (*i*) places us readers in the moment of composition by a living person, occupying a certain place, gesturing to a slave. We can imagine this person, his decision, his action: we witness his authority as the composer of the book. But the command also gives the ending a rushed, ragged edge. If we are reading literally as the poet "writes" (of course in fact he is giving lines to a proxy to write), the conceit of spontaneity comes at the cost of our readerly sense of care and finality. We might even unroll the scroll further to check if the lines being added (*haec*) by the slave follow the injunction instead of preceding it. In their move away from universality and toward the occasion, the immediate, the lines brush off the characteristic classical poet's goal of eternal fame. We are left in the particular moment, the feel, the conditions of the narrator's expression, at the very second that we are not sure to whom he is speaking, who he is, or who he wants to be.

Play of this type with the first-person voice—more specifically, with the readers' expectations about voice, which are themselves partly derived from the poet's own expectations about the readers—is a striking element of Horace's satiric style, and possibly thanks to him, Roman satire as a genre. At certain moments, and for limited stretches of lines, the book represents a coherent, authoritative persona, which may be moralistic and sincere or ironic and detached or some combination of these; then, in the course of a single poem, and repeatedly in the course of a poetry book, the persona undercuts itself, calls itself into question, destabilizes. When the second group of three poems in the book turns to the narrator himself—his poetry and his upbringing (*Sat.* 4), his friends, including Vergil, his account of a journey through the region in southern Italy where he grew up (*Sat.* 5), and his life as a man of modest means in the city (*Sat.* 6)—it will by come as no surprise to the reader that these poems repeatedly undercut the narrator's credibility and self-assurance.[24]

Horace's readers disagree over the significance and cause of this pattern. For some, the narrator is still simply Horace, a writer struggling more or less successfully to import pre-existing Greek philosophical concepts into a new Latin style of prosaic-poetic language, and the strain leaves its marks in the text.[25] Many others have approached the narrator's destabilization as a programmatic strategy. One seminal article interprets the "pure posturing" of the first person voice as a "parodic impulse" to subvert the putative ethical enterprise of the Epicurean-influenced book. Gradually, as the book unwinds, the narrator's ambiguous nature and authority undermines his gestures toward intellectual and social progress made in the earlier poems.[26] Basil Dufallo sees the wavering of the persona as an encouragement to read anti-programmatically: no systematic purpose to see here, ladies and gentlemen, now move along.[27]

Scholars have also explained the shifting persona as the expression of Horace's negotiation of social relations, focusing on how his construction of literary authority responds to class tensions and his age and inexperience (the *Satires* marks Horace's entry into the Roman literary scene). Ellen Oliensis, for instance, reads Horatian diffidence as a passive-aggressive performance of civility that is strongly colored by Horace's ironic awareness of his social status as the son of a freedman, lower than that of his patron and

24   For a review of past scholarship and a new argument about the relation of these three poems to 1.10, see Schlegel, *Satire and the Threat of Speech*.

25   Of the large literature on this point, see Rudd, "Horace as a moralist," in *Horace 2000: A Celebration*.

26   Zetzel, "Horace's *Liber Sermonum*: the structure of ambiguity," 59–70.

27   Dufallo, "Satis/Satura: reconsidering the 'programmatic intent' of Horace's *Satires* 1.1," 579–90.

many of his readers.[28] Emily Gowers sees the narrator as a "child-like" presence that moves from uncertainty to decision and back again, in a process of rebirth that may leave us disappointed, but which preserves Horace's independence from Maecenas and reinforces satire's self-imposed anti-decorum of messy incompetence. Further, she points out, the book presents its narrator as unfinished, still living "a life in transit."[29] Taking the Augustan context into consideration, Catherine Schlegel argues that Horace seeks to draw attention to the limits of free speech under the new post–civil war order; the self-parodic self-shutting-down is designed "to reassure the reader by undermining the threat of satiric speech." There's bark in Horace's book, but no bite.[30]

These interpretations treat the destabilization of the narrator's voice as intimately related to its authority (and the authority and influence of the living poet and his ideas), and further, to the nature and recognition of authority itself. They assume that destabilization is fundamentally and exclusively a problem of ethos, of identity, of the way the poet's status as a social agent affects the status of his words as they circulate in the world. Paul Ricoeur takes such an approach in his argument that literature is an experimental "laboratory" for exploring and jeopardizing the self, a mode of mimesis that exposes the non-sovereignty of the self in reality.[31]

No consideration of narrative destabilization, however, should forget that it is not only a person or even a persona but also a specific *act* that is destabilized: the satirist's trademark act of judging. As I hinted when I observed that judging people in public is an awkward thing to do, what preoccupies Horace here is less the poet's bid for recognition than the triangular subjective play that accompanies *judgment*: the play of certainty and self-questioning and accountability to both self and others. Figuring out how to judge is clearly tightly bound up with figuring out the nature of oneself and one's values and tastes. Remember Arendt's observation that "by his manner of judging, the person discloses to an extent also himself, what kind of person he is": her thought fortuitously captures the deep connection in Horatian satire between judgment and self-constitution and the (usually anxious) awareness of the self's exposure to others.[32]

---

28   Oliensis, *Horace and the Rhetoric of Authority*.

29   Gowers, "Fragments of autobiography in Horace *Satires* 1," 87.

30   Schlegel, *Satire and the Threat of Speech*, 13.

31   Ricoeur, *Oneself As Another*, discussed in Haker, "The fragility of the moral self," especially 361–62, and S. H. Clark, "Narrative identity in Ricoeur's *Oneself As Another*," in *Ethics and the Subject*.

32   Arendt, "The crisis in culture" in *Between Past and Future*, 223.

The second satire, which like the first opens with an assortment of figures who are engaged in the act of judging another person, has a lesson to offer about the limitations of both judgment and sovereign self-constitution. We are first invited to join the narrator in judging both the judges and their object, the Sardinian singer Tigellius.

> The guilds of flute-girls, the drug-sellers, beggars, actresses, buffoons,
> all this breed are grieved and upset at the death of the singer
> Tigellius. Really [they—and the narrator?—thought] he was such a
> nice guy.

> Ambulabarum collegia, pharmacopolae,
> mendici, mimae, balatrones, hoc genus omne
> maestum ac sollicitum est cantoris morte Tigelli.
> quippe benignus erat.

At first the narrator anxiously surveys the contradictory variety of judgments that get passed on the same person: "one man is praised by some and blamed by others" (11). That worry recedes under a tide of examples that presents judgment as operating according to a standard of excessiveness. This standard we are initially invited to treat as universal—isn't everyone disgusted by the spectacle of those who diverge from the middle course (*nil medium est*, 28)? But after attacking men who go to sexual extremes, either having sex exclusively with married women or with prostitutes in "greasy brothels" (29–30), the narrator slides into self-contradiction as he quotes the elder Cato's "divine wisdom" in praise of brothels, which at least restrain them from corrupting wives.

Just as the passage's comic familiarity and quotation of the famous Roman moralist has put us at ease again with the act of judging others, the narrator changes his tone. Now his theme is the violence done in the act of judging. Anyone desiring to exact severe punishment on the worst offenders, he says, "needs to listen" (*audire est operae pretium*, 37) to how they actually punish themselves (37–46): through despairing suicide, brutal retaliation, mutilation by the sword. We want our adulterers to suffer, but should we want them to suffer that much? With his reference to Galba, a figure who rejects mutilation, the narrator suggests we had better not.

Recall the way the narrator abruptly ends the first satire in a final act of self-judging that in its acknowledgment of another's possible judgment verges on disavowing the act of judging others proper to satire: "lest you think I've pillaged the works of bleary-eyed Crispinus, I will add not one more word" (120–21). We begin to glimpse judgment as a capacity one must mobilize—telling the city what's for what is the traditional task of the satirist, after all—and something that must be held at a careful distance, whose force is not to be identified with or exulted in.

Critics express frustration at the narrator's hesitation about judging, finding puzzling inconsistency between his glee in going on the attack and his air of "amiable hedonism."[33] A clue to the narrator's close-to-simultaneous embrace of and withdrawal from judging, and to the insight that led him to this stance, emerges at the end of this satire. The body of the poem, nearly seventy lines, offers recourse for the reader who wishes to avoid charges of adulterous vice: pursue an affair with a freedwoman (47–109). In a pattern we have seen before, the reader is invited to relax and take pleasure, here through the narrator's earthy catalogue of images illustrating the prospect of making love in safety to a freely available beauty. He contrasts the advantages of women who wear transparent robes so that their lovers can judge what they're really getting with those who surround themselves with "the attendants, sedan, hair-dresser, parasites, the robe dropping to the ankles," and other obstacles to sensual delight that are typical of the married woman's cultivated appearance. The narrator's language grows more explicit as the poem nears its end and he imagines the alternative to the sex-with-freedwoman choice he has just recommended:

> I'm not afraid, while I'm fucking [the freedwoman], that her
> husband's coming back from the country, that the door will crash
> open, the dog will bark, and everywhere the house will resound
> with a terrible knocking; that deathly pale, the woman will leap up,
> her accomplice will cry out in misery, this one fearing for her limbs,
> that one bewailing her dowry, and I for myself.

> nec vereor, ne dum futuo vir rure recurrat,
> ianua frangatur, latret canis, undique magno
> pulsa domus strepitu resonet, vae pallida lecto
> desiliat mulier, miseram se conscia clamet,
> cruribus haec metuat, doti deprensa, egomet mi. (1.2.127–31)

So far the clause of fearing articulates a comic vision imagined in the subjunctive mood. But in the next lines, the closing lines of the poem, there is

---

33   Rudd, "Horace as a moralist," 75, is typical.

a sudden change of mood, from subjunctive to indicative, inflected by the hasty imperative of the passive periphrastic:

> With tunic undone *I must run away*, and barefoot too, lest my
> fortune wither or my backside or my reputation, at least. It is
> wretched to be caught. Even with Fabius as my judge, I can prove
> that.

> discincta tunica *fugiendum est* ac pede nudo,
> ne nummi pereant aut puga aut denique fama.
> deprendi miserum est; Fabio vel iudice vincam.

What has happened? It is as though the poet has been caught up in his own vision of high-class adultery, and must admit that instead of enjoying his freedwoman in peace, he too indulges in more dangerous liaisons. The effect is a self-indictment. Throughout the poem, the narrator, contradicting his own warning about those quick to judge, has repeatedly rendered judgment and offered advice on how to judge. As elsewhere in the book, the reader is lulled into agreement with what are presented as judgments about adultery "obviously" deserving affirmation—only to be thrown unexpectedly into a scene that suggests that the narrator himself fails to obey them.

Catherine Schlegel is right to say that the poem is unstable, "thrown off course" by its own examples.[34] But when she says that "Horace has no real objection to adultery; his argument is against stupidity ... [and] the failings that give rise to a distorted idea of need and its satisfaction" she runs off track. This reading takes us in the wrong direction, privileging the notion of a coherent subject that has a goal of self-government through self-knowledge. We should attend more carefully to Horace's suggestion that judging others is violent and deceitfully seductive, not in so far as we fail to know ourselves but rather in so far as we trust too blindly in the redemptive power of self-knowledge.

At the end of the poem the joke is on us. We've learned to expect to keep reading a voice that knows its limits and lives by them, but this is exactly what we shouldn't get used to expecting. This conundrum is also a challenge to the reader to displace expectation. Horace's poems awaken us to our own desire to pass judgment and thus dominate the other—"the narrator insists that we worry about the other's desire," as Erik Gunderson puts it—but even as the satirist declares that the sovereign principle of judg-

---

34   Schlegel, *Satire and the Threat of Speech*, 29.

ment must be upheld, he backs away from the throne. If the scandal of satire is its "reinvestment in the scandalous," the scandal rests in the satirist's refusal to fully inhabit his rightful place (in the Roman context) as the manly teacher of virtue—as the holder of sovereignty over himself and others.[35]

My thinking about this strategy is informed in part by Stanley Cavell's famous essay on Shakespeare's *Lear*.[36] According to Cavell, the key to the resolution of King Lear is not Lear's recognition of Cordelia's love or Gloucester's recognition of Edgar's. The key is each character's fragile and temporary achievement of insight into themselves, and specifically, the insight that they have been avoiding something in themselves all along: the need for love, which Lear has concealed from everyone, including himself, by loving power. They come to understand themselves not only in their present wretched condition, but as they were in the past, and having achieved this understanding, they are in a position, temporarily anyhow, to judge and act well. Lear rejects the crown, acknowledging that his earlier will to sovereignty rested on a lack of knowledge of himself that led to the evil injustice of his treatment of Cordelia.

But Cavell insists that the tragedy does not suggest that Lear simply needed to know himself better; rather, he needed to unwind his intertwined assumptions about self-knowledge and self-rule from their very roots—because they failed him, as they must. The tragedy does not exhort us to work toward or trust in the promise of self-knowledge; it brings us face to face with the limits of our capacities of self-knowledge, and with the need to keep that knowledge of ignorance front and center as we live our lives.

So, until the end of satire 1.2, the narrator speaks with authority: he's happy to tell us in lurid detail what he likes and how he plans to get it. But we gather from the change in mood from subjunctive to indicative and the revelation of the speaker himself as the surprise target of the cuckolded husband's wrath, that the narrator, like Cavell's Lear, has failed to predict his own action in the contingencies of the future; as Markell puts it, the

35 This may better explain the narrator's anxious desire, expressed many times through the book, most frequently in *Satires* 4 and 10, to distinguish the tone of his satire from Lucilius', whose judgments (he says) were excessively harsh. On the perversity of the desire instilled by Juvenal to gaze at (sexual) desire, see Gunderson, "The libidinal rhetoric of satire," in the *Cambridge Companion to Satire*, 231.

36 Cavell, "The avoidance of love," in *Disowning Knowledge in Seven Plays of Shakespeare*; first appearance in *Must We Mean What We Say?* I was drawn to this essay, and my reading of it is influenced, by Markell, *Bound By Recognition*, 34–36, 177–85.

shape of his will is not quite determined by or aligned with his capacity to judge. In our sudden recognition of him as the adulterous criminal/victim, we realize we have misrecognized him all along, just as he has apparently misrecognized himself. The naked barefoot figure at the end of the poem, we might say, outruns the terms and norms of regulated selfhood and confident judging—which we begin to see are closely intertwined—that the speaker dictated for himself at its beginning. Through its problematization of the judging voice—as the fragile self-constitution of the voice that first laid brash claim to self-sufficiency and self-mastery is revealed—the satire warns us to distrust the satisfying confirmation of self-sovereignty that judging may seem at first to provide. After a poem full of judging, we find the narrator himself in the dock.[37]

In the end, what is most interesting about the second satire is its narrative shape, the way it represents the habit of judging others as the abrupt, even violent catalyst for the revelation of self-ignorance. As the narrator faces the world and judges it, his self-constitution occurs as a process bound up in and with others and subject to change (including change prompted by the displacement of expectation) beyond his control or expectation. The effect has already been achieved in brief in the first poem when the narrator turns the tables on the reader he imagines laughing at Tantalus (1.168–70):

Thirsty Tantalus swoops down on the waters fleeing from his lips—
why laugh? Once the name is changed, the tale is told of you.

Tantalus a labris sitiens fugientia captat
flumina—quid rides? mutato nomine de te
fabula narratur.

Only by acknowledging self-ignorance does the self have a hope of escaping the punishment of Tantalus.

---

37   Robert Kaster's conclusion in *Emotion, Restraint, and Community* that in Roman thought, *integritas* is not an "inner" state, supports this reading. He argues that we need not think that *integritas* provides a basis for acting reflectively, with reference to itself as a normative principle: *integritas* does not mean "defining an element of your self-conception and self-evaluation" such that we may think "my sense of integrity causes or forbids me to do X because X is (or is not) what a person of integrity would do"; *integritas* as the Romans viewed it "lacked the dimension of internal, reflective autonomy." Rather, it comprises a "bundle of dispositions and behaviors that anchored a person securely in the social world" (148). Knowledge of who one is as a coherent self matters differently: it turns out to be social knowledge rather than self-knowledge.

JUDGING (WITH) OTHERS

Life's burden can be better borne not if one knows who one is—no one can know himself—but if one is known by others as he knows them; and knows not as the cultivators of the inner life define knowing, but as the great poets and dramatists exemplify knowing, through their creative mimetic power.[38]

Of the poems in the first triptych, the third satire is most explicitly concerned with finding the crucial balance between passing judgment—in social, moral, erotic, parental, and legal contexts—and the importance of restraining our impulse to judge. It opens with another contemptuous account of the singer Tigellius, who appeared in the previous poem, a man "in whom there was no balance" (*nil aequale homini fuit illi*, 3.9). "Never was anyone so off-kilter to himself" (*nil fuit umquam / sic impar sibi*, 1.3.18–19). In the poem's first major transition, an unnamed interlocutor asks Horace:

> Now someone may say to me "What about you? Don't you have any vices?" "Yes indeed, but lesser ones, perhaps." When Maenius was carping at Novius behind his back, "Jeez," someone said, "don't you take any note of yourself, or do you suppose you're going to get away with this kind of talk because you're an unknown quantity?" "Oh, I forgive myself," Maenius answers. This love is *foolish* and unwarranted and worthy of (censorious) note. Since you scan your own sins with bloodshot, ointment-filled eyes, why you do examine your friends' vices as sharply as an eagle or a snake from Epidaurus?

> nunc aliquis dicat mihi 'quid tu?
> nullane habes vitia?' immo alia et fortasse minora.
> Maenius absentem Novium cum carperet, 'heus tu'
> quidam ait, 'ignoras te, an ut ignotum dare nobis
> verba putas?' 'egomet mi ignosco,' Maenius inquit.
> *stultus* et improbus amor est dignusque notari.
> cum tua pervideas oculis mala lippus inunctis,
> cur in amicorum vitiis tam cernis acutum
> quam aut aquila aut serpens Epidaurius? (1.3.19–27)

---

38   Kateb, "Freedom and worldliness in the thought of Hannah Arendt," 148 n. 35.

Critics tend to explain the narrator's sustained warning against judging others by appealing to Horace's Epicurean suspicion (explicit starting from line 94) of the Stoics' denial of any meaningful distinction among vices. This seems likely, but it is not the whole story. Since in the opening scene the narrator acknowledges room for uncertainty about his own virtue with that "perhaps" (*fortasse*, 20), and ends the poem by describing himself as "foolish" like Maenius in the earlier anecdote (*stultus*, 140), his point seems rather to echo the suggestion of the second satire, that self-knowledge is too undependable to permit us to judge others with certainty. In a provocative move, Horace smears the same "dark ointment" on his own sore eyes in *satire 5* (*hic oculis ego nigra meis collyria lippus inlinere*, 5.30–31). Of this passage Emily Gowers remarks, "this is a kind of cautionary inoculation against other people's blackening or accusations of moral shortsightedness."[39] Of course, it literally blinds Horace, who explicitly occupies the place of the narrator in that poem.

Back in the third satire, the reference to poor sight sets the scene for three more revelations about judgment. Each has to do with the presence of the other and his influence on passing judgment. The degree to which the other is implicated in the ability of the self to know and master himself is the issue that Foucault raises in his late work on selfhood and freedom. The question is: does the other contribute to the narrating self's self-mastery? Or does the other leave an "irreversible imprint" that disrupts the self's effort to establish self-mastery?[40]

The body of the third satire is a serial report on appearance and its effects: a rustic hairstyle that makes men laugh (31–32); Hagna's wart, adorable to her lover Balbinus (41); the squinting boy whose father calls him "Blinky" (45); behaviors taken as indexes to the soul (49–62); the slight offenses of slaves and drunken friends, and our proper reactions to them (80–83, 90–95). The narrator (along with the characters he describes) calls things literally as he sees them. The collective aesthetic experiences described here occur in the space of appearance, the space in which people appear to one another and are judged accordingly.

The deeper significance of the confrontation between people first begins to unfold in the middle of the series in a poignant pivotal passage where the narrator moves from the judgments of others to his own case:

39 Gowers, "Horace *Satires* 1 and 2," *Cambridge Companion to Horace*, 56.
40 Butler, *Giving an Account of Oneself*, 128, citing Levinas' and Laplanche's work on the other's claims on the self.

CHAPTER 3

If a rather simple person (my sort when I've often carelessly put
myself in your face, Maecenas), annoyingly interrupts you at
random with some kind of talk when you are reading or keeping
silent, we say "he utterly lacks common sensibility." Oh, how
thoughtlessly we wield an unjust law against ourselves! For no one
is born without faults: that man is best who works with the fewest.
A sweet friend, as is fair, should weigh my goods along with my
bads, and let him incline the scale with the latter [adding up to]
more in number, if indeed my goods are more in number, if he
wants to be loved: by this law he will be placed in the same scale.

Simplicior quis et est qualem me saepe libenter
Obtulerim tibi, Maecenas, ut forte legentem
Aut tacitum impellat quovis sermone molestus:
'communi sense plane caret,' inquimus. Eheu,
Quam temere in nosmet legem sancimus iniquam!
Nam vitiis nemo sine nascitur: optimus ille est,
Qui minimis urgetur. Amicus dulcis, ut aequum est,
Cum mea compenset vitiis bona, pluribus hisce,
Si modo plura mihi bona sunt, inclinet, amari
Si volet: hac lege in trutina ponetur eadem. (1.3.63–72)

As other readers have noted, Horace's patron Maecenas is a figure of paternal authority and security for the narrator who prompts in him both love
and painful uncertainty. Closely resembling the narrator's relationship to
his freedman father, a man whom satire 4 both praises and sets at a distance,
the relationship with Maecenas exposes the narrator's consciousness of the
degree to which his recognition as a poet—which the satires collapse into
his recognition as a self—hangs on the judgments of another.[41]
A Foucauldian reading of this scene would emphasize the internaliza-
tion of self-discipline at work in Horace's ruefully self-critical representation of himself as he tactlessly interrupts his patron.[42] The ambivalent char-
acterizations of Maecenas and, later, Horace's father, capture the anxieties at
work in the struggle of the self to judge and moderate itself—that is, to be
a certain way—as it is being judged by others and inculcated into social

41   Johnson suggests that the reference aligns Horace with the Cyrenaic philosopher
Bion, who is also supposed to be the son of a freedman in *Horace and the Dialectic of Freedom*,
27, citing Diogenes Laetrius 4.46.
42   I am grateful to Paul Allen Miller for reminding me of the relevance and importance of the Foucauldian reading of this and other scenes of self-mastery in the *Satires*.

practice. By this view, self-constitution is a public, heteronomous process that involves the "impregnation" of the self by social norms.[43] But there is another way to approach matters that does not treat the self's relation to externals in these oppositional terms. This approach recalls Dewey's injunction that we learn how to think of the "I" and "the other" not as antithetical but as intertwined and complementary.

First, the encounter between Horace and Maecenas reminds us of the limits of self-sovereignty. In the narrator's description of himself interrupting Maecenas, he worries that he is always unconsciously offending his powerful friend by behaving in a tactless way. He calls attention to his own dilemma: he is caught between the desire to bear witness to the specific flavor and feel of his character (*simplicior*: straightforward, impulsive, eager for friendship) and its formation (divulged through the exploration of his background in the sixth satire) and his inability to control the way his appearance adversely affects the social recognition he longs for. Who is the narrator in this scene? He recognizes here that he is as he is known and judged by others, just as they are what they are known to be by him. A political truth is peeking out: that in social relations the self is always profoundly compromised by the judging presence of the other—a compromise harshened and made uncomfortably perceptible by conditions of systematic inequality.

Second, a point that will become clearer in the sixth satire: Horace's self-relation—his assessment of himself as far as he knows himself—is knotted into his relation to the other, especially to his father and to Maecenas, but also to his friends. How necessary the other is is made clear at the end of the third satire. The last scene but one attacks the Stoic philosopher, who allows for no distinction among human faults and thus treats others unjustly. With heavy irony, the narrator addresses the Stoic in the second person, imagining him at the center of a jeering crowd who pluck at his beard and jostle him while he howls in futile rage (1.3.133–36). And then:

> . . . So while you, a king, go to bathe for a penny, and no escort will
> follow you, moron, except moron Crispinus, if I (a fool) do
> something wrong, my friends will forgive me, and in turn I will
> freely suffer their transgressions, and as a private man I will live
> more happy than you, a king.

> . . . dum tu quadrante lavatum
> rex ibis neque te quisquam stipator ineptum

43   Haker, "Fragile self," 359.

praeter Crispinim sectabitur, et mihi dulces
ignoscent, si quid peccaro stultus, amici,
inque vicem illorum patiar delicta libenter,
privatusque magis vivam te rege beatus. (1.3.137–42)

This philosopher is alone, though he is in a crowd, because he has placed himself outside the bounds of humanity by making all crimes equally vicious: the petty thief is as bad as a bandit (1.3.121–23). This judgment erases human individuation. When the philosopher looks at others and judges them by a single abstract rule, he does not see them as individuals. By contrast, in the last scene (1.3.138–41), the narrator is surrounded by his friends, who know his crimes as well as he knows theirs, but who forgive him nonetheless, as he forgives them. This is a provocative idea. The narrator's recognition of his friends' effect on him, and his reciprocal effect on them, guides his choices, including the choice whether or not to judge. Here judging not only takes place under the eyes of others; it takes on an intersubjective quality. The narrator's choice to be the man who he is occurs in and through friendly exchanges that let him "live more happy than you, the king" (*privatusque magis vivam te rege beatus*, 1.3.142).

The poem's contrast between the wrathful solitary philosopher and the self-aware social narrator draws attention to the need to be aware of the way we need each other in order to know ourselves, at least as best we can, and to choose our lives accordingly. This is Stanley Cavell's point, once again: that the avoidance of the other is a "distortion of one's own self-relations, an avoidance of something unbearable about oneself."[44] If we follow the arc tracking the limits on judgment set by the limits of self-knowledge laid out in the first three poems, we see that the unbearable truth the Stoic philosopher appears to avoid is the limit of self-knowledge.

The scene of intersubjective relations raises a third issue that speaks to their promise rather than their burden. Common sense, which the narrator refers to as a touchstone in Maecenas' circle of friends, is the public sense of judgment that evolves through the conversations of which Horace's *sermones* are a part. To write satire is to acknowledge that one's judgments, and thus the spontaneous reactions and secondary deliberations that compose our sense of the world and our sense of ourselves in it, are *common—*

---

44   Cavell as quoted and discussed by Markell, *Bound by Recognition*, 35. I am also thinking of Kimberly Curtis' point in "Aesthetic foundations of democracy politics" about the "fragility of our capacity to sense reality, to be present to 'what is' . . . [and] the way we need each other" (46).

in the sense that they orient people in the world they have in common with the people whose company they share.[45] The narrator affectionately details the advantages of this reciprocal sensibility in his relationship with Maecenas, overdetermined several times as a relation of equality (*amicus dulcis, ut aequum est,* 69; *aequum est,* 74), and again in his Lucretian and Ciceronian accounts of the primeval invention of law and order (99–104):

> When animals crept forth on the primeval earth, a mute and brutish herd ... they fought ... until they invented spoken words and names with which they might express words and feelings.

> cum prorepserunt primis animalia terris,
> mutum et turpe pecus ... / pugnabant ...
> donec verba, quibus voces sensusque notarent,
> nominaque invenere ...

In Cicero (*Inv.* 1.5) and Lucretius (*DRN* 5.1011–27), after language comes the constitution of law. But with its many anecdotes about minor improprieties, the rest of Horace's poem tells us that law cannot govern the sinews of human relations, the connections between friends that ease everyday life and allow a modest private man to think himself happier than a king. Only being responsive to common sense does that. And while this compels us to acknowledge that we are vulnerable and dependent (in the narrator's self-questioning turn to Maecenas), the support of intersubjective existence is also felt as sweetness (*dulces,* 139). To be a good judge and a good man, in the terms of this poem, is to be alive to the other and constantly alert to the ways the other might judge us.[46]

FROM SATIRIC TO POLITICAL JUDGMENT

Consider all this in the larger political context. As every Romanist knows, appearance matters intensely in Roman social and political practice. "Ar-

---

45 I draw here on Kirstie McClure's remarks on common sense in "The odor of judgment: exemplarity, propriety, and politics in the company of Hannah Arendt," in *Hannah Arendt and the Meaning of Politics,* 78.

46 David Velleman offers an account of moral action that begins with our desire to follow rules of behavior defined by our sense of what others expect of us, in *How We Get Along.* A very differently oriented approach that in some ways parallels Velleman's may be found in Haker, "The fragility of the moral self," a review of accounts of the moral self in Foucault, Butler, Ricoeur, and Levinas.

range your face," advises Thomas Cromwell in Hilary Mantel's novel *Wolf Hall*, a pithy reference to Baldesar Castiglione's *Il libro del cortegiano*, the early modern rewriting of Cicero's and Quintilian's rhetorical treatises. We can easily find many more examples of face-arranging in Ellen Oliensis' work on Horace's *persona* or Maud Gleason's study of the gendered significance of deportment in rhetorical education. In his *de Oratore* Cicero instructs readers how to attack people with unusual looks or habits, lessons manifest in speeches like *pro Caelio* and the *Philippics*. The lesson reverberates in the well-documented preoccupation of Roman historiography with physical appearance: Sallust's detailed descriptions of Jugurtha and Catiline, Tacitus' pictures of Tiberius and Sejanus, the obsessive return of Livy and Valerius Maximus to scenes where leaders appear before the people in the forum.

The intertwining of judgment and selfhood in these passages and many others like them that represent the legal, judicial, and social experiences of the *res publica* transcends its specific propositions and their purely social implications. It suggests that in these texts aesthetic perception, sensation, and judgment lie at the heart of all the moments where the non-violent negotiating of conflict takes the place of physical violence—that is, at the heart of politics. Cicero's business in his rhetorical project (to draw a phrase from Jacques Rancière) is identifying moments of "sensory intensification where power lies in the sensations it actively elicits."[47] He represents his audiences as eager to judge the orator's claims on their attention through performance and as only minimally committed to judging the reasons anchoring his arguments. This is why in his rhetorical treatises he prefers the orator to acquire not intimate knowledge of dialectic or the law but a strong grasp on collective taste and passion (e.g., *de Orat.* 1.224–39), and why he attends so carefully to the orator's *actio* or self-presentation, which has visual and aural aspects. Sometimes this is a matter, literally, of *sensus communis*, the "common sense" we have already discussed (*Sat.* 1.3.66): the effective speaker relies on his own judgment of taste to guess at popular opinion (*Orat.* 1.221 and elsewhere). At other times, when the matter in question is uncertain or simply if the speaker is sufficiently eloquent, the orator's projection of his sense of (not argument for) what is right wins the day (*Orat.* 1.237). Either way, public standards of reasoning are low: the point of public speech is less to lead the audience through a deliberative process than to invite them into a collective sensory experience of judgment that takes

---

47   Rancière, *The Politics of Aesthetics*, 20.

place through the messy conglomerated action of reason, instincts, taste, and emotions.

If political judgment inevitably (and perhaps unsettlingly) escapes the bounds of reason, it is still necessary. And the Horatian narrator does not wriggle out of the judging role or try to evade its consequences or to undermine the notion of judgment wholesale. When the friend-betraying critic Maenius admits that he forgives himself (*egomet mi ignosco, Sat.* 1.3.23), the narrator calls him a fool in love with himself. We remember that the verb *ignoscere* connotes ignorance as well as forgiveness, and there is no question that the narrator thinks ill of Maenius. He thinks equally ill of the philosopher types, especially Stoics, who try to regulate human behavior with laws that are insensitive to concrete situations and conflicts, against which our "senses and customs fight back" (*sensus moresque repugnant*, 1.3.97).

Other philosophical schools offer a contrasting vision of moral judgment grounded in the notion that virtue is not a matter of following codifiable rules. Aristotle says in the *Nicomachean Ethics*: "To say to what point and how much someone is blameworthy (for diverging from the correct and good) is not easy to determine by a principle" (1109b20). Greek and Roman literary critics and rhetoricians developed Aristotle's thinking further, agreeing that there were limits to rules (*parangelmata*, or in Latin, *praecepta*). In the case of aesthetic judgment, the proper supplement to critical taste was thought to be an irrational (*alogos*) sensibility (Dion. Hal. *Thucydides* 27).[48]

What constitutes a good judgment? To answer the question, I need to turn back to the fourth satire, which describes the figure who most profoundly influenced the narrator: his freedman father (described literally as *libertino patre*, 1.6.6, 45, 46).[49] If the satirist cannot answer the question by articulating rules, it turns out that he may at least be able to model practices. The fourth satire aggressively (and thus ironically) defends the narrator from charges of harshness, exaggeration, and inflexibility—charges which, as many readers have noted, scarcely seem credible in the first place, since the first three satires eschew the assertive attacks of iambos. In defend-

48   For a provocative phenomenological critique of Aristotle's teleological rationality and Alasdair MacIntyre's purposive rationality, both of which indirectly spur my thinking here, see Werner Marx, *Towards a Phenomenological Ethics*, 112.

49   For the seminal treatment of Horace's father and his citizen status, see Williams, "Libertino patre natus: true or false?" Michèle Lowrie points out to me that if Williams is right to argue that Horace's family did not come from a long line of slaves, then Horace becomes paradigmatic for those Romans who suffered in the Social Wars (personal communication).

ing himself, the narrator turns those charges against his critics. "If I speak too freely or too whimsically," the narrator says, "grant this to me," because he has a valuable lesson to impart, even if it sometimes expresses itself awkwardly. The lesson is the narrator himself, an exemplum who has been taught by exempla who now lays himself open, as Lucilius had done, to his readers' evaluative gaze.

> The best of fathers taught me this, that I might flee vices by noting examples of each.

> insuevit pater optimus hoc me,
> ut fugerem exemplis vitiorum quaeque notando.(1.4.105–6)

The narrator's father teaches common sense through examples: Albius, Baius, Scetanus, Trebonius, and more (107–29). Drawn from past custom and present observation, they push the narrator (and us) into the meaty middle of human affairs, and push against the rules of philosophers, especially the Stoics Horace attacks for ignoring the messy plurality of human life. Exemplarity, which Arendt followed Kant in calling "the go-cart of moral judgment" is not rule-following but something one appeals to. As for the standards the father establishes, they are specific to the southern Italian context, located in common knowledge, yet universalized by their presence in moralistic discourse and comedy—in Kirstie McClure's phrase, "a recombinative distillation of past particulars."[50]

In a key narrative juxtaposition, the narrator recalls how his father used his own young instincts as the basis on which he learned to shape his maturing opinions, and then moves to his adult experience of silent self-constitution that is later expressed in writing, in a scene we have encountered before (131–39). The suggestion is that the narrator continues to follow his youthful learned habit of observation, judgment, and selective imitation, but where with his father paternal judgment was the standard and fear the motivation (126–28), the narrator now appeals to his friendly crowd of like-minded poets to enforce his judgments with the power of their collective tastes (141–43):

> Let a great band of poets come who will bring help to me (for we are the majority by far), and like the Jews we will compel you to join our crowd.

50   McClure, "Odor of judgment," 56.

multa poetarum veniat manus, auxilio quae
sit mihi (nam multo plures sumus) ac veluti te
Iudaei cogemus in hanc concedere turbam.

Who are these poets? From the narrator's sharp dismissal of rival poets earlier in the poem, these are the men who share his tastes and values, who (to return to an earlier idea) compose his world, with whom the narrator can communicate his judgments and presumably listen in turn. In a burst of comedy with profoundly serious implications, the narrator describes the tiny group as "a majority" (*multo plures*), a "band" (*manus*), a "crowd" (*turbam*).[51]

In her later work, as we saw at the start of chapter 2, Arendt came to believe that Kant unlocked a new way of thinking about political judgment— because in his separation of judging from pure and practical reasoning, he discovered a distinctive characteristic of judgment that Arendt took to be crucially important for imagining how moral and political beliefs can exist in the basic, irrefutable condition of human existence: plurality. To Kant, the peculiar characteristic of aesthetic perception that distinguishes it from pure reasoning and moral judgment rests precisely in the relationship between the plural and the singular. Each of us has aesthetic perceptions, and Kant insists that these are subjective: the Cézanne is beautiful not in any objective sense, but because we find it to be so. Yet even as we experience subjective aesthetic perceptions, and we sense them as precisely that, subjective, our own—we still expect, paradoxically but reasonably, according to Kant, that everyone else will agree with us. "You don't find the Cézanne beautiful? How not?" I ask. Kant argues that the distinctive thing about aesthetic judgment is that it is neither rational nor moral yet prompts a reasonable expectation of universal agreement.

This argument prompted Arendt to suggest that understanding aesthetic taste would illuminate our moral choices: "Is our ability to judge, to tell right from wrong, beautiful from ugly, dependent upon our faculty of thought? Does the inability to think [about these things] and a disastrous failure of what we commonly call conscience coincide?"[52] She concluded that "imagination alone enables us to see things in their proper perspective, to put that which is too close at a certain distance so that we can see and

51   This group may anticipate the men described in the following unusually realistic poem, the so-called "journey to Brundisium" with Vergil, Maecenas, and others. The usual scholarly move is to treat the "crowd" references as a play on contemporary Latin poets' allegiance to Alexandrian notions of vulgarity and refinement (see Dufallo and many others).

52   Arendt, "Thinking and moral considerations," in *Responsibility and Judgment*, 160.

understand it without bias and prejudice, to bridge abysses of remoteness until we can see and understand everything that is too far away from us as though it were our own affair. This 'distancing' of some things and bridging the abysses to others is part of the dialogue of understanding."[53] Arendt's account gives the judging self a role in producing and reproducing a common world through the reciprocal exchange of common sense.

In Horatian satire, satire itself is the site for this exchange. The narrator recognizes that its "common sense" risks being exclusive or distinct: hence his joke about the Jews. But his tenacious refusal to fully or consistently inhabit the role of judge, his constant questioning of his proper capacity to render it thanks to his inability to fully know and govern himself, his recognition of the violent underpinnings of judgment, and his acknowledgment of the role of others in shaping his judgments—and thus, in an important sense, of himself as an agent in the world—all work against the assumption of exclusion. If satire refuses to escape the violent structure of judgment altogether, it establishes itself as an imaginative discourse where reflection tempers certainty and where the standards of judgment are constantly subjected to a brand of common correction that is attuned to the local.[54]

IMAGINATIVE SELF-ACCOUNTING

Satires 1.7, 1.8, and 1.9 are markedly different in style from the rest and are often treated together. Eduard Fraenkel suggested that the poems were casual add-ons designed to help the book meet the (presumably then fashionable) ten-poem format set by Vergil's *Eclogues*. Catherine Schlegel has argued that the poems undertake an extended experiment in aesthetic release, as the poet explores the harsher elements of satiric and comical jesting that he has carefully excluded from the earlier poems in the book, and which he will shut down again in poem 10.[55] Recent readings like hers typically affirm social norms as Horace's main concern.

---

53 Arendt, *Essays in Understanding*, 323.

54 I mention, but cannot address here, the tough questions raised by the perpetuation of "common" standards that do not serve the common good, because they are not truly "common" but rooted in inequality; or by situations when communal standards change radically to accommodate evil. On the latter question, see David Velleman's and Herlinde Pauer-Studer's discussion of the "common" distortion of morality under the Nazis, "Distortions of normativity," 329–56.

55 John Henderson sees the triptych as a "serial progression from the past and distance of Brutus' war-torn Asia, through the pivotal work of reconstruction of Rome under way in Maecenas' Esquiline gardens [where a wooden Priapus statue frightens two witches away], to the forensic present of Maecenas' cosmopolis," "Be alert," 222.

The radically altered voice of the narrator from poem to poem in this group dramatizes and celebrates the unsettled progress of the self. Since these three poems stand apart from the rest, a puzzle that prompts specula-tion, I will close with a reading of them that is grounded in Arendt's discus-sion of imagination before returning to the themes of judgment and sover-eignty in the last poem in the book. This is satire 1.10, a poem that picks up on the fourth and sixth satires' articulation of Horace's deep anxieties and hopes about his work and critical reaction to it.

Each poem in the third triptych locates its readers in a distinct and vividly imagined place: a chaotic law court in Asia Minor (7), a shabby garden on the Esquiline Hill (8), and the Sacred Way (9). Their characters are equally memorable, standing out vividly from the other characters in the book: the rich "hybrid" Persius who takes vengeance on the foul and poisonous Ru-pilius Rex; the Priapus statue who narrates 1.8, and who describes the shriek-ing Canidia and her friend Sagana, carrying magical dolls of wax and wool; and the parasitic "pest" of 1.9, comically familiar in his obsequious, tactless questions and his refusal to let Horace go his own way. In these three poems Horace makes trial not only of the range and effect of his satiric voice, but his powers of *enargeia*, which make chaotically alive the human and more than human plurality he has only gestured toward in the earlier poems. Where they were set in familiar contexts and company, now at every turn the poems draw our attention to what is involved in imagining that which is absent, how the poem has the power to move us into different places and into different identities. Satire 1.7 opens in a sudden, even shocking transi-tion from the familiar maxims and autobiographical anecdotes of 1.6: we land, with no explanation, in Brutus' law court. Then, 1.8 opens in a totally unique way: the speaking voice is not even human, but belongs to a piece of wood (*inutile lignum*) that has been carved into a Priapus statue. And 1.9 leads us back to the social center of Rome and to figures we have met before, but in a vividly imagined dialogue that invites us to identify with Horace even as we grow uncomfortably aware of our affinities with the poor pest.

What is involved in being a sensible reader of these sudden transitions? The exempla work by inviting us to identify with or against worldly particu-lars in all their variation, from non-Roman Greeks fighting over a matter of law to a wooden Priapus to Horace and his unwelcome pest. In the vivid description of each, the text elicits a peculiar mode of judging: judging by way of, in Arendt's suggestive phrase, "thinking ourselves into identities where we are not." We might say, recalling Horace's expression of sympathy for a frustrated Jupiter early in satire 1, that the poems themselves, as the speaker imagined Jupiter to do, offer us the opportunity to switch lives, temporarily at least. In these poems our attention is directed to how particulars achieve a vivid "thisness" that provides imaginative engagement with the vicissitudes of human experience. If we are not the Romanized Greeks cat-fighting in Brutus' law court, or the wooden Priapus, or the pest, we are asked to measure the distance between us and them, and to reflect on why they are here, alongside the greedy man, the miser, the adulterer, and the other stock representatives of vice in the first half of the book. This is the practice of the "enlarged mentality," in which Arendt sees the promise of animating truly civil judgments.

Here for the first time judging appears as an art. To read the sudden transitions of this triptych, and to develop the habit of readerly flexibility with the shifts and changes of the narrating voice, is to gain skills in the play of faculties that ward against the fixedness and misleading sense of stability that Horace warns against in the opening poems of the book. They suggest that to be at home in and responsive to a world that changes, often unpredictably and uncontrollably, we change as well, eluding the temptation to make a fatally self-deceiving bid for self-sovereignty. Horace is deeply concerned with the formation and preservation of shared sensibility, but his games with authorial persona, his carnival and corporeal imagery, and ironic attitudes toward authority express ambivalence about the regulatory, disciplinary, homogenizing effects of moralistic "common sense." In a vast empire encompassing many ways of being in the world—and I am thinking now about us as well as the Romans—the satirist's uneven performance of a moral discourse suggests that judging ourselves and others is an art we need to learn and refine through the experience of de-centered self-awareness, of free play within the constraints of meaningful dialogue. This is the exemplary experience satire provides.

FACING THE OTHER

Earlier I made three claims about the first triptych—that the self represented in it seeks the imprinting judgment of the other; that self-accounting is bound up with others' accounting of the self; and that the relation to the other is a source of pleasurable consolation as well as responsibility. Before concluding, there is more to say about the relations of self and other as they emerge in satires 4, 6, and 10—and in the Roman poetic habit of direct address in general.

Each poem is a conversation that blends the act of writing poetry with living a certain style of life, with the connecting glue between ideas being the attendant relations of friends, fellow poets, and patron. The fourth satire is a conversation with a second person (who is never named but who is addressed repeatedly) about the narrator's judgments of poetry, both others' and his own. Starting halfway through (1.4.78), the poem gradually transforms itself from an apology for the narrator's work to a defense of his upbringing and character. The first line of the sixth satire addresses and acknowledges Horace's patron Maecenas for his willingness to overlook Horace's unknown birth (*ignotos*, 1.6.6), unlike many who disdain his freedman origins (45–46), and explains the narrator's preference for a modest, simple life. The tenth poem also addresses itself to an unnamed interlocutor who appears to be a poet, or so it is suggested by the narrator's emphatic turn in his direction: "When you make verses—I'm asking you straight . . ." (*cum versus facias, te ipsum percontor*, 1.10.25).

Consider Horace's framing of these works as conversations in light of Emmanuel Levinas' reflections on the significance of the other to the self. Levinas is an ethical thinker best known for his claim that ethics is primary, that nothing is more primary than ethics—in other words, that social life incorporates ethics within itself, because ethics is what occurs between people when they encounter one another. He starts from the particularity of individuals, which comes into being as an ethical issue when one individual faces another. When the other presents his face to the self, he makes a claim on the self that is both authoritative and vulnerable. This, for Levinas, is the starting point of thinking about ethics: not with rules or laws or the habit of privileging either reason or faith, but with the social encounter and the particularity of the individuals involved in it. "In social life, I am always confronted by another particular person, who is near or far, friend or foe, present or absent, but always in the world with me and more importantly over against me or before me."[56] Levinas' point is that we live in relation with others' faces.

Satire 4 begins with praise of the Greek comedians and iambic poets, identified as forebears of Lucilius, who in turn inspired the narrator. First, in the self-undermining mode we saw in the first triptych, the narrator declares that no one reads his work, which is closer to prose than poetry (22–24, 40–42). In the middle of the poem the narrator rebuts the accusation that he rejoices in others' pain (*laedere gaudes, / inquit*, 78–80). On the contrary, he pleads that unlike false friends who make insinuations, he tells the truth openly; and even this he may cease to do if it seems right:

56   Michael L. Morgan, *Cambridge Introduction to Levinas*, 39 of 260 (Kindle edition).

Perhaps even from this a long life, a free-spoken friend, and good
counsel may take away; for when my couch or the colonnade takes
me in, I do not desert myself: "this is the right thing: I will live
better if I do this: thus I will make happy the friends I meet: that
certainly was not a nice thing: some day, might I foolishly do
something similar?"

> ... fortassis et istinc
> largiter abstulerit longa aetas, liber amicus,
> consilium proprium: neque enim, cum lectulus aut me
> porticus excepit, desum mihi: 'rectius hoc est:
> hoc faciens vivam melius: sic dulcis amicis
> occurram: hoc quiddam non belle: numquid ego
> imprudens olim faciam simile?' (1.4.131–37)

Here the narrator's imagination of a future move away from the judgment
of others to self-reflection (*neque ... desum mihi*) still ends by turning to the
other. As he wanders the portico or meditates in bed and mulls over the
right course of action, thinking about the act he dislikes and fears imitating
in spite of himself, his concern is focused on friends and their happiness.
The narrator knows the social rules: the pretense of the poem is that he is
free by virtue of his withdrawal into the couch or portico, but this is a refuge that lasts him only one line before he is back to reflecting on the encounter with his friends. He displays himself as split in several ways: between friends and solitude; between social rules and isolation; between the
pleasure of having friends and the anxiety of offending them; between the
awareness of the need to maintain a face and the worry that his face is the
wrong one. Nonetheless he continues to return to the scene of address—a
scene of interconnection, obligation, responsibility, worry, pleasure—everything that goes into constituting the free but non-sovereign self.

As Levinas might say, the solitude of the I in the world is never complete
or consistent: the I is never alone. "It is as though the self, being too full of
itself with a sense of the ceaseless, meaningless activity of its own being,
with its own insomnia, takes a leap outside itself, calls a halt or at least suspension to such activity, and finds the elements of its own gratification, its
own desires, in that which is 'other' to itself. Originary to the self, in sum,
originary to the formation of its ego, is a splitting or fracturing of self-
identity which conditions receptivity to what Levinas will call 'otherwise

than being."[57] In Horace's satire there is always another whose face the narrator confronts, whose presence compels a process of self-reflection that is self-reflexive, even automatic. "I see myself," said Sartre, "because somebody sees me."[58] The philosopher Simon Critchley, a close reader of Levinas, refers to what he calls "dividual" ethical subjectivity, a subjectivity divided against itself by the other's demand that unmoors the self from its temporary anchorage even as it reifies the self as necessary for the other.[59] This poem oddly exposes the subject, as a vulnerable entity, to the beholder: there appears to be a tension between longed-for absorptive, solitary states of independent self-reflection and the sociality of relations with others.

In Roman elegy, lyric, epic, and pastoral, making an address to another is almost a reflex. The relation of the writing self to the other, expressed in the vocative, has obvious social functions: the poet addresses friends and patrons, the more influential or well-born the better, and grants them social recognition in the act of claiming social recognition for himself. But the addresses and references to others in Roman poetry also deserve to be considered in light of Levinas' thinking, where the face "says 'no' to the I, but not an angry no; it is a no to my unchecked desire, to unbridled self-interest. The I has the power of its sheer presence, and the other stands over against it as a plea for acknowledgment, permission, assistance, concern."

Satire 6 places the role of the other in a specific social context: upper-class Rome. It dwells on the encounter between the narrator—closely identified with Horace, given the references to his freedman father, and the poem's narrative building on satire 5—and Maecenas and other well-off Romans, some of whom disdain the narrator's low birth. The narrator remembers tiny details of his first meeting with Maecenas: Vergil's introduction, his own shy greeting, Maecenas' quiet response followed by an invitation nine months later, their growing friendship (54–62). The narrator's acknowledgment of his vulnerability is followed by his acknowledgment of the limits of his capacity to shape himself, the limits of his self-sovereignty, in a move we have seen before: "even if I am dear to my friends," the narrator remarks, "my father is the cause of this" (70–71). This is a refusal to claim that the element of his character he most treasures is truly all his own doing.

---

57   Henry McDonald, "Aesthetics as first ethics: Levinas and the alterity of literary discourse," 26.

58   Cited in Stroup, *Catullus, Cicero, and a Society of Patrons*, 123.

59   Critchley, *Infinitely Demanding*, 23. Quotation in next paragraph, Morgan, *Cambridge Introduction*, 68.

Confident in himself, he nonetheless acknowledges that he is not fully responsible for being the man he has become.

So far we might still be tempted to consider the narrator's self-positioning as a social strategy, a career move, a bid for status. The pre-eminent analyst of relations of face in Horace, Ellen Oliensis, observes of the second book of Horace's *Epistles*: "[I read] Horace's poems as preeminently 'polite' acts, in the broad sense of acts oriented toward face needs."[60] This reading (which otherwise sheds much light on Horace) does not explain the next stage in the poem, where the narrator contemplates living a life other than his own, a life of wealth and privilege. Like the men in satire 1, however, who when Jupiter offered them a different life refused it, the narrator dismisses this vision: "If nature commanded us to go back . . . and choose other parents . . . content with my own, I would refuse to accept noble parents with the rods and chairs of state" (*nam si natura iuberet, / . . . remeare . . . / atque alios legere ad fastum quoscumque parentis / fascibus et sellis nollem mihi sumere*, 1.6.93–95). Why? Because this choice would not affect the fundamental human condition of non-sovereignty. The narrator would be encumbered by people and by obligations that would limit his freedom. "Immediately my affairs would have to be increased, more men would call on me, one or more companions would have to be led by me lest I go alone abroad or to the country" (*nam mihi continuo maior querenda foret res / atque salutandi plures, ducendus et unus / et comes alter, uti ne solus rusve peregreve / exirem*, 100–103). Neither the modestly well-off nor the rich can escape the condition of responsibility to others.

The end of the poem appears to offer an account of a simple, self-sovereign narrator who does precisely what he likes: lie in bed for hours, stroll around the city, get rubbed down with sweet oil, go to the baths (122–27). But the simplicity of the self-display, climaxing with the closing reference to ancestry (*quaestor avus pater atque meus patruusque fuissent*, 131) reminds us that the narrator is addressing Maecenas, the man who overlooks his lower-class ancestry but whom he worries about offending with his simplicity, as we have already seen (*simplicior . . . molestus*, 1.3.63, 65). The whole book closes with a list of people the narrator wants as readers and friends:

Let Plotius and Varius, Maecenas and Vergilius, Valgius and
Octavius, best of men, and Fuscus and each of the Viscus family
praise these verses! With ambition set aside I can speak to you,

60   Oliensis, *Horace and the Rhetoric of Authority*, 4.

Pollio, and you, Messalla, along with your brother, and at the same
time you, Bibulus and Servius, and also with these you, bright
Furnius, and many other learned men and friends whom I
prudently pass over: for whom I want these poems, whatever they
may be, to entertain, and I would grieve if they pleased you less than
I hope. Demetrius and you, Tigellius, I order you to complain
among the chairs of your young students!

Plotius et Varius, Maecenas Vergiliusque,
Valgius et probet haec Octavius optimus atque
Fuscus et haec utinam Viscorum laudet uterque!
ambitione relegata te dicere possum,
Pollio, te, Messalla, tuo cum fratre, simulque
vos, Bibule et Servi, simul his te candide Furni,
compluris alios doctos ego quos et amicos
prudens praetereo: quibus haec, sint qualiacumque,
adridere velim, doliturus, si placeant spe
deterius nostra. Demetri, teque, Tigelli,
discipularum inter iubeo plorare cathedras. (1.10.81–91)

This passage is often read as Horace's claim to authority via the social standing or literary accomplishments of his friends—their authority and *existi-
matio*—and a cruel dismissal of his rivals.[61] But it is also a plea. It acknowledges the primal vulnerability of a writer whose book has exposed the
constitutive interdependence of people and the limits of sovereignty.

CONCLUSION

On the "republican" view ... politics is constitutive of the process of
society as a whole. It is conceived as the reflective form of substantive
ethical life, namely as the medium in which the members of somehow solitary communities become aware of their dependence on one
another and, acting with full deliberation as citizens, further shape
and develop existing relations of reciprocal recognition into an association of free and equal consociates under law.[62]

61   Bramble tracks this dynamic in *Persius and the Programmatic Satire*, 190–204.
62   Habermas, "Three normative models of democracy: liberal, republican, procedural,"
Questioning Ethics, 135.

In 1711, Joseph Addison and Richard Steele began to publish the *Spectator*, a magazine aimed at the increasingly lively London coffeehouse scene. In *The Structural Transformation of the Public Sphere*, Jürgen Habermas identifies the emergence of "moral weeklies" like the *Spectator* as key players in the emerging notion of the "self-enlightened self" that helped spur the progressive social and political movements of the later eighteenth century and beyond. The *Spectator* modeled for its readers a droll, ironic, educated, sharply self-aware critical style. It couched its polemics against religious fanaticism and its calls for subsidized education in sentences crammed with classical references. The choice of epigraphs indicates the texts Addison and Steele found most congenial: *Spectator* 1 opens with a passage from Horace's *Ars Poetica*; #2, Juvenal; #3, Lucretius (a rare choice); #4, Horace's *Epodes*; #5, the *Ars Poetica* again; then Juvenal, Horace's *Epistles*, Virgil, the Neronian satirist Persius, Ovid. These, the usual suspects of the eighteenth-century Latin canon, are punctuated by the occasional quotation of Homer. But Horace has by far the lion's share—many hundreds of references in epigraph and body text in the magazine's 555 issues. Why? And what might political and social progressives find worthy of consideration in Horace today?

One issue I have not addressed so far is humor, but it is too important to go unmentioned. As Adam Thurschwell points out in his assessment of Simon Critchley's argument for the role of humor in moral thought: "Rather than self-lacerating or self-aggrandizing (in a heroic-tragic mode) humor is deflationary in a self-revealing manner. It is a relation of self-knowledge that permits the subject to transform its self-violence into a chastening self-understanding."[63]

Horatian satire undoes the claim to sovereignty that usually partners claims to moral judgment. It presents us with an exemplary voice, a humorous, ironic, self-critical voice that does not privilege the finitude of selfhood for its own sake, but rather sees it as a comic truth of the human experience. This is the Horace Addison and Steele enrolled in their battle on behalf of liberal values—a Horace fully cognizant of the inescapable constraints of intellectual capacity and social relations, but fighting back, with wit and in the company of others, not against moral commitments but moral certainty—even within himself. This fight, I think, makes the fighter free.

---

63   Thurschwell, review of Critchley, 303.

4

DIVIDUAL ADVOCACY

C LASSICAL POLITICAL THOUGHT is often understood as hostile to the disruptions, irrationalities, and banalities of quotidian experience: unity and order are taken to be its goals. In a much-quoted passage in Plato's *Republic*, musical harmony is used as a metaphor to describe the self and the city (401d–e, 432a); Aristotle praises genteel moderation and confines political theory to the variegated but contained sphere of rule; Cicero wrote his own *Republic*, which had its own memorable musical metaphor for concord (2.69). But as we saw in chapter 1, Cicero also theorizes political action as a contest, seeing the republic as a political association riven from the moment of its foundation by dynamic conflict on at least two fronts: the intra-elite competition for glory, and the "struggle of the orders," the haves and the have-nots. Like Cicero, we persist today in talking about ideals of concord (though we tend to redescribe concord as a pluralistic consensus based in mutual trust or friendship)—at the same time that we treat politics as contest, a field where deliberation leads to decisions and policies with real winners and real losers.

In this chapter, I work toward a clearer normative but non-prescriptive, non-telic account of the play of concord and discord in the politics of a democratic republic, and an account of being a citizen that incorporates both the will to harmony ostensibly adopted by much classical writing and the presence of experiment and self-division that characterizes all our lives.[1] I want to think about the citizen as a paradoxical unity of multiple possibilities, resistance and consensus, improvisation and institution, habituated to and expressive of the irreducible plurality of the world. This citizen lives amid institutions, traditions, and moral prescriptions in a style that encourages pushing against them. Here I build from the argument made in chapter 1 about Cicero's dialogues and speeches—influential texts that knit together productive instabilities where the parts usually fail to cohere—in

---

1   On play, passion, and radical experiment, see Don Herzog on Emma Goldman: "Romantic anarchism and pedestrian liberalism," 313–33.

order to sketch out the kind of citizen who can live in a world where the drive to achieve *concordia* or *consensus* thrives within a framing of politics as conflict. This citizen is a virtuosic speaker *of* and *to* an acknowledged multiplicity, and the patterns of thought and action modeled by oratory have consequences for deliberative and judicial political institutions.[2]

ENTANGLED SILENCES: THE SPOKEN WORD AND THE CONSTITUTION

By contrast with the Greek city-states, in Rome no formal "constitution" was ever written—until the 1870s and 1880s, as the joke goes, when Theodor Mommsen wrote it, in his *Römisches Staatsrecht*. Again by contrast with Greece, where a plethora of stories about the origins of rhetoric and drama gave rise to a flourishing biographical tradition about Homer, the archaic lyric poets, and the inventors of rhetoric Corax and Tisias, all collected by Aristotle in his *Rhetoric* and *Poetics*, no canonical Roman history of the spoken word existed until the era we now refer to as the end of the republic. At that time Cicero composed the first history of Roman oratory, *Brutus* (incorporating a few comments on poetry) and scattered a few comments on the origins of Roman poetry and drama in the *Tusculan Disputations* and other works.

The scenes of literary history that Cicero provides sketch speech and strife in mutually supportive relations. In the first book of *Tusculans* Cicero recalls the elder Cato's stories about the Romans' earliest form of poetry: banquet songs honoring heroic deeds to the accompaniment of flutes (1.2). This nostalgic portrait of celebratory song in a closed aristocratic circle locates the origins of Latin poetry in myth; this is a Homeric early Rome. Cicero's other references to the first moments of poetry's performance in public, by contrast, link art to strife: he claims the earliest production of state-sponsored drama to have occurred in 240 BCE (in fact an improbably late date), during the public games celebrating the end of Rome's first imperial war with Carthage—soon to be re-engaged in two more violent cycles. Here, song is a publicly funded celebration of the public war machine that the First Punic War formally inaugurated (*Brutus* 72–73). In *Brutus*, the earliest orators at Rome succeed in putting down popular discontent—an

---

2   See Geuss, *Philosophy and Real Politics*, on understanding power, not fantasizing around it: "politics is more like the exercise of a craft or art, than like traditional conceptions of what happens when a theory is applied. It requires the deployment of skills and forms of judgment that cannot easily be imparted by simple speech, that cannot be reliably condified or routinized, and that do not come automatically with the mastery of certain theories" (15).

idea Cicero must have found attractive after the mob scenes and gang wars of the 50s.[3]

A generation after Cicero, Livy in his *Ab Urbe Condita* represents the evolution of political speech into dramatic forms in archaic Rome. In the cultural memory he traces, the young men of the past incorporated a seductive new foreign form of dance into their Roman tradition of exchanging witty public abuse. Through this synthesis their jokes become drama, then satire, then farce, genres ultimately dominated by professionals.[4] A tradition that initially reminds us of the political invective of later centuries is thus purified (paradoxically) by the adoption of foreign (Etruscan) practices that mutate a political practice into early comic drama and remove it from the sphere where it originated. When the young Romans take their games elsewhere, these too are soon penned in by the conventions of a different dramatic genre, Atellan farce. Avenues of stylized verbal performance with a political valence open up only to be foreclosed by the conventions of dramatic mimesis; abuse is appropriated and transformed into imitation; by processes Livy does not specify, the forces at play within this scene of youthful public competition are channeled and controlled, aestheticized into a "play."

Horace offers a slightly different account of the relationship between stylized speech, the social order, and the law (*Epistle* 2.1.139ff). He describes post-harvest celebrations featuring sacrifices and feasts, during which men began to engage in

> the Fescennine licentiousness, which in alternating verses poured forth rustic tauntings; and this liberty, welcomed each returning year,

---

3   Again, these orators are too late in date to deserve Cicero's historical distinction as the "earliest" orators: this is a fictive history.

4   To stop a plague in 363 BCE, the senate introduced "scenic shows, a novelty for this warlike people, which up until then had known no spectacle except the circus contests.... Dancers were summoned from Etruria and they danced gracefully in Etruscan style to the strains of the pipes, without any songs or any gestures in imitation of songs. The young citizens took to imitating them, at the same time exchanging among themselves jokes in improvised verse, with gestures to match their words. The innovation was a success and grew in favor after frequent repetition. The native [Roman] artists received the name *histriones*, *ister* being the Etruscan for actor. They then performed *satura* [related to satire or satyr drama], rich in meters, written with music for pipes, and with appropriate movements. After the new method governing plays had replaced merriment and uncontrolled jesting, and the 'game' had gradually turned into the dramatic profession, the young citizens left the performance of plays to actors and returned to the old custom of exchanging jokes set in verse; their performances were later called after-pieces, and were worked into plays, especially Atellan farces. These Atellan entertainments were derived from the Oscans and were kept by the citizens in their own control, unpolluted by the actors." (7.2)

played affectionately, until the jokes, now growing cruel, turned into open rabid madness, and stalked honorable homes without fear of punishment. Men were mauled by a tooth that drew blood; even for those who escaped, the problem seemed in need of a common solution; and at last a law was passed, including a penalty, forbidding the portrayal of anyone in abusive song. The style changed, and in fear of a beating, men were led back to speaking well and graciously.

Here a mysterious story about the harm done by abusive public speech is interwoven with a turning point in Rome's legal history—the Twelve Tables' prohibition of public verbal abuse—reminding us of the significance of speech to the evolution of a polity "governed by laws, rather than men" (Livy 2.1).

The informal, scrappy, anecdotal quality of Roman histories of the original conditions of public utterance suggest the historians' collective desire to tame and minimize the role speech plays in the foundational history of the city, and I have suggested that this is best explained by the historians' troubled awareness that speech (certainly not written texts or laws or ideology) is precisely that through which the republic was constituted.

This evidence should make a difference to the way we approach Roman political thought. Roman political thought is figured not through static concepts but through a variety of other scenes to which writers return repeatedly, even obsessively: the scene of the virtuous exemplar (*passim*); the scene of class conflict (Sallust, Cicero, Livy, Plutarch); cultural change and decline (*passim*); the delegation of emergency powers in time of war (Cicero, Sallust, Livy); and persuasion, in the public assembly, the senate, the law court, and the school (Cicero, the elder and younger Senecas, Petronius, Tacitus, Pliny).

THE ROMAN SUBJECT:
VISIBLE, MULTIPLE, EMBEDDED IN CONFLICT

Elsewhere I have made the case that Cicero presents the republic as a "state of speech," and defends the orator as a model for the republican citizen.[5] We find in the Ciceronian orator a resource for our political imagination as we seek a repertoire of perspectives and tactics that will assist us in negotiating the terrain of civic discord—especially if we seek (as I do) to preserve the field of political difference and contestation without permitting it to solid-

5   Connolly, *The State of Speech*, especially 145–57, 161–65.

ify into irreparable divisions of distrust, fear, and contempt—and without ourselves embracing unrealizable ideals of civic trust or self-sacrifice.[6] I will focus on three related issues: visibility, the orator's reflection of the multiplicity of the political community, and contest.

As Cicero describes him, the orator is an object of aesthetic judgment. In the first few pages of his ambitious three-book dialogue *de Oratore*, or *On the Orator*, Cicero rehearses what will become a constant theme: that the orator is visibly active in public, and that this dictates his mode of engagement with the world, for he must speak a popular language: "it is the worst possible fault to deviate from the ordinary mode of speaking" (1.12). *De Oratore* also argues that the orator fashions his virtuosic self-display in response to the communal gaze; this means that he is not entirely his own man, but his value and sense of self is utterly entangled with his status in public (1.18). His virtuosity provides the chief basis "for his own dignity and for the safety of countless individuals and for the state at large" (1.34). No orator exists in isolation from the community, and this awareness of community is always reflected in his style. Lastly, contest. The interlocutors in *de Oratore*, Marcus Crassus and his friends, begin their conversation under a plane tree compared to the tree in Plato's *Phaedrus*; the stage is metatheatrically set for another scene in the ongoing Roman contest with Greek intellectual history. And as in Plato's dialogues, *de Oratore* begins with an argument among its participants. But Cicero diverges from the Platonic dialogue structure in constructing two alternative versions of Socrates, Crassus and Marc Antony, and the two never cease their debate; the dialogue flirts with, but refuses to offer a single node of allegiance, dwelling always in the realm of doubles. It's no accident that Cicero dedicates *de Oratore* to his brother Quintus, thus invoking the Romans' ambivalent associations with fraternal relations, where brothers are always at once partners and rivals.

What kind of a character best copes with a polity riven by such entrenched division? What values and perspectives are at stake in his formation? We have seen the interrogative ethos narrated in Sallust's histories, and the self-aware, shifting, ironic ethos in Horace's *Satires*. Are there worthwhile dispositions to reflect upon in Cicero, or is Cicero's orator, as many critics have concluded, mostly a model for oligarchic domination, a driver

6   It will become clear that I share Bonnie Honig's belief that "to keep the contest going requires a commitment to a politics of self-overcoming, a politics that contests closure" (*Political Theory and the Displacement of Politics*, 209) rather than Danielle Allen's praise of sacrifice, though I am intrigued by her discussion of rhetorical strategies for civic action (*Talking to Strangers*, 39, 156–59).

of false consensus that enacts the will of the rich and noble senatorial order? To arrive at the latter opinion requires ignoring the way Cicero frames the formation of the orator in terms of struggle, that is, the disavowal and externalization of dissonant impulses that are understood as never fully erasable. As Cicero elaborates it in *de Oratore*, rhetorical education instills habits of creative, productive reflection, establishing a kind of self-government in the speaker even as it unleashes the passions that individuate the self and incorporate it into the community. Cicero's speaking self is thus not conceived as wholly autonomous; in the course of fashioning himself as a self committed to the instruction, moving, and charming of the populace, he is multiply constituted yet ordered and bounded; the possessor of one tongue yet not univocal. Cicero's citizen must speak with authentic passion on behalf of others, necessarily engendering dissonance in himself; this dissonance is always to be moderated but not erased, because it produces a dynamic energy inherent in performance.[7]

The notion that the advocate embodies and enacts resistibility underlies the Ciceronian defense of rhetoric and oratory. In treatises like *de Oratore* and especially *Orator*, Cicero has much to say about the orator's mastery over his audience, but it is often forgotten that his talk of mastery always assumes that his ideal orator devotes himself to a life of conflict. The role of the advocate is so important to Cicero's claim that oratory is the quintessential act of citizenship that he devotes most of his prescriptive discourse not to deliberative but to forensic oratory, the better to articulate and explain the best techniques of agonistic argument.

Cicero's rhetorical theory presumes a plurality of voices in the Forum, and he views the orator-statesman as an advocate, partisan but reasonable, divided in his sensibilities (the proems to various speeches of prosecution and defense). He speaks to all, he speaks for those who have no voice; he has a passionate link to the causes of those on behalf of whom he speaks; he has

---

7   Persuasion involves neither mastery over, nor regard for, but the acknowledgement of the relation between self and other in the context of agonistic competition. This is acknowledgement of the type Stanley Cavell has in mind (as Patchen Markell has noted in *Bound by Recognition*), where the direct object of acknowledgement is not the other but the self. The orator's acknowledgement of his audience is not a recognition of their identity and interests, but an acknowledgement of the self. This explains Cicero's interest in the orator's self-understanding; as Markell says, "to acknowledge another is in the first instance to respond to, to act in the light of, something about oneself; and conversely, the failure of acknowledgement, the avoidance of the other, is crucially a distortion of one's own self-relation, an avoidance of something unbearable about oneself" (35). To paraphrase Markell's reading further: what has value and meaning, Cavell says, is not the recognition of another in itself; this has no intrinsic value. What matters is what we do in the presence of the other, how we act in the light of what we do know about them, and about ourselves.

autonomy of judgment that he characterizes as responsive to the people but also reasonable.[8] Cicero's orator is best understood along the lines of Simon Critchley's notion of dividual subjectivity, where one's sense of identity as a person is formed around the moral experience of assenting to a demand from another that is placed upon the self. This is a circular structure where the person feels himself to be most himself when he agrees to speak and act on behalf of the other who has made the demand on him: but Critchley argues that this circle is an accurate description of the mutual constitution of our selves.[9]

The advocate's adversary is somebody whose ideas or beliefs the advocate neither shares nor condones, but who is treated as a legitimate opponent—a "legitimate enemy" with whom the advocate has as common ground a shared adhesion to a set of ethico-political principles. Rational resolution of disagreement, whether over principle or implementation, is rarely possible, but compromises may be reached. Nothing in Cicero's account suggests that anything further is at stake. As we have seen, he believes that his "side," the senatorial elite, should consistently dominate the people, but his own history of Rome underlines the ineradicability of antagonism between senate and people and the necessity (suggested by historical experience) of popular intervention in cases of senatorial over-reach—an overreach that is all the more likely due to the very high value the senate places on the achievement of individual glory. Senatorial domination is not authoritarian or eternal; it is one condition of agonistic confrontation.

Cicero models the antagonism that is constitutive of politics in his own orations, where he presents himself as split in two or caught between two desires or wills, never quite identical to himself, a literally partial voice that is distanced and analytical of the whole. He explains the split in various ways: as born from his wish to speak a different way or to remain silent, from conflicted personal loyalties, from a decision about rhetorical strategy (for example, conflict over dealing with last-minute information), or from his sense of propriety. Cicero introduces the *pro Caecina* of 69 BCE with a theatricalized account of his last-minute change of heart: he had been planning to plead the case one way, but he has discovered an alteration in the prosecution's strategy, so he leans "now" toward a new approach (1–2). In

---

8   Nadia Urbinati's notion of representativity is useful here: "a condition that lies in between transcendence and adhesion, defining relationships of control (on the part of the represented) and responsibility (on the part of the representatives) that are eminently political and moral but not juridical and legal": *Representative Democracy*, 74.

9   Critchley, *Infinitely Demanding*, 23–25; see also Thurschwell's illuminating review, especially 301.

the speeches for Sestius, Plancius, and Marcellus, and the speech against Caecilius, Cicero begins with an extended apology for speaking at all when he wishes to put his voice to other uses, or to be silent.

In 56, not long after Cicero's return from exile, he frames his defense of Sestius as delivered under compulsion: he is forced to exert his voice to ward off danger from men he should rightly be using his voice to thank. The sense of split will he cultivates here is deepened in later passages recounting Cicero's decision to reveal only half of himself, his emotions rather than his talent (2–3), and his contradictory desires simultaneously to express his fury and to control himself (6–7). Similarly, speaking against Caecilius, Cicero begins his assault on Caecilius' ability to prosecute Verres by reminding the jury of his own preference for defense; he is profoundly "anxious and distressed" at the need to prosecute Caecilius, but he will do it for the good of the republic (3). The exordium of the *pro Plancio*, delivered in 54, lays emphasis on the internal conflict arising from Cicero's awareness that Plancius' opponent Iuventius Laterensis has been a staunch friend in the past, particularly during his persecution by Clodius. The speech on behalf of Marcellus (a special case) dramatizes Cicero's reluctant decision to break the long silence of the civil war.[10]

Is Cicero's recurrent choice to cast himself as a conflicted voice an artful part of his plea, a *captatio benevolentiae*? They are not particularly interested in the theme of conflict, but John Dugan and Elaine Fantham have recently explained Cicero's thematization of self-fashioning as the product of his desire to advance himself while minimizing the disadvantages of his status as a *novus homo*. I argue rather that Cicero's construction of himself in these and other speeches resonates with his representation in his rhetorical works of the orator as a political *exemplum*; the speeches thus model a political subjectivity. These moments are microcosms of the notorious contradictions in self-presentation in his letters and the speeches, where Cicero portrays his enemies, friends, associates, and commitments in radically different ways, according to his assessment of his audience's expectations and judgments. Especially marked here is the contrast between the epistolary voice of Cicero the *optimate* and the rostra voice of the *consul popularis* in the *contio*, especially the two speeches against Servilius Rullus' agrarian laws and the Manilian oration 17–18 (see also *Rab. Perd.* 5), where Cicero em-

---

10   Ultimately, Cicero's defense of Marcellus is an apologia for oratory, for the perpetuation of the field of political action: it anticipates his *Philippics* as much as the younger Pliny's *Panegyricus* of Trajan. The troubling availability of republican-style speech for both resistance *and* collusion with autocratic power is precisely the heart of the moral problem I treat in closing.

braces tribunician aggressiveness and popular heroes like Marius, and bitterly attacks consular arrogance (*Leg. Agr.* 2.1–10, 14). In the wake of work by Iris Young and others thinking about deliberation and recognition or acknowledgement, we might conclude that Cicero's divided self serves to acknowledge the existence of other points of view, of other paths to judgment.[11] But better justice is done to the overarching concern with conflict and advocacy in Cicero's thinking, I suggest, if we see the divided self as a figure that imaginatively embodies the resistance to Cicero's argument. By preserving traces of his own resistance to his choice of case or line of thought, Cicero flags the resistance of others and weaves antagonism as a central theme in the speech.

Consider the *pro Sestio* and the *pro Plancio*, where Cicero presents himself as caught between his desire to play two roles at once. In the *pro Sestio*, Cicero wishes to be both the panegyrist and the protector of Sestius. So keenly aware of his obligations to the man is he that he concludes the speech with a parallel conflict: his intense desire to remain in Rome and his sense that he should depart again in order to ease the pressure on Sextius and his friends—but then, of course, he could not defend them. The spectacle of Cicero's dilemma, his desire to do the right thing, to give back to his protectors what is due, provides the climactic image of the peroration.

But since the roles of panegyrist and protector normally work together in a defense speech (for example, in the *pro Archia*), it is remarkable that Cicero disarticulates them so carefully here. The evocation of a self divided creates a marked distancing effect, drawing attention to the dramatically constructed nature of the orator's ethos. So the overdetermined apology contributes to two key strategies in the speech: first, it shifts the conflict from between the two litigants into the field of Cicero's own character: Cicero internalizes (and particularizes) the contest. Second, it makes moral propriety, the question *quod decet* (what is fitting?), central to the defense; and Cicero explores the theme throughout the speech in terms that draw attention to appearance and the communal judgment of visible appearance. He exhorts the jury to consider the appearance of his rivals (explicit at *Sest.* 18–22); he argues that he has always approached his life with *dignitas* in mind (48).

In the *pro Plancio*, Cicero constructs another embarrassed and internally conflicted Cicero, a Cicero keenly sensitive to the competing demands of friendship, of the need to appear to behave in the right way toward people.[12]

11   Young, *Inclusion and Democracy*, 53–70.
12   Christopher Craig, "Cicero's strategy of embarrassment in the speech for Plancius," 75–77.

As he stages his inner conflict of loyalties as a drama of ethos that reflects and amplifies the conflict between prosecutor and defendant, Cicero recasts the claims of the law as competing claims of propriety.

The perceptible contradictions that emerge are symptomatic of an agonistic politics arising from plurality, that is, from a multiplicity of interrelated and conflicting individuals, perspectives, values, claims, and attachments.[13] The workings of agonistic politics necessarily leave behind "remainders" and "excesses"—necessarily, because of the irreducible plurality of the polity, which means that any consensus at any given time inevitably involves the rejection or exclusion of some people or groups. Cicero's self-dramatized internal conflicts speak to these remainders. While he does not intend to signal agreement with the excluded, it is key to his success as a speaker in the republican agon that he acknowledges dissent or "thinking otherwise," that he recognizes (in Iris Marion Young's sense of the word) others' sense of alienation, conflict, difference, and loss, accepting these experiences into his own ethos and thus welcoming the excluded back into the body politic.

Agonistic politics shapes what I have elsewhere called oratorical "performative ethics." This emerges most clearly in *de Oratore*, where Cicero sidesteps the notion of a perfectly unified self in favor of a discursively constituted subject who, to use a phrase of Helen McManus, "is never quite identical with" himself.[14] There is much talk in the dialogue about the importance of actors as models for the orator, so long as the orator "keeps it real." One speaker, Marcus Antonius, defends his ability to stir up his emotions on behalf of his client, insisting that there is no "art" involved; his feelings as he speaks are utterly genuine. A pleader's lack of authenticity is easily perceived, and the case is lost (2.102). The mode of subject formation outlined in *de Oratore*'s rhetorical pedagogy starts from and never lets go of a norm of unity and mimetic consistency, but it also insists that the developing and practicing orator transcend the norm, cultivating flexibility and responsiveness to externals.

The orator must "taste" the senses of his audience; he must know human character through and through; this allows him to appeal to the *sensus communis*, the communal sensibility, of his listeners (1.218, 223, 2.182–86, 337). Since audiences differ in nature and quality, the orator must change his style

---

13   My original inspiration for thinking along these lines was sketched by Bonnie Honig's arguments for agonism in her *Political Theory and the Displacement of the Political*.

14   See further Helen McManus, "Enduring agonism: between individuality and plurality."

accordingly. Cicero's speaking self is thus not conceived as wholly autonomous; in the course of fashioning himself as a self committed to the instruction, moving, and charming of the populace, he is multiply constituted yet ordered and bounded; the possessor of one tongue yet not univocal. Cicero's citizen is, as Étienne Balibar might say, "unthinkable as an isolated individual, for it is his active participation in politics that makes him exist. But he cannot on that account be merged into a total collectivity."[15]

It is well known that pleaders in the Roman law court tended to frame questions of legal conflict as questions of moral judgment: the facts or the truth of the case scarcely mattered.[16] In Cicero's presentation moral judgment is not precisely replaced, but enabled by aesthetic judgment, the communal evaluation of appearances. In his speeches, he enlarges the scope of the judgment so that it includes himself. Here is a master orator who is profoundly concerned with proper relations between persons. Cicero couches his arguments not with a view toward justice, but in terms of appropriateness, decorum, appearance—encouraging the audience to judge himself and his client by terms that collapse the difference between the moral, the political, and the aesthetic.

To speak in conditions of pervasive conflict exposes the orator to the contingency and fragility of all unity; it forces him to recognize his own internal divisions. Cicero offers a sensitive account of the division-conscious, agonistic self in the first book of *de Legibus*, where he takes up the theme of self-knowledge, beginning from the Delphic Apollo's command *gnóthi seauton*, "know yourself." Knowledge of ourselves, in his account, begins with the recognition of irreducible difference, indeed eternal contest, since each self has a divine element within him and self-knowledge involves a process of observation and examination (*se ipse perspexerit totumque temptarit*, "he scrutinizes himself and thoroughly tests himself," 1.59). Once the self ab-

---

15   Locating violence in the enforcement of (naturalized) unequal relations of power, Balibar argues that to understand these relations, it is necessary to see how their history is intertwined with the way identities emerge, are fixed, and change. He treats identity as "fundamentally transindividual," as a process of identification, not an essential static product, and as ambiguous, multivocal. Selves are overdetermined from the perspective of the viewer yet internally decentered, fragmented. The self is never identical with the self, or rather, "the self." The object of political thought, Balibar suggests, is that which regulates the ambiguities of our identifications, the inevitable conflicts that spring from our simultaneous identification with, say, a nation and a religious community—a regulation he calls "civility." Lastly, in his writing on the citizen-subject, Balibar suggests that the subject, "(which the citizen will be supposed to be) contains the paradoxical unity of a universal sovereignty and a radical finitude," being constituted from "both the point of view of the State apparatus and that of the permanent revolution" (55).

16   See Andrew Riggsby on the Roman lawcourt, *Crime and Community*.

jures slavery (*obsequium*) to bodily pleasures (without eradicating desire for them), *exacuerit illam, ut oculorum, sic ingenii aciem*, "it sharpens the keen edge of its critical faculties, just as one may seek sharper vision," and finally it may seek knowledge of multiplicity: it examines "the heavens, the earth, the seas, the nature of the universe," finitude and immortality, "and when it realizes that it is not shut in by walls as a resident of some fixed spot, but is a citizen of the whole universe, as it were of a single city, then in the midst of this universal grandeur, and with such a view and comprehension of nature, how well it will know itself" (1.61).

At this point in its development, the self has learned to discount conventional values for their own sake, but it will then seek to improve convention by entering into public life, where "it will conclude that it must use not only the customary subtle methods of philosophical debate, but the more resourceful, broadly ranging continual style of speech," which allows the self not only to consider best how to establish and enforce laws, but how to "persuade" its fellow citizens (*ad persuadendum . . . suis civibus*, 1.62). Properly equipped with these intellectual and affective resources, the speaker's own plurality permits a bridging, through speech, between himself and the plural community. This model of ethical formation proposes a durable, dialogic self capable of incorporating the necessary contradictions that arise as the subject shapes himself to understand, address, and persuade a multiplicity.

Cicero's move anticipates the conception of political discourse in the work of Nietzsche and Hannah Arendt, common critics of what they read as Plato's devaluation and degradation of appearance, aesthetics, contingency, and multiplicity in favor of essence and truth. As Arendt saw it, in dialogues like *Gorgias* and *Republic* Plato constructed an epistemology, ethics, and political theory—an integrated vision of philosophy and its proper ends—that dismissed appearance and action in favor of a self-destructive "ideal of uncompromising self-sufficiency and mastership." Plato's philosopher-king first identifies the nature of the good, then contemplates the proper ends of the good; he *sees* the product he aims to create before he takes action. Relegating action to the realm of the necessary, Plato emphasizes the *end* of action and the eternal values that underwrite that end. As Arendt puts it, Plato cuts knowing and doing in two, in a separation that becomes reified into the "natural" hierarchy of theory and praxis.

Cicero, too, found Plato's contemplative identification of a single end, whether it be "justice" or "the good," to be fundamentally hostile to the human condition of plurality and, further, to the contingency and creativity of human action. In *de Oratore*, Cicero attacks Socrates for having cut the intellect from the tongue, the acts of analysis and reflection from the *actio* of persuasion (3.60–61). Cicero defines the best orator by contrast to the philosopher.

The orator is an expert in the realm of opinion, not truth; he is the master of the realm of appearance; he fashions himself like a work of art; he seeks to project simultaneously consistency and adaptability. He can live with and negotiate political difference, because he has examined the fundamental conflicts in his own soul; he understands his history as a series of violent struggles; and he employs a strategy of self-acknowledgment that exposes the internally contradictory fragments of the speaking self, which in turn opens unexpected avenues of identification between the speaker and those who oppose him. This is an exemplary civic ethos.

As we saw in chapter 1, the importance of contestation in political history and in the self has profound implications for Cicero's thinking about the nature and legitimacy of political authority. In *de Republica*, *de Legibus*, the speeches *pro Sestio*, *pro Flacco*, and the fourth speech against Catiline, Cicero describes the fundamental challenge of republican politics as attaining the proper balance between the authority (*auctoritas*) of the senatorial haves and the power (*potestas*) of the popular have-nots (most succinctly at *de Leg.* 3.28). Cicero's representation of the orator as symbiotically dependent on the community for the shaping of his present and future identity (the eternal life of communal memory) makes his striving for recognition a condition for representing the greater struggles between mass and elite. Citizens' struggle for approval in the public eye attunes them to the struggle of the people and the senate (*potestas* versus *auctoritas*). The resulting performative play of character mimics the core struggle that defines republican politics and through which the republic is constituted: the struggle of SPQR, between the senate and the people of Rome.

This interplay occurs in and on the body: the dynamic energy native to the body must be channeled by the authority of reason and practical wisdom, but in such a way that the performance remains authentic and the speaker's emotions are not erased but directed. The charm of popular appeal must be woven into the speaker's sense of himself as constantly accommodated to the public gaze, constantly put to the test in the public arena. His performance speaks to the eternal struggle that constitutes the republican order. But the law court and assembly are more than pressure valves for class struggle. By the forceful logic of Cicero's association of resolving violence with re-foundation, the republic is repeatedly reconstituted through the mediated, channeled violence of forensic and deliberative argument.

In a fascinating analysis of his letters to friends in the year 46 BCE, Elea-nor Leach appeals to Lacanian theory to account for Cicero's "anxieties of personal identity," first during the years of civil war and later under Caesar's tyrannical domination.[17] Having declared rhetorical ethos a "rational en-deavor" that assumes "integrity of self for which consistency of observable public conduct is the sign," she argues that the desire for such a self can never be satisfied, because the self perceives the discrepancy between "its source within the individual 'ego' and the subjectively conceived objects toward which it tends." The awareness of alienation from power makes Ci-cero "virtually paradigmatic of the Lacanian subject of desire," so that his self-presentation in his letters comes to look less like a set of stable portraits than "mirrors wistfully reflecting an absent self through the very gesture of assimilating that self to another."

To read Cicero's mounting of multiple persona as a strained sign of his "obsessive desire for self-fulfilling recognition" and a direct response to Cae-sar's usurpation of traditional authority (as compelling a reading as it is) misses the extent to which the habit of multiplicity characterizes his writing and oratory from the start of his career. The embattled, internally contested self he mounts suggests that ethos itself is a response to the agonistic condi-tions of republican politics.

CONCLUSION

Cicero's performance-oriented account of good oratory is a theory of action essential to the preservation of the conflict that constitutes the polity; his aestheticization of the orator's action, his construction of the orator as the voice of multiples, defies the Platonic instrumentalization of action. Does this mean that Cicero is not committed to senatorial leadership, or that he seeks to speak for the people in all their diversity? Cicero does make speak-ing to the diverse collective of the citizen audience a priority (contrast his treatment of Greeks or Gauls in the *pro Flacco* and the *pro Fonteio*). He ad-dresses "the people" (*Leg. Agr.* 2.1–10, *Sest.* 91ff.) and a multiplicity of fac-tions and interests (e.g., the *Verrines*). But my point is not Cicero's personal political commitments. Bonnie Honig has remarked that "the perpetuity of contest is not easy to celebrate."[18] I am not interested in values but in the repertoire of strategies that make the perpetuity of contest easier to bear.

---

17   Leach, "Ciceronian bi-Marcus," 140; for the quotations in my next sentences, 143 and 145–47.

18   Honig, *Political Theory*, 14.

Yet the nagging question remains: what is the anchorage of the orator's ethos? If Cicero sees politics as a contest, what prevents him from simply spurring on his fellow elites' will to power? When the self must be capable of speaking in more than one voice, what grounds and legitimates his performance? Why shouldn't we see his orator as a leader and the audience as sheep, vulnerable to seduction and misinformation? How can Cicero claim moral legitimacy for his performative confection?

I will sketch two answers to this question. Let me approach the first via a short digression. In her book *Eichmann in Jerusalem*, as we have already seen, Hannah Arendt concluded that Eichmann's crimes were due to his loss of the ability to think.

> He merely, to put the matter colloquially, never realized what he was doing. . . . In principle he knew quite well what it was all about, and in his final statement to the court, he spoke of the "revaluation of values prescribed by the government." He was not stupid. It was sheer thoughtlessness. . . . The longer one listened to him, the more obvious it became that his inability to speak was closely connected with an inability to think, namely, to think from the standpoint of someone else. No communication was possible with him, not because he lied, but because he was surrounded by the most reliable of all safeguards against the words and the presence of others, and hence against reality as such.

Picking up this last point, Arendt argued that Nazi Germany was an environment where legal, social, and moral norms were systematically inverted. The inverted order "hindered people from understanding their consciences aright, creating an obstacle to moral reasoning"—in particular, the capacity of self-reflection.

Eichmann and his contemporaries' confusion of criminality with duty left Arendt deeply suspicious of people who cited moral principles in the conduct of everyday life: as she said of the Nazis, "this 'new order' was exactly what it said it was—not only gruesomely novel, but also and above all, an order." Many say "I *ought not* to do this," Arendt observes, but she adds, "morally the only reliable people when the chips are down are those who say 'I can't.'"[19] Where does the "I can't" come from? The beginning of the answer is self-examination: "I cannot do certain things, because having done

---

19   Insightfully discussed by J. David Velleman and Herlinde Pauer-Studer, "Distortions of normativity."

them I shall no longer be able to live with myself." But self-examination, as historians of the Holocaust have shown, is only part of the story; on its own it cannot guarantee virtue. The communal reinforcement of values is the other, crucial part: it provides the necessary context, providing (mutable) norms for individual self-confrontation and regulation.

This brings us back to the exemplary orator, especially the forensic orator of Cicero's rhetorical works and his own speeches. In order to win his cases, and more, in order to win glory and eternal memory in the community, this figure consistently thinks himself into the other position, and he believes in his performance, in a practice that is not empathy, but something closer to what Hannah Arendt calls "thinking in my own identity where actually I am not." The audience, ever watchful on the front of taste, on the alert for signs of mendacity, is the other that monitors the performance in keeping with communal norms.

As Cicero says in *Orator*, his last treatise, the *prudentia auditorum*, "the prudence of the listeners," is the *moderatrix eloquentiae*, "the moderating force of eloquence" (24). By now, we are in a position to see that as the orator seeks to guide, lead, even dominate the jury, the senate, or the assembled *contio*, he is also bound to respond to the community's multiple desires and values. The agonistic performance of values—expressed in the basic language of "what feels right" to the plurality—is one bulwark against pure vice. The aesthetic categories in *de Oratore*, *Orator*, and *de Officiis* ground virtuoso political action and the world of appearances in a communal contest that is both beyond good and evil and a constant challenge to the meaning of those terms.

Rome has played an important role in the post-political work of Michel Serres, Giorgio Agamben, Michael Hardt and Antonio Negri, and others concerned with the violence of the state; they speak of autocratic consensus, the collapse of politics into policy-making and from there into policing. Jacques Rancière argues that the police is defined as the existing order of things, a partitioning off of the arena of the political; by "police" he refers to the activities of the state, which sees that citizen bodies are assigned to particular places and tasks, which authorizes certain activities as visible and others as lawless, which defines some speech as discourse or deliberation and other speech as noise. As conceived by the police, "society is a totality comprised of groups performing specific functions and occupying determined spaces."[20] As I have said before in this book, according to thinkers

20   Rancière, "Dissenting Words: A Conversation with Jacques Rancière," with David Panagia, 124.

like Rancière, Žižek, Hardt and Negri, and Simon Critchley, the left's historical emphasis on distribution of wealth has become the essence of policing, the policing of normalization: the distribution of peoples, names, functions, jobs, places to live. In response these thinkers have called for a redefinition of the political itself. Alain Badiou argues that politics should concern itself with inventing new and hitherto unauthorized modes of disagreement and disorder. Rancière argues that "the political" is about dissent, rupture, disruption, "demanding the part for those who have no part." He critically dissects the "scandal of democracy," pointing out that it is radically split into two: the oligarchic police process on the one hand, the principle of equality expressed through activism on the other. Summarized, his definition of "politics" is: reminding the police that their order is not political.

As we saw in chapter 1, Cicero theorizes political authority as part of a broader conception of political action that privileges the virtuosic display of the speaker whose authority must be resistible and whose legitimacy is subject to public consensus. The legitimacy, indeed the inevitability of resistance is thus built into Cicero's understanding of republican authority and order. If he has a lot to say about tradition, honor, and glory, he is equally alert to the fictionality of these qualities, and their inadequacies in the face of injustice.

In Cicero's framing of political history as violent conflict and the polity as a field of difference I have sought and found a scene into which the kind of citizen I am thinking about may be interpolated. This citizen is one whose proper action is the making of demands, the scrutiny and checking of institutions and institutionalization. This citizen pays close attention to the gritty processes of political action; if s/he does not deliberate more, s/he injects dynamism into institutions, scrutinizes the actions of representatives, demands accountability, minimizes the circulation of private property as an instrument of political persuasion. I hope to have shown that the process of citizen action is naturally never finalized, and its unfinished aspect is the crucial point.

In Cicero's speech on behalf of Marcellus, the subject of the next and last chapter, I will argue that Cicero advocates a tragic clearsightedness that required both Pompeians and Caesarians to take up responsibility for civil violence and, with that memory in mind, to make a path forward in difficult new political conditions. As Cicero frames it, clearsightedness in the future rests on the senators' acknowledgment of past failures. His account of the suffering in civil war and his hyperbolic praise of Caesar make an urgent memorial for those who died—an exhortation to acknowledge the finitude of human efforts to live a certain way, and to try, with that acknowledgment in mind, to invent another mode of life where the quest for individual glory and masterful self-sovereignty is tempered by another one, the acknowledgment of the need for self-recognition as a collective with shared values and purpose.

5

IMAGINATION, FINITUDE, RESPONSIBILITY, IRONY

CICERO'S *PRO MARCELLO*

Our judgments concerning the worth of things, big or little, depend on the feelings the things arouse in us. Where we judge a thing to be precious in consequence of the idea we frame of it, this is only because the idea itself is associated already with a feeling. If we were radically feelingless, and if ideas were the only things our minds could entertain, we should lose all our likes and dislikes at a stroke, and be unable to point to any one situation or experience in life more valuable or significant than any other. Now the blindness in human beings of which this discourse will treat, is the blindness with which we all are afflicted in regard to the feelings of creatures and people different from ourselves.[1]

ARE THE RESOURCES of premodern thought adequate to modernity? George Kateb argues that to understand the scale of modern horrors we must come to grips with the human imagination—specifically, the tremendous new capacity of the imagination of one or a few people to unleash itself on the world. Leaders construct society or law afresh in their minds with an energy that Kateb calls "hyperactive"; they go on to sway their followers to make the stuff of their imaginations real. In cases when change leads to atrocity, imagination is once again responsible—this time, the stunted imaginations of the followers, which blind them to alternative ways of thinking and doing and to injuries suffered by others. Unfortunately for political theorists, according to Kateb, the premodern canon has traditionally paid little attention to imagination. As a result its capacity to illuminate or improve our situation today is seriously reduced.

1   William James, "On a certain blindness in human beings," 841.

173

The problem is not that canonical thinkers do not understand the capacity of humans to imagine harm or to do it. They are notoriously pessimistic about human nature: for every virtue catalogued by Plato and Aristotle there is a vice. But for Kateb their gloom only throws a deeper shadow on already obscure terrain.[2] He acknowledges that the canonical vices like immoderation index and to a degree illuminate the "irritants" that nudge the leaders' hyperactive imaginations into motion while keeping the followers' imaginations sluggish. Yet the canon fails to account for vice as it operates in a world where, as Ulysses S. Grant said, space is annihilated.[3] From televisions and trains to remote prisons and weapons of mass destruction, modern technologies make it possible for the visions of hyperactive imaginations to be transmitted almost instantly to a mass audience, and for atrocities to be committed at a distance over an extended period. Silent complicity and habit allows atrocities to accrue their own reasons and justifications and even to become normal.

Here the real horror of the situation emerges. The "sense of possibility" among both leaders and masses "develops its own momentum; if it is abstract or fanatical enough, it can eventually supply its own motivation. The momentum is experienced as destiny or mission, that is, as a necessary pattern that must be taken to completion."[4] Committing atrocities or major acts of injustice becomes partly a matter of aesthetics. In the imagination of the perpetrators, the world comes to *appear* and *feel* a certain way—as an organism that requires the purging of a particular type of people in order to survive or stay pure, in the minds of Nazis and American segregationists; as an arena where flattery, submissiveness, and pretense form the constraints of manners, in the courts of various autocrats; or as a battlefield where messy considerations of justice "necessarily" take second place to expediency, to cite the terms openly used by the planners of the American occupation of Iraq. Having become familiar, this appearance of the world—all white, or well-mannered, or pragmatic and efficient—becomes worth preserving, even dying for, in its own right.

To further clarify Kateb's portrait: an idea in a person's head—at first a mere figment of thought, a fiction—has entered others' heads, taken on existence in common lived experience, and changed that experience, and

2   Kateb, "The adequacy of the canon," 495. Augustine is the only Roman member of his canon: "Plato, Aristotle, Augustine, Aquinas, Machiavelli, Hobbes, Locke, Rousseau (in spite of himself), Kant, probably Hegel, Mill in his stoical moods, Nietzsche in his way" (485).
3   Speaking of the twelve-mile-per hour railroad: Grant, *Personal Memoirs*, 428 of 12185 (Kindle edition).
4   Kateb, "The adequacy of the canon," 488.

even, perhaps, the conditions of life itself. While the change is happening, the ideals and values developed in the past, appropriate for the past, continue to hold. If the change is traumatic, it may even become more urgent for people to insist on the past's survival and relevance. Over the course of time, what people imagine themselves to be and what their actions reveal them currently to be significantly diverge. This is the pattern traced, if not acknowledged in so many words, in Thucydides' account of the Peloponnesian war. The Athenians praised as models of freedom and justice in Pericles' funeral oration become, within a few years, the men who vote to massacre the Mytilenians and the Melians. (Meanwhile the Melians briefly become the new Athenians: they make their final appeal to Athens in defiant language that recalls the city's resistance to the Persians as reported by Herodotus.) But the Athenians' image of themselves and the possibilities that lie open to them, never entirely accurate in the first place (as Thucydides implies), proves difficult to abandon, which contributes to their undoing in the Sicilian invasion.

At the heart of Kateb's critique is not so much the political canon's scanting of imagination in the abstract, but its failure to grasp the role played by the imagination in making and remaking the world and in our experience of making judgments in it. One way to summarize the problem is that premodern thinkers tend to draw too thick a dividing line between fiction and reality or fiction and truth. Plato's Socrates, for instance, takes care to constrain the making of fiction in his ideal constitution described in Plato's *Republic*. Though his return to mythos-making at the end of the dialogue strongly suggests that matters are more complex than they first appear, Socrates' disparaging account of non-philosophers as people who prefer to live with fictions, like the inhabitants of the cave entranced by their shadow-show, is impossible to dismiss. Even if we understand the return to mythos in *Republic* 10 as a subtle acknowledgment of the central place of shared fictions and projected imagination in collective life, it is still true that nowhere in Plato's work or in the Greek tradition of political thought is that place explicitly discussed.[5]

With the late speeches of Cicero, we move onto unfamiliar terrain for the political canon, at least the post–nineteenth century philosophical version of it. His speech *pro Marcello* was popular in the late medieval and early modern periods, mainly because it provided a model for panegyric and for

---

5   The careful arguments of Jill Frank and Christina Tarnopolsky have gone a long way to convince me that the return to myth (and comparable moments in the Platonic corpus) reveal Plato as a political thinker who is deeply concerned with appearances and fictions.

a highly figured style. It was delivered in 45 BCE under exceptionally diffi-cult conditions. Julius Caesar had recently won the civil war; his rival Pom-pey was dead. Cicero, whose support of Pompey was never as strong as his futile hope to avoid armed conflict, spoke to a senate reduced by war and still deeply divided over the recent past and the future. He spoke, according to the first line of the speech, under pressure, and it is commonly assumed that the pressure came from Caesar, who wanted to be publicly thanked for giving clemency to a prominent Pompeian, Marcellus, who had abandoned Rome in protest and established himself in exile. Now, thanks to Caesar's policy of clemency, a hallmark of his behavior throughout and after the war, Marcellus was free to come home.

I end the book with this currently little-read speech that Cicero gave at a time that is now identified as the end time of the republic for two reasons. Ostensibly written in response to the newly dominant Caesar's clemency toward the defeated Marcellus, the *pro Marcello* is a good example of the kind of text avoided by political theorists and classicists whose preconceived notions of republican ideals and norms exclude it from serious consider-ation as an exercise in political thought. More importantly, it illustrates at least five issues that Cicero, an insightful participant in republican politics, believed worthy of careful thought and advocacy. First, the imagination: Cicero prompts the senators to reflect on what kinds of men they could and should imagine themselves as being in the new political atmosphere estab-lished by the victor in the war. Second, a notion we have encountered be-fore, which Jacques Rancière calls *aesthesis*: by memorializing the death and suffering experienced during the recent civil war, the speech also establishes the terms of collective action in the postwar present—in the case of this speech and this audience, shared pain. Third, acknowledgment, and specifi-cally acknowledgment of limits, familiar from Horace: Cicero diagnoses his senatorial audience's complicity in the war, and sketches values and habits of self-regard that will help the senators preserve themselves and their com-munity (32–33). Fourth, contingency, and the capacity to think well and act well given the unpredictability of others' actions. Fifth, and closely related to the third, sovereignty: the speech probes the delicate transition between resistance and submission to an external power.

These ideas are not the kind of thing that is celebrated by Polybius or Valerius Maximus or their modern interpreters as republican virtue, but nor are they new to Cicero's audience. They make up, I think, a silent and unac-knowledged but persistent element of the republican experience of politics.

Cicero's speeches entered the Western curriculum in the earliest stages of modernity because they were considered to be a vital part of civic education. They are not histories or philosophical treatises but texts designed to be spoken aloud—at least they operate on that conceit. As such, they do not (only) transmit ideologies, values, and dispositions; they do not make philosophical arguments. They open up space for critical reflection on moral dilemmas and uncomfortable spaces of politics, especially compromise and deceit and other tensions that inject political life with tragedy.[6]

While this chapter stands on its own as an analysis of the *pro Marcello* (with brief reference to Cicero's two other "Caesarian" speeches), it also serves to summarize and reflect on the topics of earlier chapters. Imagination, aesthetic experience as the frame for political judgment and action, acknowledgment, and sovereignty and its discontents have been the main themes of this book.

THE MODERN DISCOMFORT WITH PRAISE

This speech makes for a painful experience for many of Cicero's modern readers, and to understand its complexity we need to understand the reasons for their discomfort. These days most scholars working on Roman poetry dating from the civil war and the Julio-Claudian period avoid trying to squeeze their texts into one box titled "reconciliation" and another one called "resistance." In poetry criticism, the bipolar pro- or anti-Caesar approach appears to be dead.[7] But scholarly discussions of prose tend to hold fast to the old binaries. This is notably true of readings of this speech and the two other "Caesarian orations" of 46 and 45 BC, the *pro Ligario* and the *pro rege Deiotaro*, which are considered by some to be the first significant Roman experiment in the genre of panegyric.[8]

In general, panegyric is an uncomfortable genre, and contemporary scholarship on these speeches continues to avoid approaches that allow for deep and unresolved ambiguities in favor of comparatively straightforward

6   On the early modern investment in reading a morally complex Cicero, see Virginia Cox, "Ciceronian rhetoric in Italy, 1250–1360," and "Ciceronian rhetorical theory in the *Volgare*: a fourteenth-century text and its fifteenth-century readers," 201–2; also Jennifer Richards, "Assumed simplicity and the critique of nobility: or, how Castiglione read Cicero."

7   See Duncan Kennedy's influential essay, "'Augustan' and 'anti-Augustan': reflections on terms of reference": "Augustus was more significant as an idea. The power of Augustus was a collective invention, the symbolic embodiment of the conflicting desires, incompatible ambitions, and agressions of the Romans, the instrument expression of a complex network of dependency, repression, and fear. 'Power' emerges from this discussion not as something immanent, an attribute of an individual, but as an analytical term" (35). More recently, Michèle Lowrie, *Writing, Performance, and Authority in Augustan Rome*, esp. 342–48.

8   On the place of the Caesarian orations in the history of Latin panegyric, see Susanna Braund, "Praise and protreptic in early imperial panegyric," 53–76.

questions about Cicero's intentions and credibility. In 1802, Friedrich August Wolf set the tone for modern criticism when he found the flattery in the *pro Marcello* so insupportable that he published an edition denying its authenticity. As the author of the Notes in the 1813 *Classical Journal* anxiously reports:

> Markland had already suspected some of the orations to be apocryphal, but the learned began to murmur when M. Wolf, with more hardihood, attacked the celebrated oration *pro Marcello*, on which the admirers of Cicero found his strongest claims to immortality. It was in 1802, that M. Wolf printed, at Berlin, this oration, with a preface, in which he boldly stated his reasons for doubting its authenticity. M. Olaus Wormius, the Danish Professor of Eloquence and Ancient Literature, at Copenhagen, first undertook to answer M. Wolf.... M. Kalau, of Frankfort, next entered the lists in 1804. The Literary Journals at first gave an account of the controversy with reserve, and a kind of fear. At length, in 1805, an adversary worthy of Wolf appeared: M. Weiske published his 'Commentarius perpetuus et plenus in Orationem Ciceronis pro Marcello.' In his preface, M. Weiske indulges in some pleasing raillery against the world of his adversary, and endeavours to demonstrate, in a happy strain of irony, that the world of M. Wolf, on this very oration of Cicero, could not be written by him, but by one who had assumed his name. In a graver tone, however, he proceeds to show, that we might on the same grounds dispute the authenticity of the oration *pro Ligario*, which M. Wolf himself admits, is genuine beyond all question.

Defending the speech against Wolf, Michael Winterbottom interprets it as a frank expression of thanks, or *gratiarum actio*, for Caesar's clemency. Giovanni Cipriani sees it as a didactic speech modeled on the pedagogical exercises known as *suasoriae*, and argues that it was intended to encourage Caesar to exercise his power honorably. This is panegyric as Erasmus would eventually define it, as the *speculum principis* or "mirror of princes." Taking the opposite tack, Paola Gagliardi ingeniously argues that Cicero seeks to veil his exhortation to tyrannicide with flattery. R. R. Dyer goes so far as to suggest that the speech, a supreme exercise in irony, celebrates (and was perhaps even composed after) the killing of Caesar on the Ides of March in 44 BCE.[9]

9   Michael Winterbottom, "Believing the *pro Marcello*"; Giovanni Cipriani, "La *pro Marcello* e il suo significato come orazione politica"; R. R. Dyer, "Rhetoric and intention in

What are the costs of interpreting the speech in these pro- and anti-terms? William Batstone probes the epistemological and ethical consequences of modern judgments passed on Julius Caesar.[10] Call Caesar a "visionary," he points out, and one ascribes to the Roman dictator an uncanny awareness of history before the fact. Call him a "precursor" and a more troubling suggestion emerges that Caesar is one of a chain of figures locked in place by immutable and ineluctable forces of history. For Batstone, neither approach holds much historical or humanistic interest: not only do they "always lie outside the evidence to the extent that they require access to Caesar's desires, intentions, and self-knowledge" but worse, they take for granted a coherence and predictability in human psychology and relationships that we would do better to suspect.

For the same reasons that Batstone questions the utility of evaluating Caesar's intentions, I want to close the door definitively on the reductive habit of reading a text like the *pro Marcello* as either authentic or insincere, pro- or anti-Caesar. Like the rest of us, who cannot know and are unable to control the consequences of our actions, including our speech and writing and others' interpretations of our words, Cicero could exert only limited power over his utterances and their effects. Better to reflect on how and why the speech has presented such a hermeneutic puzzle—why, that is, the speech appears to keep both options decisively open: praise and blame, celebration and critique.

It does so, I think, because it is a deliberative speech about the future, an exercise in political imagination. As Kateb notes, canonical thinkers and the scholars who work on them are often reluctant to consider the role that imagination plays in politics, but drawing on work on political fantasy by Jacqueline Rose, Slavoj Žižek, and others, I understand it as the capacity by which we project our desired relations with others.[11] Consequently, far from being strictly opposed to our public, political, social, "real" existence, imagination plays a central role in the real world, or to put it more precisely, in making the world comprehensible to its inhabitants.

Cicero's *pro Marcello*"; Paola Gagliardi, *Il dissenso e l'ironia: per una rilettura delle orazioni 'cesariane' di Cicerone.*

10   William Batstone, "Caesar's republican rhetoric and the veils of autocracy."

11   See, for example, Jacqueline Rose, *States of Fantasy*, Donald E. Pease, "States of fantasy: Barack Obama versus the Tea Party movement," and Slavoj Žižek, *Living in the End Times*. In an earlier version of this chapter, I used the word "fantasy" exclusively; but "imagination" is usefully free from the association with psychoanalysis that the other term carries, and "imagination" better suits an argument influenced by Adam Smith, Arendt's work on Kant, Merleau-Ponty, and Stanley Cavell.

The entwined fantasies of revenge, obedience, and future security that Cicero articulates in the *pro Marcello* do not offer an escape from reality. Nor is it the case that this speech is an "imperial" text. Big Men had come and gone before in Roman republican politics: this is a speech about crisis, but not one that imagines autocratic rule as the permanent norm. Woven together and expressed in terms that underscore the aesthetic language of perception, especially seeing and hearing—Cicero's very first sentence describes his rising to speak after a long period of silence—these fantasies compel their audience to acknowledge the real traumas of civil war and defeat, and incorporate this trauma into a vision of future peace in the *res publica*. Ironically, as we know, this vision will never come true. But in the world limned by Cicero's speech, both the victor and the vanquished, the triumphant and the guilty, are imagined to have a share in it.

The *pro Marcello* confronts head-on the challenge of Caesar's victory and the question of what the Pompeians will do in response by acknowledging the responsibility of both senatorial factions in the recent civil strife. Cicero's exhortation to his fellow senators to join him in praise of Caesar reminds them of their role in the Pompeian cause and in its failure. This acknowledgment is not passive and it does not look exclusively backward in time. It calls for action and orientation toward the future, for Cicero suggests that efforts to preserve the sovereignty of action as it ostensibly existed under the old republican order can end only in that order's utter destruction.

Recent work in political theory over the past half century has borrowed the term "sovereign" from the statist frame and transferred it to the realm of the self. Drawing on this work, we may say that, by sharp contrast with his later *Philippics*, Cicero does not play at being sovereign in the *pro Marcello*.[12] Instead, by repeatedly returning to the trope of panegyric incapacity ("I cannot praise Caesar as he deserves"), Cicero pursues an uncomfortable experiment in articulating his acknowledgment of the new limits on sovereignty. He replaces claims of self-determination and freedom (in Roman terms, the cluster of characteristics and capabilities captured in the terms *dignitas, auctoritas*, and *libertas*) with a self-consciously ironic embrace of unpredictability—the literal unpredictability of what Caesar will do next, and the further,

12 See further, chapter 3. Relevant work on sovereignty and its limits: Hannah Arendt, *The Human Condition* (Chicago 1958), esp. 234; Isaiah Berlin, "Two concepts of liberty," in *Four Essays on Liberty*, Melissa Orlie, *Living Ethically, Acting Politically*, esp. 143–68; Michel Foucault, *The Government of Self and Others*, esp. 61–73. I borrow the phrase "play at being sovereign" from Patchen Markell, *Bound By Recognition*, esp. 34–38 and 183–89.

inherent unpredictability of speech, which is the type of action Cicero proposes to pursue in the new conditions of Caesarian domination. Cicero urges his audience to adopt discourse over the contest of arms, whose tragically finite outcomes his audience knows all too well. This is a speech about how the republic can continue to exist in such a way that it will not tread the path of civil war once again.

THE AESTHESIS OF HYPERBOLE AND PAIN

With its title, the *pro Marcello* suggests that it is pressing the argument for Marcellus' return from exile, but in fact this is not the case. Caesar has already guaranteed the safety of the Pompeian partisan, who was living in self-imposed exile on the island of Lesbos, so Cicero is praising and thanking Caesar for a deal already done. He opens by giving an account of himself, explaining his choice to speak after a long silence (*diuturni silenti*), not because of fear (*timore*) but rather pain and shame (*dolore, verecundia*)—an important theme, as his audience will soon realize. The second sentence introduces a frequent tactic throughout the speech: using hyperbole as a response to the challenge of expressing that which is impossible to express. Cicero praises Caesar's "unusual, unheard-of clemency" (*tam inusitatam inauditam clementiam*), his "incredible wisdom, practically divine" (*tam incredibilem sapientiam paene divinam*), which is so overwhelming that Cicero does not have the capacity to ignore it (*praeterire nullo modo possum*)—though, he will soon add, and repeat, he cannot describe it either (4, 9, 12).

Hyperbole is exceptionally difficult to analyze as a mode of expression that illuminates serious thought. But it is not impossible. Consider this programmatic paradox seriously for a few moments. The central thesis of the opening paragraphs, and indeed of the speech as a whole, can be summarized in these two expressions of the impossible. It is important for me to distinguish here between the kind of flattery that records a truth to which the audience can easily testify (for example, *Caesar is praiseworthy because he has not killed all the Pompeians*) and the kind that veers into the literally false. Cicero is uttering a literal falsehood when he says it is not possible for him to describe Caesar's greatness, since of course he proceeds to describe it in the following sentences. But he is making a surprise sound like a falsehood when he says of Caesar that it is not possible that Caesar can act in this way, granting clemency to his defeated enemies, but he is nonetheless doing it. It is virtually a rule of the panegyric genre to acknowledge the speaker's incapacity in the face of the difficult task of praise (cf. Isoc. *Evagoras* 8–10). What bursts forth as unusual here is the way Cicero ties the impossibility of describing Caesar with the impossible scale of Caesar's achievements—above all, his clemency. "I cannot be saying these things; he cannot be doing these things": in the repetitive statement of the two linked impossibles, rhetorical form conveys shock at Caesar's action and the sense of profound confusion it has generated among those opposing him.

Caesar's clemency is not just a welcome surprise, it is "unheard-of," and Cicero's incapacity to describe it is not just his, it applies to everyone in the present and even the future. Caesar's achievements are so far beyond belief that they prompt insanity: "And if I did not admit that these deeds are so great that virtually no one's mind or cognition is able to grasp them, I'd be crazy: but there are things even greater" (*quae quidem ego nisi ita magna esse fatear, ut ea vix cuiusquam mens aut cogitatio capere possit, amens sim: sed tamen sunt alia maiora*, 6). Cicero's shock at this greater deed, the granting of clemency, gives rise to one of the most convoluted passages in the speech (12):

> And indeed all the other victors in civil wars you had already vanquished in fairness and pity: this day, you vanquish yourself as well. I fear that what I am saying cannot be understood when it is heard as thoroughly as I understand it myself as I reflect on it: you appear to have vanquished victory itself, since you have given up those things that are taken away from the vanquished. For although, by the condition of victory itself, all of us who had been vanquished fell into ruin, we have been preserved by the judgment of your clemency. Rightly, then, you alone are unvanquished, by whom the condition and power of victory itself have been utterly vanquished.

> Et ceteros quidem omnis victores bellorum civilium iam ante aequitate et misericordia viceras: hodierno vero die te ipsum vicisti. Vereor ut hoc, quod dicam, perinde intellegi possit auditum atque ipse cogitans sentio: ipsam victoriam vicisse videris, cum ea quae illa erat adepta victis remisisti. Nam cum ipsius victoriae condicione omnes victi occidissemus, clementiae tuae iudicio conservati sumus. Recte igitur unus invictus es, a quo etiam ipsius victoriae condicio visque devicta est.

In these sentences, Cicero makes Caesar's clemency into something, as a contemporary American might say, "unreal."

This tortured hyperbole is the style of expression that made Friedrich Wolf want to exile the speech from the legitimate Ciceronian corpus. But before we file the passage away as an exceptionally excessive example of flattery, let us ask: what political vision is this speech articulating?

The imperial rhetorician Quintilian, writing a century after Cicero's death, reminds us that there is meaning in hyperbole. He defines it in the following terms (*Inst. Orat.* 8.6.75–76):

> And so hyperbole is a virtue when the thing of which we speak exceeds the natural limit: for we are allowed to amplify, because the exact extent cannot be described, and speech is better when it goes beyond than when it stops short.

> tum est hyperbole virtus cum res ipsa de qua loquendum est naturalem modum excessit: conceditur enim amplius dicere, quia dici quantum est non potest, meliusque ultra quam citra stat oratio.

By Quintilian's definition, hyperbole is the proper figure for the state "exceeding natural limits" in which Cicero's audience finds itself. Cicero asserts that he must speak with no limit (*nullo modo*, 1); he suggests no one will ever be able to praise Caesar adequately; he compares Caesar to a god (*simillimum deo*, 8); he says he thinks of Caesar day and night (22). Such hyperbolic terms constitute a discourse of simulation. They disclose the world anew in terms that are not strictly, simply true; and in their excess of truth, as Quintilian says, they better represent an "unreal" reality that no one expected, though everyone ought to have expected it, for it is the reality of autocracy experimented with by Marius and Sulla half a century earlier. Hyperbolic speech assumes the task of absorbing the shock of living in the end times of the republic—and further, its unreal dimension propels its listeners into new identities and relations in a world where identity and relations have profoundly changed. By adopting hyperbole as the governing figure of this new style of senatorial speech, Cicero holds out the promise not of a morally legible universe, but of a recognition that every Roman now lives in conditions virtually "impossible to believe": the emergence of one ruler, under whom the chains of traditional obligations do not consistently hold. Hyperbole is the supremely appropriate figure for the state of emergency "exceeding natural limits" in which Cicero's audience finds itself.

Here we may usefully turn for insight to Peter Brooks' work on French melodrama, which examines the Parisian theater after the suspension of the moral and legal order in the Revolution and suggests that its hyperbolic style is born of "the anxiety created by the guilt experienced when the allegiance and ordering that pertained to a sacred system of things no longer obtains."[13] In the Roman postwar context, hyperbolic praise summons an unusual kind of consensus, one based not on a logical, sensible order, but rather on disbelief and irreducible uncertainty. (Uncertainty and chance is a central theme in Sallust's historical writing, as we have seen in chapter 2.)

Oddly enough, hyperbolic fantasy is a profoundly inclusive rhetorical strategy. Cicero's image of Caesar is an image in which each part of his partisan audience may invest in different ways: pleasure and pain, glee and envy. In the space of hyperbole everyone is invited. Of course Cicero's Caesarian audience will share in the hyperbolic celebration of their leader, even as they are reminded of the costs of his victory.

But there is real pleasure here for the Pompeians in the audience, too. Recall Quintilian's statement that hyperbole knows that it asserts that which is not, from the consciousness of falsehood: that is, it is always accompanied by irony. Paul De Man, commenting on irony, argues that irony splits the self into two, "an empirical self that exists in a state of inauthenticity and a self that exists only in the form of a language that asserts the knowledge of this inauthenticity."[14] Hyperbole enables the self-delusion not only of Caesar, but of the resistant listeners, whose envy and resentment are eased by their ironic awareness of it. Hyperbole preserves a space in which they may say "I don't believe this" without saying "I will not obey." The double consciousness by which the irony of hyperbole allows the acknowledgement of inauthenticity mediates the experience of domination by reinstating the speaker and the listener as agents even as they give up agency. It allows the resistant listener to distance himself from the assent to power at the same time that he assents to limits on his political sovereignty.

By harnessing the power of fantastical untruth, Cicero becomes what Shelley calls the poet, an "unacknowledged legislator," exercising the power he and his audience have to remake the world in light of the new understanding of it which his literally, self-consciously false words unlock.[15] By enjoining the senators to do something that will offend or disturb most of them—praise Caesar—the speech enters the realm of self-conscious fictionalization. Philippe Lacoue-Labarthe points out that the political, in the West, is an actualization of values and norms that are "otherworldly"; the body politic is shaped in accordance with an ideal and thus is fictional in the highest sense. Fictionality is the very essence of the community's being

13   Peter Brooks, *The Melodramatic Imagination*, 4, 12, 200.
14   Paul De Man, *Blindness and Insight*, 214.
15   Further remarks on Shelley in Pease, "States of fantasy," 100.

a community: it is a made thing.[16] Recognition of the fact that it is made, and that the making begins with the acknowledgments of responsibility and of shock that Cicero is exhorting through his excessive, ironic speech here, is the first step to controlling its future. Cicero asks the senators to confront the appearance of Caesar as the victor of the civil war: he introduces Caesar into the field of the senators' experience, which must now modify "the regime of the visible," that is, what they are accustomed and able to see as politics.[17] Reality is split and reconfigured, at least temporarily, as double: the reality of Caesar, holding nearly unlimited power over life and death, and the reality of the senators as the leading men of the republic, who must somehow map out a way forward.

We also begin to see how the speech aims not only to praise Caesar, but to bury civil war. As he speaks in the aftermath of the bitter zero-sum game that the Roman senatorial order had made of republican politics by the middle first century, a game that had produced Big Men with big armies on a scale never seen before, Cicero's grief at the collapse of republican *libertas* vies with his desire to negotiate the uncertain future under the current Big Man. His speech reveals how praise may heal past and present breaches in the body politic. It does this not simply by establishing conditions for the formation of consensus ("now we must all praise Caesar, and woe to those who don't"). Rather it configures the politics of the new postwar era by summoning up images and emotions in which each part of his partisan audience may invest. The hyperbole and pathos of his language make it possible for his audience to "feel" the shock of life in the new world of Rome after the civil wars.

The long and the short of it is that Cicero creates a collective *aesthesis*—what Jacques Rancière calls the "sensible texture" of the community.[18] *Aesthesis*, because it involves the generation of affective reactions, is multivalent by nature, even within the bounds of the experience of the individual self. Each of us may feel pity, fear, and many other things in the course of a single experience, like going to a play or seeing a man beg on the street. The complexity of the *aesthesis*, the sensible texture, of the *pro Marcello* transcends the classical generic categories of praise and blame as well as the late antique and modern interpretive categories of sincerity and "figured" irony.

---

16   Lacoue-Labarthe, *Heidegger, Art, and Politics: The Fiction of the Political*; see also Frederick Dolan, *Allegories of America*, 30.

17   Rancière, *Disagreement*, 99.

18   Rancière, *The Politics of Aesthetics*; also, "Thinking between disciplines: an aesthetics of knowledge," 10–12.

But we have not yet exhausted the significance of the programmatic prologue. The second theme introduced in the proemium is suffering, *dolor*.
Suffering is the motivation for Cicero's decision to speak (*dolore*, 1). His suffering derives from his recognition that Marcellus was suffering unjustly: "I
was intensely grieving and feeling violent pain, senatorial fathers, that such
a man, though he had stood on the same side as I, was not in the same
happy condition" (*dolebam enim, patres conscripti, et vehementer angebar
virum talem, cum in eadem causa in qua ego fuisset, non in eadem esse fortuna*,
2). The theme recurs repeatedly, most memorably in the images of the devastation caused by the civil war.

In her subtle reading of the *pro Marcello*, Paola Gagliardi argues that
Cicero's emphasis on *dolor* is a central element of his "figured" ironic strategy. For her, the juxtaposition of praise for Caesar's clemency with repeated
reminders of the suffering he caused, both in making war against Pompey
and offering clemency to the losers, makes a "sincere" reading of his panegyric impossible. I see other dynamics at work here. First, suffering is part
of the consensual aesthesis of the speech: it unfolds as an experience that
links the Roman community, inside and outside the senate. Marcellus has
lost many members of his family (*iam ad paucos redactam*, 10); Caesar suf-
fers from his own clemency because it requires him to put aside private
resentments (*doloribus*, 3); the Roman people suffered in the war (18; cf. 23,
24, 31, 34); Cicero himself feels pain repeatedly (*doleo*, 16, 22). By suggesting that the experience of suffering ties the entire audience together, Cicero installs suffering at the heart of the identity of the post–civil war senate, both Caesarian winners and Pompeian losers. This tactic (a classic of
identity politics) works to stabilize a collective whose "traumatic formation" would otherwise render it unstable; it forges a "politically coherent,
continuous, and conscious identity" out of past and present antagonism
and shared pain.[19]

This scene of trauma goes on to become the heart of the historical narrative that reduces autocracy to an ethical and personal crisis for the senatorial order, best known to us from Tacitus. But the later narrative of trauma
and subjective crisis rests on a longstanding habit of republican thinking
that places individual and collective feeling at the heart of political sensibility and action. Feeling bundles sensation (here, the sense of loss or absence)
and emotion (grief, regret, and anger; or triumph and vindication). Together
they trigger a new aestheticized sense of how the world could and should
be—in other words, a new sense of judgment and a motivation for action.

19   Wendy Brown, *Politics Out of History*, 55.

Second, as Cicero explains when he compares Caesar's clemency to his past fearful anticipation of the excessive form Pompeian vengeance might take (18), it becomes clear that his suffering also derives from the pain of recognition that Caesarian clemency bears out his fears about the limits of the Pompeians' virtue. So his praise is also an expression of guilt at his collusion with an order in which the dominant element abandoned its concern for the common good, and thus ended up "rushing on, without desire or hope, prudently and knowingly, to voluntary death" (*nulla non modo cupiditate, ne spe quidem, prudens et sciens tamquam ad interitum ruerem voluntarium*, 14). As Cicero makes guilty accommodations to power, he acknowledges that guilt for his past failures spurs his desire for security—while still trying, painfully, to do a certain justice to the doomed Pompeian resistance by memorializing it. In chapter 2, we saw how *aesthesis* operates in Sallust, who also directs his readers' attention, in unexpected ways, to suffering and death.

Cicero complains in a number of letters from the 50s through 44 that the republic is being lost or has been lost. The foundation of the political frame to which he and many of his peers are committed has been shown to be weaker than the forces of competition that originally enabled the frame and have now created the conditions under which autocracy has become thinkable. While the republican ideal is a site of desire—that which Cicero and his senatorial audience identify and wish to preserve—it is also a site of failure. Love for the republic is thus love for a flawed system, so it is an illicit love; and in Caesar's presence, it is an explicitly illicit love. The system of elite competition for *gloria* has failed its participants, whose defeat now compels them to discover that the world to which they are devoted does not esteem them; their identity as senators "occurs" at a point where the promise of *gloria* is found to be impossible and hollow. This is why Cicero dwells so long on the topic of Caesar's glory, the site of trauma for thwarted competitors on the field of *gloria*.

To return briefly to the question of the old binary opposition between sincerity and deceit in interpretation of a panegyrical text: the *gloria* passage reveals questionable assumptions about integrity, literally the fantasy that the text is *in-teger*, untouched. The etymology suggests that when we say a text is sincere, we mean that it floats free of contact with contingencies and constraints that could mar or stain it. But it should be clear by now that Cicero's speech reminds readers repeatedly of the conditions that "touch" it, constraining it, its speaker, and its audience. The self that speaks without constraint is barred from this text. That is the truth it has to offer, and the source of discomfort we feel when we read it.

Freud draws a careful contrast between mourning and melancholy.[20] Mourning, he believes, is a normal emotional process that signifies acceptance of a loss; melancholy is a pathology that occurs when the subject persists in his narcissistic identification with the lost object. The melancholic link allows both attachment and legitimation of what destroyed the object in the first place. Freud's portrait of melancholy explains the traumatic intensity of Cicero's passion for the republic as well as our own fascination with Cicero: we are caught up not in the organic immediacy of republican freedom but the immediate experience of the loss itself. This intensity of feeling is part of what later theorists have called "patriotism": the temporal context of loss and gain, desire and fulfillment, is built into the pendulous movement of republican politics.[21]

ACKNOWLEDGMENT AND A NEW VISION OF SOVEREIGNTY

We'd be good instead of being so harsh,
If only our relations were not as they are!

Wir wären gut anstatt so roh,
Doch die Verhältnisse, sie sind nicht so!

—Brecht, *Threepenny Opera*

The question Cicero poses now is what the Pompeians will choose to do. This brings us to the other *laudandus* in the speech, Marcellus, to whom no one is "superior in good birth, or honesty, or in zeal for study, or purity of life, or any other excellence" (4). Cicero repeatedly assimilates Marcellus to himself: at the beginning, when he identifies him as his rival and imitator (*illo aemulo atque imitatore*, 2); throughout the speech, when he identifies Marcellus as the beneficiary of Caesar's favor (*nam num M. Marcellum deprecantibus vobis rei publicae conservavit, me et mihi et item rei publica . . . reddidit*, 13, 33–34); and most importantly, when he contends that he and Marcellus

---

20   Freud, "Mourning and melancholia," *The Standard Edition of the Works of Sigmund Freud*, vol. 14 (1914–16), 237–58.

21   Pocock, *The Machiavellian Moment*, 471–72, discusses the temporal swing of republican politics, where the cycle of effort and failure to achieve perfect virtue constitutes a perpetual motion machine, endlessly justifying its own existence and its own failure. On Hume and the exposure of commercial politeness as a form of vice, see his *Virtue, Commerce and History*, 132.

agreed in hating violence and loving peace (16). But this is another element of the speech's unreal aspect: this Marcellus is scarcely recognizable. As Giusto Picone has pointed out in an essay that examines the letters between the two men as well as the younger Seneca's account of Marcellus in his *Consolation of Helvia*, Marcellus is no Cicero.[22] He resisted accepting Caesar's clemency and resisted returning to Rome. Seneca describes him as "nobly enduring his exile; his change of place made no change at all in his mind" (*Cons. Hel.*, 9.6–10.2). Cicero falsifies his Marcellus, tendentiously transforming the ex-consul into another Cicero capable of sacrificing his Pompeian convictions in the name of the collective good.

When Cicero identifies himself with Marcellus as a lover of peace while speaking in conditions that identify himself as Marcellus' opposite—the one who quickly accepted Caesar's offer of clemency—Cicero both acknowledges and displaces the problem of his own submission: praising Marcellus as inferior to none and punishing Marcellus by falsifying his identity. The suggestion is this: to resist is to die, or live in exile, to lose yourself; to accept clemency is to be Cicero. But when Cicero assimilates Marcellus to himself in front of an audience who knows the truth of the matter, they see that the consequences of accepting clemency are the same as resisting: either way, you lose yourself.

The second significant doubling in the speech links Cicero and Caesar. Like Cicero in *Catilinarians*, Caesar is the savior of the day who must guard himself against assassination (this is the main theme of the longest sustained passage of the speech, sections 21–32); Cicero assimilates Caesar to himself at the beginning of the *Post Reditum Populo*, when he "got back the republic when it was almost lost" (5). There is some self-glorification here, but the pattern of assimilation also draws attention to men's resemblances to, relations with, and responsibilities toward one another. The doublings of Cicero and Marcellus, Cicero and Caesar, highlight the lines of communal interdependence even, and especially, after civil war. It also puts an Arendtian question mark after these actors' self-sovereignty: none of us can be in perfect control of who we are, and we can rarely be quite what we say we are, under conditions of severe political stress.

Cicero writes in his letters to Marcellus that though Marcellus refused to see out the end of a hopeless civil war, he yet retained his allegiance to the old order (*Fam.* 4.8 *et al.*). In the *pro Marcello*, by falsely assimilating Marcellus to himself, Cicero suggests that no one is as he once was: the civil war and Caesar's victory have changed everything. Marcellus and the Pompeians

---

22   Giusto Picone, "Il paradigma Marcello: tra esilio e *Clementia Caesaris*."

cannot depend on old political identities or relationships—and there is pain and guilt in Cicero's acknowledgement of this, particularly in his reference to the diminution of Marcellus' family (10)—but they can invent new political identities and relationships.

To learn to be subjects, in the sense of selves as well as subordinates, Cicero exhorts his audience to look clearly at their political situation.[23] They must *see* the present situation and the immediate past. Here is the explanation for the repeated emphasis in this speech on *seeing* the present situation and the immediate past: "As for you whom we gaze upon, present among us, whose mind, feelings, and countenance we at this moment see to be such . . ." (*te vero, quem praesentem intuemur, cuius mentem sensusque et os cernimus*, 10), "I saw, along with you, the tears of C. Marcellus" (*lacrimas modo vobiscum viderem, omnium Marcellorum meum pectus memoria obfudit*, 11); "For which reason your generosity ought to be more welcome to us, who have seen (*vidimus*) these things [the violence of civil war]. We saw (*vidimus*) your victory. . . . We did not see (*non vidimus*) your sword unsheathed in the city" (16–17). Caesar, too, must look into the dark spots in the souls of those who might wish to kill him (*in animis hominum tantae latebrae sint et tanti recessus*, 22) so that he may fully understand his role and duties.

Cicero uses the world-disclosing capacity of language to "loosen the hold" of the familiar machinery of identity and action.[24] Once his addressees see the post–civil war world clearly, they must act accordingly, with a view toward themselves and others. The senators must understand their past, the pitfalls of the system they used to live by, which led them "knowingly" to ruin (14). They must then look to the future without immediate recourse to violence; they must think of themselves anew. Remembering that they are preserved by the choice of Caesar, a fact Cicero repeats several times, he and the senatorial audience are compelled to proceed from that fact, with a sense of ironic good fortune. To maintain both moral and political sovereignty in exile in Athens or Mytilene is not supportable, because it is a lie: "wherever you may go," Cicero bitingly reminds Marcellus in a private letter, "you are under that man's power" (*Fam.* 4.7).

The situation demands some abdication of self-mastery: the senators must refuse the violent defense of self-sovereignty as they once conceived it.

---

23   The horrors and dangers of moral and political blindness and the urgent necessity of recovering "stable markers" in a world devoid of them is a central theme of Hammer's discussions of Livy, Seneca, and Tacitus in his *Roman Political Thought and the Modern Imagination* (see esp. 109–20, 165, 198–99). See further the discussion of *enargeia* in Sallust in chapter 2.

24   Stephen White links this capacity with the ability to loosen the self from the familiar, "Post-structuralism and political reflection," 196.

Caesar is offering clemency, not a traditional response to defeated enemies in war, and the senators must reciprocate by showing some measure of recognition of Caesar's power. Here Cicero picks up and transforms the language of his *post reditum* speeches, where he acknowledges his reliance on others for help in returning to Rome and giving him back his sense of self, and he promises to fulfill his obligation by serving the state. "I (as was necessarily so) was born of my parents as just a little child; it is of you [the People] that I am born a consular (*a vobis natus sum consularis*).... Wherefore your kindness towards me is so much the greater, in that you restored me not to a crowd of relatives, but to myself" (*nobis met ipsis nos reddidistis, Post Red. Quir. 5, 3*). Cicero here underscores the necessity of replacing the old republican ideal of self-sovereignty—individual striving for glory—with a new model of collective identity and collective endeavor. As the senate had begged for Cicero's return, now Cicero and Marcellus' brother and other senators have worked collectively to influence Caesar and secure Marcellus' return.

The task of understanding how to become subjects is not as simple as recognizing Caesar as victor and dictator and perhaps a future king and god.[25] As recent work on self-sovereignty emphasizes, exploring alternatives to traditional conceptions is as risky and painful as it is necessary. In the context of the fatal but apparently eternally recurrent cycle of civil war, Cicero's hyperbolic act of praise replaces an idealized ethico-political code that inscribes the individual at its center with another one. Just as Marcellus and the senators must attend to their capacity to see clearly, they must modify their desire to be seen, to be recognized, to receive the high-stakes acknowledgment of *dignitas*—which is also to say that they will bear the risks of a new politics.

The code implicit in the *pro Marcello* puts first the relations of *amicitia* and obligation among the senators, relations facilitated by the exchange of communication, from which Cicero withdrew during the war:

> To a long silence, senatorial fathers, which I have taken advantage of
> in recent times—not due to any sort of fear, but partly due to suffer-
> ing, partly to a sense of shame—this day has brought an end, and
> similarly it has brought the beginning of saying what I like and what
> I think, according to my old habit. For such mildness, such unaccus-
> tomed and unheard-of clemency, such moderation in the exercise of

25   David Levene discusses the divine references in the speech in "God and man in the classical Latin panegyric."

the highest power over all, and finally, such unbelievable wisdom, nearly divine, I am in no way capable of passing over in silence.

Diuturni silenti, patres conscripti, quo eram his temporibus usus— non timore aliquo, sed partim dolore, partim verecundia—finem ho- diernus dies attulit, idemque initium quae vellem quaeque sentirem meo pristino more dicendi. Tantam enim mansuetudinem, tam inus- itatam inauditamque clementiam, tantum in summa potestate rerum omnium modum, tam denique incredibilem sapientiam ac paene divinam, tacitus praeterire nullo modo possum. (1)

Returning to speech is not (only) a celebratory strategy, though Cicero col- ors his return to speaking in celebratory terms. It also involves painful loss—the abandonment of the old code and the ethical exemplars that em- bodied it, most prominently, as we shall see, the younger Cato and every- thing he represents. Here and in his letters to Marcellus, Cicero redefines the role of the senator from seeking glory and defense of *dignitas* to a much more limited role: seeking to contest authority when it is exercised unjustly. He raises what must have been a deeply uncomfortable question for his audience, namely: Where to turn in a world where their desire for freedom has proven less emancipatory than bloody, the spur not for justice but for the broad violence of civil war? This speech in praise of a man who chose to preserve another man's life reconfigures republican politics as a system of mutually responsive "relations of dependence" where the question is not *what do I gain?* but *to whom I am responsible?*[26] This is a question that preoc- cupies the poet Horace, as I have already shown in my discussion of the problem of sovereignty and intersubjective responsibility in his satires in chapter 3.

Cicero refuses to adopt Cato and his suicidal sacrifice as an exemplary model. This wariness of absolutes is also a central theme in Horace's *Satires*. "As for the *Cato*," Cicero writes to Atticus, referring both to the book and the man, "it's a problem for Archimedes" (*Att.* 12.4.2). To Papirius Paetus, he writes, "Cato died well; let's die well too, but let our death be not so neces- sary to us as it was to him!" (*Fam.* 9.18). Cato kills himself: he embraces ne- cessity and wilfully chooses to end the play of chance. He responds to the experience of vulnerability before Caesar like an actor in a tragedy, deciding on a permanent end in favor of the constant struggle of life. He does not

26   Markell, *Bound By Recognition*, 188.

acknowledge his limits but chooses to overcome them, and when they cannot be overcome in real life he overcomes them in death.

Given what he has to say about sight in the *pro Marcello*, it is no surprise that Cicero casts Cato as a figure who literally *cannot see* the new conditions of Caesarian politics. In *de Officiis*, he cannot "look upon the face of tyranny" (*Off*. 1.112). Writing to Atticus, Cicero remarks, "but really, that man cannot be praised sincerely unless these things are mentioned, namely that he saw the way things are now and will be in the future, and he struggled lest they come about, and he gave up his life so that he would not see them done" (*ad Att*. 12.4.2). He warns Marcellus in similar terms: "You preferred being absent perpetually than to see those things which you did not want to see" (*ut abesse perpetuo malles quam ea quae nolles videre, ad Fam*. 4.7). "Perhaps you may see many things that you do not wish to see, but they are no more than what you hear daily. And it is not your habit to be affected by the sense of sight alone.... You may not be able to say what you think, but you may certainly be silent" (*multa videbis fortasse, quae nolis, non plura tamen quam audis cotidie. non est porro tuum uno sensu solum oculorum moveri...*, *Fam*. 4.9).

With regard to Cato, Cicero takes Adorno's stand in *Problems of Moral Philosophy* (163): "We may say in general—and this is what is valid about this critique—that it is right to feel a certain wariness toward people who are said to be of pure will (*die sogennante reinen Willens*) and who take every opportunity to refer to their own purity of will. The reality is that this so-called pure will is almost always twinned with the willingness to denounce others, with the need to punish and persecute others, in short, with the entire problematic nature of what will be all too familiar to you from the various purges that have taken place in totalitarian states." The *pro Marcello* turns instead to the difficult encounter with a new form of power and a venture into "making an uncontrollable future."[27]

As I argued earlier, the figure of impossibility, hyperbolic adynaton, embodies Cicero's sense of risk and disbelief moving forward in an uncertain world: in a darker tone, the speech's operatic gestures of submission to Caesar suggest Cicero's and his fellow senators' self-disempowerment. Cicero draws to his conclusion by reminding his Pompeian audience that he, like them, owe their lives to Caesar. I suspect that part of the resistance to Ciceronian authorship among readers like Wolf derives from this part of the

---

27   Brown, *Politics Out of History*, 46, discusses freedom and trusting to the future in these terms.

speech, because it openly acknowledges the limits on Cicero's sovereign agency that have arisen out of his vulnerability to Caesar's unpredictable actions. This is not to say that Cicero is invested in submission or self-fragmentation for its own sake. Rather, he sees that avowing the impossibility of full sovereign agency, an impossibility signified by Caesar's role in fixing the terms of his life, amounts to a sort of abdication of self.[28]

The effort to find a way forward requires the construction of an ironic sensibility that acknowledges the falsity and the necessity of praise, as well as the incapacity of the one doing the praising. When Cicero bitingly and obsequiously refers to the fact that "all dissension is crushed by the arms and extinguished by the justice of the conqueror" (31), his irony does not express or speak to the standpoint of resistance, but rather to what the philosopher Ruth Smith calls "the capacity to identify illusions that overstate the social-moral goods human beings have to offer."[29] His speech is "world-disclosing" in Rorty's sense: its language of praise loosens the hold on us of the world we desire, by calling attention to the ways our own unrecognized or unacknowledged fictions structure that world.

Before closing, I want to point out that understanding the *pro Marcello* in these terms may help us better understand certain aspects of Augustan poetry—specifically, the appeal to Bacchic poetics in Horace's odes, especially the Roman odes of book 3. Consider Horace *Odes* 3.25:

Where, Bacchus, do you tug me,
　　full of you? Into what groves and what caves am I brought,
fast, in a novel mood? In what
　　caves shall I be heard
practicing to graft the everlasting glory of pre-eminent Caesar
　　into the stars and the council of Jove?
Let me speak of what is great and new and as yet
　　unspoken by another mouth. Just as on the ridges
the unsleeping Bacchant gapes,
　　gazing at the Hebrus, and white with snow
Thrace, and Rhodope marked
　　by barbarian tread, so I delight
in gazing at off-road riverbanks and the quiet grove.
　　O ruler of Naiads

28　I was first prompted to consider the relationship between finitude and abdication of sovereignty by Markell, *Bound by Recognition*, 36.
29　Smith, "Morals and their ironies," 379.

and of vigorous Bacchants
  with hands that uproot tall ash trees,
let me say nothing trivial or humble,
  nothing merely mortal. It's a sweet risk,
o Lenaeus, to follow the god
  binding our temples with green vine-tendrils.

Quo me, Bacche, rapis tui
  plenum? Quae nemora aut quos agor in specus
uelox mente noua? Quibus
  antrum egregii Caesaris audiar
aeternum meditans decus   5
  stellis inserere et consilio Iouis?
Dicam insigne, recens, adhuc
  indictum ore alio. Non secus in iugis
exsomnis stupet Euhias,
  Hebrum prospiciens et niue candidam   10
Thracen ac pede barbaro
  lustratam Rhodopen, ut mihi deuio
ripas et uacuum nemus
  mirari libet. O Naiadum potens
Baccharumque ualentium   15
  proceras manibus uertere fraxinos,
nil paruum aut humili modo,
  nil mortale loquar. *Dulce* periculum est,
o Lenaee, sequi deum
  cingentem uiridi tempora pampino.   20

After the scene-setting in the forest and caverns, the panegyrical reference to "pre-eminent Caesar" (*egregii Caesaris*) at line 4 comes as a shock. Commentators have accounted for the appearance of Augustus in a poem initially "about" Bacchic frenzy as a sign of intense excitement at a new theme, a protreptic excuse of divine madness for any missteps Horace might take as he embarks on the challenging new task (*nova mente*) of panegyric, and as a bid to establish the grandiose aesthetics of Horace's new Augustan poetics.[30] If we read 3.25 against 2.7, a different set of concerns emerges. In 2.7, Horace welcomes his friend Pompeius back to Italy after Philippi. Nisbet and Hub-

***

30   The views of Gordon Williams (excitement), Fraenkel and West (apology), and Schiesaro (aesthetic stake-claiming).

bard find little to admire in Horace's "whimsical" greetings to a friend in such uncomfortable conditions. Tarrant remarks more sympathetically on his "frantic jollity," especially in lines 26–27:

> ... no more sane than
> an Edonian, I will run wild like a Bacchant.
> It's sweet to go mad at the return of a friend!

> ... non ego sanius
> bacchabor Edonis. recepto
> *dulce* mihi furere est amico.

Horace never speaks of Philippi with open regret or anger. He represents civil war in a different register. The "sweet" madness described in both poems describes the symptoms of a body afflicted by trauma. To begin with, this body belongs to the poet, but the invocations of Bacchus and his implied invitation to his friend suggest that the social body of his readers is implicated too. When this inspired body speaks, it uses the hyperbole and irony of Bacchic poetics to redirect the pain of defeat at Philippi evoked in 2.7 toward imagining a new world ruled by *egregius Caesar*. Horace creates ironic dissonance by practicing panegyric in a Bacchic frenzy and by inviting a partner in civic disaster to join the poet in mad drunkenness—a dissonance that expresses the shock of a world turned upside down by the emergency of Augustan autocracy. "To turn into a singer of Caesar's great deeds," Alessandro Schiesaro observes, "Horace does have to metamorphose, politically as well as stylistically, and Bacchic energy can help him in this major enterprise."[31] Like Cicero in the *pro Marcello*, Horace puts ironic hyperbole to work in accommodating this new world. His technique emerges from a republican sensibility attuned to the existence of an aesthetic field for *feeling* power, and feeling through one's negotiation of it.

THE PRIORITY OF SPEECH

In her postwar novel *The Mandarins*, Simone de Beauvoir explores the moral and psychological dilemmas of intellectuals who, despite their good intentions, frequently act in bad faith to their friends, their political allies, and

---

31   Schiesaro, "Horace's Bacchic poetics" 64. See also Lowrie, *Horace's Narrative Odes* (317–21), a reading from which I have learned even though she sees Horace's Odes as the expression of a newly developing autocratic discourse that has decisively if painfully set aside republican habits.

themselves. The two characters she fleshes out most fully, writer Henri Per-
ron and psychiatrist Anne Dubreuil, confront what is for de Beauvoir the
key point about human action: that one acts always in conditions that are
not and cannot be fully known, so actions resemble wagers or leaps in the
dark—but one is responsible for them nonetheless. The novel returns repeatedly to action's unforeseen consequences, especially unexpected or un-
wanted obligations of love, family, and friendship.

Alongside these familiar existentialist concerns, *The Mandarins* bril-
liantly illuminates how the choices of its characters, which they discuss
with one another almost exclusively in political terms, are shaped by other
powerful forces they tend to overlook, ignore, or dismiss as "private" concerns. Most significantly, Henri and his friends repeatedly long for (but in
postwar Paris only occasionally secure) good food and wine, fashionable
clothes, reliable transportation, and other comforts; they pursue painful,
sometimes deeply damaging love affairs. Though they almost always brush
off their deprivations and erotic distractions with self-deprecating humor,
the frequency of scenes of frustrated desire and its effects on the plot make
it clear that the characters' most pressing political dilemma—the choice of
whether to throw support behind a French alliance with the United States
or with the USSR—is intimately bound up with their personal tastes and
frustrations. As we follow Anne's passionate, doomed affair with an American and Henri's abandonment of his bohemian lover for a much younger
woman with whom he has a child, de Beauvoir suggests that the notional
line between political sensibility and personal desire is not easily maintained, and that the way Henri and Anne actually *see* the political landscape
is not so much in tension with their personal concerns as it is a product of
them.

The Mandarins ultimately rewrites its characters' choice between com-
munism and capitalism into a richer and more ethically challenging narrative about the field of action under the conditions of modernity, where
radically expanded access to goods and services creates new modes of empowered, individual selfhood whose realization depends heavily on consumption. Henri and Anne neither explicitly acknowledge this development, nor take it seriously as a major force in their political vision and life
choices. But the novel's foregrounding of desire and consumption subtly
suggests that the source of their struggles lies precisely here: not in a choice
between conflicting pure ideologies, but in an unresolved, unexamined,
vain hope of reconciling old belief systems with the bourgeois, consumer-
ist, individualist worldview that has engulfed them. By showing how her
characters fail to see the true challenges of modern politics, de Beauvoir

prompts us to examine more closely the ways we understand the crises through which we live, to see how certain values, habits, and purposes we blindly adhere to may incubate the drive toward political or social conflict, and to imagine how we may *be* differently, for a secure future.

I have argued that the *pro Marcello*, the first speech in the Roman panegyric tradition, defies attempts to define it as "pro-" or "anti-" Caesar. Its praise for Caesar as a peace-bringer is sincere; it is also resentful, guilty, collusive, quietist, sarcastic, resistant. The speech is inclusive in its quiet insistence on the remainders left behind in the construction of a new consensus. It is visionary in its refusal to play at the old republican game of claiming sovereignty—recognizing that to do so in the face of tyrannical power means death (the death Cato chose) or more violence. It works in both directions at once: it relies on, and works the interval between, registers of sincerity and irony, praise and blame, in its effort to speak to all parties across the fractured political spectrum within the senate: the Caesarians, the Pompeians, and the rest. This is a eulogy that attempts to come to terms with the loss of the republic; it is an attempt to fix a certain tragic memory of the republic; it clarifies to Cicero and his audience his view of the shared situation and their duties in it; it is also an attempt to remind Caesar of what Cicero is, and what the other senators are, in an effort to define his responsibilities and to demarcate limits to Caesar's potentially tyrannical freedom of action. This is all to say that the speech acknowledges the significance of imagination—above all, the senators' imagination of themselves—in the composition of political experience.

The irony in the speech may strike us as insupportable over the long term. Richard Rorty acknowledges that irony is not well suited to the public sphere because it undermines hope. Many, perhaps most, people do not like to continuously occupy a position of doubt and conscious double-think, just as most people do not want to experience the kind of contested, conflictual self-consciousness that Cicero seems to undergo. "What binds societies together are common vocabularies and common hopes," Rorty says. "To retain social hope, members of such a society need to be able to tell themselves a story about how things might get better."[32] But Rorty also "depends on ironists for the solidarity that is required for public morality, because ironists are sensitive both to vulnerability as the orienting point of solidarity and to the limitation that nothing can be guaranteed in public moral life."[33]

32   Rorty, *Philosophy and Social Hope*, 86.
33   Smith, "Morals and their ironies," 377.

The speech also contains provocative normative claims. It calls on its audiences to cultivate two habits that pull in what first appear to be opposite directions: sharing in a collective act of imagination, fantasy if you will, as a tactic in healing breaches in the civic order; and seeing conditions of Caesarian power for what they are. It suggests that how we understand what divides us is important to moving on—and that excessive acts of acknowledgment are at times necessary for the first few steps to be taken. It establishes the moral imperative to respond to current conditions with a new form of self-envisioning that preserves within itself potential practices of future liberation, namely the spoken word, which Cicero implicitly claims as his central weapon in the ongoing republican struggle against domination.

The speech itself is a stroke in this battle. It powerfully articulates the view that speech, even under repressive conditions, preserves the potential power to resist repression and violence. It underscores the necessity of preserving a space for politics, even when—perhaps especially when—the conditions for politics are unsettling and distasteful. (Chapter 1 showed that its opening account of internal conflict has deep roots in Cicero's sense of what the republic is and where politics begins in it, and that communication is the only way to prevent conflict from turning into violence.) Here, Cicero repeatedly reminds his listeners of the value of speech and the threat of silence (*diuturni silenti*, 1). He emphasizes speech as the medium of Roman memory, ironically underscoring Caesar's desire to preserve his *gloria* for eternity (*celebrabuntur ... audimus aut legimus*, 9, 29) but also stressing Cicero's risk-laden efforts to persuade his friends (and) the excessively violent Pompeians to avoid war (*semperque dolui non modo pacem sed etiam orationem civium pacem flagitantium repudiari*, 14, cf. 15, *etiam otiosis minabantur*, 18). Courting the risk of Caesar's anger, Cicero plays with terms and values, declaring that the field of discourse in the future will be wracked by disagreement (*magna dissensio*, 29) and that there is danger that the Pompeians' futile refusal to surrender will be interpreted in the future as the virtue of *constantia* (31). He stresses the necessity and propriety of speech even when the speaker prefers silence (*sed quia non est omnibus stantibus necesse dicere, a me certe dici volunt, cui necesse est quodam modo, et quod fieri decet*), and finally ends with the suggestion that silence is dangerous (33).

Cicero's defense of Marcellus is an apologia for speech itself, an advocate's argument for the perpetuation of the field of political action over and against violence. Violence is not resistible.[34] Caesar's *clementia*, while politi-

---

34   I explored the theoretical background to this claim in chapter 1.

cally and socially repugnant, nonetheless preserves a space, not quite of re-sistance, but for resistibility, where Cicero may take the part of Marcellus "who has no part."[35] Homi Bhabha remarks that the "forces of social author-ity and subversion or subalternity may emerge in displaced, even decentred strategies of signification ... positions of authority may themselves be part of a process of ambivalent identification. Indeed the exercise of power may be both politically effective and psychically affective because the discursive liminality through which it is signified may provide greater scope for stra-tegic maneuver and negotiation."[36] Cicero's strategy of ambivalence is a risky one, and historically speaking, it was fatal to him. Eighteen months after delivering this speech, according to his own *Philippics*, his name was shouted like a dedication by the conspirators as they drove their daggers into the body of Caesar. For all the fence-sitting complained of by histori-ans, he seems to have been understood at the moment of the assassination to symbolize the freedom the conspirators sought to recapture.

Cicero is punished for the *pro Marcello* at the hands of Wolf and others who cannot *see* the speech because it disobeys the rule of republican ethics. But we might say that Cicero himself anticipates this response in this speech when he articulates the irreducible play of pleasure, desire, rage, and hope that characterize a community wounded by but still in love with an out-dated model of itself, uncertain as to what the future will bring, and divided on the rightness of consensus itself under conditions hitherto unthinkable in the republic—unthinkable, that is, before Cicero speaks out. Cicero sum-mons up images in which each part of his partisan audience may invest in different ways; he stages emotions that some will watch with pleasure and some with pain, including the glee of Caesarian triumph, and Pompeian grief at defeat and even vengeful rage at the victor, the object of praise. It is Cicero's inclusive acknowledgement of these various mental and political states that makes his speech worthy of study, because it reveals the accom-modations Cicero believes both losers and winners must make in order to live under new conditions of politics.

35 Rancière, *Disagreement*, 14. See further Kirstie McClure, "Disconnections, connec-tions, and questions: reflections on Jacques Rancière's 'Ten theses,'" sections 31–33. Indeed, in his effort to speak to all factions in the senate, it is possible to argue along with Dyer, "Rhetoric and intention in Cicero's *pro Marcello*," that Cicero's extended treatment of the possibility of tyrannicide is an example of ironic *oratio figurata* (20ff.) designed to appeal to senators enraged by Caesar's victory and especially his *clementia*. I disagree with Dyer that the speech speaks *only* to them; his praise of Caesar is designed to flatter Caesar's supporters too.

36 Bhabha, *Location of Culture*, 162.

This is not an "imperial" move. As we saw in detail in the first chapter of this book, republican politics revolves around conflict and its negotiation. Resolutions are temporary; one or some people win, while others lose. This fact is immured in the grain of the political experience. Cicero is facing a highly unusual situation: the victory of a single man in civil war. But it is far from unprecedented. Caesar is the third in a string of Big Men who left their mark on Rome over a generation, following Marius and Sulla (and Cicero would probably add Catiline to the list). And even before the convulsive conflicts of the late republic, the psychodynamics of accommodation to power were a central aspect of the experience of the law court, assembly, and senate. If the civil war and Caesar's victory represented an extreme case, living in conflict—with the palpable absence of ideal self-sovereignty—and preparing for re-foundation was familiar. This is a habit worth recovering.

CONCLUSION

THE REPUBLIC REMASTERED

A T THE CORE of most classical and contemporary approaches to politics—including the recently fashionable Carl Schmitt and his epigones—lies the commitment to the concept of sovereignty and the tendency, dominant since the nineteenth century emergence of sociology and economics, to treat human beings primarily as rational calculators or creatures of practical reason. But it is not clear that the Romans who think constructively about politics privilege either sovereignty or reason as starting or end points—or indeed that they believe that politics can yield much to systematic analysis.

This book has tried to recover the concept- and virtue-focused tradition's entwined but distinctive counterpart—what I think of as the suppressed history of republican thought. This history departs from the insight enshrined in Roman myth discussed in chapter 1: that the republic first takes shape as the regime of Romulus and Remus, eternally twinned and twinning, a two-faced sign. Just as the self-sacrificial republican hero has been understood as exemplary of both the human and the inhuman, as both the defender of the common good against tyranny and a symbol of noble contempt for common goods (think of the suicidal younger Cato in Cicero and Lucan), so the republic's ideal condition has always been understood both as a harmonious like-minded unity where the senatorial order governs the people (the Guicciardinian story), and as a state of relentless conflict among citizen contestants, where hierarchies of power and value are not neatly arranged orders that exist prior to the interaction between agents but, as Machiavelli suggests, emergent in action.

John Rawls says in *A Theory of Justice* that "conceptions of justice must be justified by the conditions of our life as we know it or not at all." This raises two questions: what if the conditions of life are such that they seem to make justification and reason-giving about justice extremely difficult, if not impossible—say, if one lives in a state of war, or in a state of conflict and instability that approaches the violence and upheaval of war? And as Robert Pippin asks, what counts as knowing the conditions of life, anyway?[1]

---

1   Rawls, *A Theory of Justice*, 454, quoted and discussed by Robert Pippin, *Hollywood Westerns and American Myth: The Importance of Howard Hawks and John Ford to Political Philosophy*, 20.

The suppressed history of republican political thought bursts forth in a series of texts invested in grappling with life under highly unstable conditions wrought by imperial expansion and unusually violent conflict within the traditional ruling order and between that order and the people, conditions under which a culture of rational deliberation was difficult if not impossible to sustain or even imagine, and possibly viewed as undesirable by parties on both sides (certainly by senators like Cicero). These texts are linked by concern for how men in such conditions come to know the world, how they make judgments about it, and how they communicate knowledge and judgment to others. These thinkers obtain knowledge of the human condition relevant to politics by focusing on *aesthesis*—our sensory perceptions and experience of emotions—and its sometimes uncomfortable distance from reason and reason-giving. Knowing and judging are outcomes of sensory and sensual intersubjective experience, that is, bundles of aesthetic as well as cognitive perception that tend to blur into "feeling." ("This word *feele* explaneth the whole," Lodowick Bryskett explained to his friend Spenser.[2])

In the formation and transmission of this suppressed history rhetoric and poetics play a central role, predominating over texts that self-identify as "philosophical" in the Greek sense. When Romans write "philosophy," they tend to self-consciously highlight their difference from Greek practice, and not just for reasons of cultural differentiation—as in Cicero's *Republic*, where the interlocutors in what at first resembles a Platonic dialogue praise the Socrates-like Scipio for inventing an ideal republic that, unlike Plato's, is grounded in human experience (or so they say, *de Rep.* 2.21–22). From Cicero and the *Ad Herennium*, Sallust, Livy, Valerius Maximus, the Roman satirists, Tacitus and Quintilian, the tradition evolves through the late medieval and early modern rhetorical tradition out of which developed the handbook of manners and the philosophically minded genre of civil dialogue. Lodowick Bryskett, whom I quoted above, was an Anglo-Italian friend of Spenser who rendered Giraldi Cintio's 1565 Ciceronian *Tre dialoghi della vita civile* into his *Discourse on Civil Life* (1606): this habit of translation underpinned later eighteenth century research into the civil passions, exemplified in *Cato's Letters* by John Trenchard and Thomas Gordon and Adam Smith's *Theory of Moral Sentiments*. The group of texts is neither static nor exclusively Latinate: in the seventeenth century, Dionysius of Halicarnassus, Plutarch, and Longinus take on central importance.

2   Quoted by Edward Armstrong, *A Ciceronian Sunburn*, 70.

Forms of expression bound up with imagination, sensation, the non-normative and the a-rational, with rhetoric and poetics, are not primarily concerned with citizens as rational calculators nor with constitutional arrangements regarding the balance of power. When we exile them to the margins of theory and intellectual history, we hobble our ability to explore the republican tradition for ways to refresh our thinking about contemporary questions, historical and theoretical alike.[3]

This is plain in one recent and in many ways successful attempt to rethink approaches to the republic. Karl-Joachim Hölkeskamp shows how twentieth century Roman historians used methods and language that established the republic as a static entity to be studied in terms of concepts and values, first by carrying out Mommsen-style analyses of the so-called Roman constitution, then by doing prosopographical studies of the familial alliances behind aristocratic factions.[4] In critical response, drawing on the past quarter-century of scholarship, Hölkeskamp convincingly presents Roman politics as a plurality of political connections, an acutely volatile "shifting of coalitions, constellations, and for that matter, lines of confrontation" between agents and classes with fragmented and internally conflicted interests. Quoting Christian Meier, who describes the republic as a "fissility" fueled by internal tension, he draws on Clifford Geertz and Pierre Bourdieu to call for subtler readings of Roman political culture as "an ensemble of texts, themselves ensembles" "suspended in webs of significance" "embodied in symbols."[5] This broad range of phenomena embraces not only moral concepts but the "entire range of images of reality, a system of 'making sense' of: that is, perceiving, interpreting, and evaluating" one's environment. But then Hölkeskamp revives the old categories. The "deeply rooted knowledge" that is "pre-theoretical and unreflected, [which] makes it very hard to grasp," takes our attention away from *actual politics*, such as the decisions and actions of magistrates" (my emphasis). Appealing to comparative studies and a "systems-theoretical model" of institutions, Hölkeskamp dismisses the symbolic, the affective, and the aesthetic elements of politics as somehow not "actual" politics. He undercuts the radical critical gesture made by his own analysis of the limitations of conventional historiography, and ends up seeing the republic through the superimposed frame of modern constitu-

---

3   See Hannah Arendt on intellectual history as pearl-diving in her introduction to Walter Benjamin, *Illuminations*, 7–58.

4   Karl-Joachim Hölkeskamp, *Reconstructing the Roman Republic*, 4–43 and passim.

5   Ibid., 53; he quotes Meier, *Res Publica Amissa* 15 and 163 on p. 38.

tionalism and institutionalism, thus losing precisely those dynamic elements of republican practice he began with a view to recovering.

To study Roman political thought following the lines I have sketched requires us to analyze Roman accounts of *aesthesis*, specifically, how one's sense of self is bound up in aesthetic experience of the world, and how aesthetic judgments get organized and habituated in ways that create shared conditions for sense-making.[6] This is prior to deliberation in the strict sense (whether it works in tandem with the making of linguistic sense is a matter of phenomenological debate beyond my scope). It occurs as a self-reflexive mental and corporeal process, because it involves spontaneous reactions of (for example) delight or disgust that humans experience as corporeal reactions.

In terms of thinking critically about our political practice, our attention to the role of aesthetics in judgment might leave us with the ironic sensation that the earth is falling out from under our feet. I do not mean to dismiss cognition and reason from the scene.[7] I would say rather that the suppressed history of republicanism compels us to take aesthetic experience seriously, both as a constitutive element of political experience in the world and as a field in which meaningful theoretical work gets done in specific works of art. It thus valuably challenges normative liberal assumptions about our habitual methods of analysis and the objects of our critical attention in ancient political theory, which extends to our habits of reading certain kinds of texts and excluding others—like satire.

It is well known—Roman practicality was already a truism in antiquity, carefully fostered by Romans and Greeks alike—that Roman writers tend to sidestep the traditional concerns of Greek political thought: definitions and evaluations of civic virtues and constitution types, the proper distribution of justice, and the nature of rule. If no Roman author undertakes sustained analysis of the Roman regime, this is not for lack of familiarity with such analysis from the Greek philosophical tradition since the third century BCE.[8] Roman thinkers treat politics in modes that mirror their topic, which exists in action, not text or inscription or anything else resembling a formal

6   I draw here on Linda Zerilli's account of judgment in *Feminism and the Abyss of Freedom*, 127–31.

7   For more on this defense, see Linda Zerilli, "'We feel our freedom': imagination and judgment in the thought of Hannah Arendt," 158–88.

8   Rome is not Athens, and as Dean Hammer notes, it has paid a price for that in postphilhellenic modern intellectual history (*Roman Political Thought and the Modern Theoretical Imagination*, 23ff.). But as Nadia Urbinati points out, modern liberal democracy is not Athens either. She shows that theorists on the left complain about contemporary electoral democracy (and especially representation) in terms that closely resemble modern critiques of Roman re-

"constitution": as we have seen, they view politics as rhetoric, as dynamic action in the realm of speech, as the constant, contested formation and undoing of consensus: in sum, as a discourse that defies the narrativization of Greek philosophical analysis.

Roman writers usefully break down the generic and intellectual barriers signified by the term "philosophy." That is, they pursue political thought in history, oratory, epic and pastoral poetry, and (arguably the most important genre for modern images of Rome) satire. This makes their work a provocative object of study for contemporary political theorists, whose field is similarly opening up to include works that are neither traditionally philosophical nor theoretical.[9] They figure political thought through a variety of other scenes to which they return repeatedly, even obsessively, from the scene of the virtuous exemplar to class conflict, cultural change and decline, and persuasion in the public assembly, the senate, and the law court. Roman thinkers write fantasies, but they rarely write utopias; they are concerned primarily with authority and its legitimacy, and they never assume that authority is stable. They address a politics "involved in the condition of subjects collectively confronted with the limits of their own power."[10] This is the moment to note, however, that one topic on which I have been more or less silent is the possibility that the collective's confrontation with the limits on their power might descend into violence. If my silence responds to a gap in Roman texts, it needs flagging here as a topic for future reflection.[11]

The ongoing retrieval and recuperation of Athenian democratic ideals places an exceedingly high value on the virtue (intrinsic or instrumental) of political participation. What I have tried to do in this book is show how reading Roman texts can reshape our habits of political thinking, our ethos of civic being. Beyond this goal lies my hope that close attention to these texts has the capacity to reshape the way we think about civic wisdom—the way schools teach history, literature, civics, and philosophy—about public discourse, especially public commentary on political oratory, and about the conversations we citizens hold among ourselves. I have no intention of calling modern democratic citizens to imitate the Romans' electoral, legisla-

---

publican government—as elite-dominated, anti-populist, and vulnerable to moneyed influence (*Representative Democracy*, 38–39).

9   James Farr, "The history of political thought as disciplinary genre," and Jodi Dean, "Political theory and cultural studies" thoughtfully survey changes in the discipline (*Oxford Handbook of Political Theory*). Latour and Weibel's sprawling collection and gallery exhibition *Making Things Public* is a good example of political thinking that crosses generic boundaries (appropriately focused on the crisis of representation, both political and aesthetic).

10   Étienne Balibar, *Politics and the Other Scene*, 26.

11   I am grateful to Michèle Lowrie and Andrew Riggsby for insisting on this point.

tive, or (such as they were) deliberative practices. Nor do I wish to sketch a program of neo-Roman civic virtue in which citizens are exhorted to live moderately, limit their consumption through sumptuary laws or self-restraint, love their country, run for office, and vote responsibly.[12] These are all admirable practices, but it is not the job of political theorists to preach on their behalf. As Annette Baier observes, "lists of productive virtues do not tell us how to bring those virtues into being."[13] Will Kymlicka adds that many studies of civic virtue may be reduced to a platitude: "namely, society would be better if the people in it were nicer and more thoughtful."[14]

I have sought to offer practical tools for civic education by articulating learnable *practices of knowing the world* that characterize late republican texts. These practices arise from close reading, and I hope it is clear that the purpose of laying out my own readings in detail is to put the interrogative ethos that fuels them on display as much as to advocate for their content. We learn from Roman writers, the closest of close readers of the Greek and Latin texts that came before them, that techniques for reading texts and for reading the world overlap. The republican tradition that I have explored, and in the exploration, composed, is distinctive because of the ways it focuses our attention—on class antagonism, on corporeal knowing, on the privileging of process over ends, on the dangers of self-sovereignty. Cicero, Sallust, and Horace compel us to evaluate our priorities—that which we as citizens choose to treat as primary matters of civic concern.

---

12   The citizenship movement often invokes the list of virtues outlined fifteen years ago by William Galston: the general virtues of courage, law-abidingness, and loyalty; the social virtues of independence and open-mindedness; the economic virtues of a work ethic, self-restraint, and adaptability; and various political virtues, from respecting the rights of others to willingness to engage in public discourse (Galston, *Liberal Purposes: Goods, Virtues, and Duties in the Liberal State*, 221–27).

13   Baier, *Moral Prejudices*, 222.

14   Kymlicka, *Contemporary Political Philosophy*, 316.

BIBLIOGRAPHY

Acemoglu, Daron and James A. Robinson. *Why Nations Fail: The Origins of Power, Prosperity and Poverty*. New York, 2012.

Allen, Danielle. *Talking to Strangers: Anxieties of Citizenship Since Brown v. Board of Education*. Chicago, 2006.

Ando, Clifford. "A dwelling beyond violence: the uses and disadvantages of history for contemporary republicans." *History of Political Thought* 31 (2010) 183–220.

Arendt, Hannah. *Between Past and Future*. New York, 1963/2006.

———. *Eichmann in Jerusalem*. New York, 1963.

———. *Essays in Understanding*. New York, 1994.

———. *The Human Condition*. Chicago, 1989.

———. "Introduction" to Walter Benjamin, *Illuminations*. New York, 1969/1999.

———. *Lectures on Kant's Political Philosophy*. Chicago, 1982.

———. *The Life of the Mind*. New York, 1971.

———. "Personal responsibility under dictatorship." In *Responsibility and Judgment*. New York, 2003.

———. *The Promise of Politics*. New York, 2005.

———. "Some questions of moral philosophy." In *Responsibility and Judgment*. New York, 2003.

———. "Thinking and moral considerations: a lecture." In *Responsibility and Judgment*. New York, 2003.

Armstrong, David. "Horace's Epistles 1 and Philodemus." In *Vergil, Philodemus and the Augustans*, ed. David Armstrong, Jeffrey Fish, Patricia A. Johnston, and Marilyn B. Skinner. Austin, 2004.

Armstrong, Edward. *A Ciceronian Sunburn: A Tudor Dialogue on Humanistic Rhetoric and Civic Poetics*. Columbia, 2006.

Asmis, Elizabeth. "A new kind of model: Cicero's Roman constitution in *de Republica*." *American Journal of Philology* 126 (2005) 377–416.

Badian, Ernst. Review of Antonio La Penna, *Sallustio e la "rivoluzione" romana*. *American Journal of Philology* 92.1 (1971) 103–7.

Baier, Annette. *Moral Prejudices: Essays on Ethics*. Cambridge, MA, 1994.

Balibar, Étienne. *Politics and the Other Scene*. London, 2002.

Batstone, William. "The antithesis of virtue: Sallust's 'syncrisis' and the crisis of the late republic." *Classical Antiquity* 7 (1988) 1–29.

———. "Caesar's republican rhetoric and the veils of autocracy." In *Cesare: Precursore o Visionario?*, ed. Gianpaolo Urso. Pisa, 2009.

Bauman, Zygmunt. *Intimations of Postmodernity*. London, 1992.

Beiner, Ronald. "Hannah Arendt on judging." In Hannah Arendt, *Lectures on Kant's Political Philosophy*. Chicago, 1982.

Benhabib, Seyla. "From redistribution to recognition." In *The Claims of Culture: Equality and Diversity in the Global Era*. Princeton, 2002.

Berlin, Isaiah. "Two concepts of liberty." In *Four Essays on Liberty*. Oxford, 1969

Bhabha, Homi. *The Location of Culture*. New York, 1994.

Boren, Henry. "Cicero's *concordia* in historical perspective." In *Laudatores Temporis Acti: Studies in Memory of Wallace Everett Caldwell*, ed. M. F. Gyles and E. W. Davis. Chapel Hill, 1964.

Bramble, John. *Persius and the Programmatic Satire*. Cambridge, 1974.

Braund, Susanna. "Praise and protreptic in early imperial panegyric." In *The Propaganda of Power: The Role of Panegyric in Late Antiquity*, ed. M. Whitby. Leiden, 1998.

Braund, Susanna and Christopher Gill, eds. *The Passions in Roman Thought and Literature*. Cambridge, 1997.

Brooks, Peter. *The Melodramatic Imagination: Balzac, Henry James, Melodrama, and the Mode of Excess*. New Haven, 1976/2008.

———. *Reading for the Plot*. New York, 1984.

Brown, Wendy. *Politics Out of History*. Princeton, 2001.

Brunt, P. A. "Fall of the Roman republic." In *The Fall of the Roman Republic*. Cambridge, 1988.

———. "*Libertas.*" In *The Fall of the Roman Republic*. Cambridge, 1988.

Burgh, Thomas. *Political Disquisitions*. Philadelphia, 1774.

Butler, Judith. *Giving an Account of Oneself*. New York, 2005.

Calhoun, Craig and Derluguian, Georgi, eds. *Business as Usual: The Roots of the Global Financial Meltdown*. 3 vols. New York, 2011.

Calhoun, Craig. "Evicting the public." Published online at ssrc.org (accessed November 2011).

Cavell, Stanley. "The avoidance of love." In *Disowning Knowledge in Seven Plays of Shakespeare*. Cambridge, 2003.

Cipriani, Giovanni. "La *Pro Marcello* e il suo significato come orazione politica." *Atene e Roma* 22 (1977) 113–25.

Clark, S. H. "Narrative identity in Ricoeur's *Oneself As Another.*" In *Critical Studies: Ethics and the Subject*, ed. Karl Simms. Amsterdam and Atlanta, 1994.

Coarelli, Filippo. *Il foro romano*. 1983.

Coleman, Janet. "El concepto de república: continuidad mitica y continuidad real." *Res Publica* 15 (2005) 27–47.

Combet-Farnoux, Bernard. "Fabius Pictor et les origines du thème de la concordia ordinum dans l'historiographie romaine." *Ann. Fac. Lett. Nice* 11 (1970) 77–91.

Connolly, Joy. *The State of Speech: Rhetoric and Political Thought in Ancient Rome*. Princeton, 2007.

———. Review of Dean Hammer, *Roman Political Thought and the Modern Theoretical Imagination. Political Theory* 40.6 (2012) 847–50.

Constant, Benjamin. "Speech given at the Athénée Royale: the liberty of the ancients compared with the moderns." In *Political Writings*, trans. Biancamaria Fontana. Cambridge, 1988.

Coole, Diana. *Merleau-Ponty and Modern Politics After Anti-Humanism*. Lanham, 2007.

Cox, Virginia. "Ciceronian rhetoric in Italy, 1250–1360." *Rhetorica* 17 (1999) 239–288.

———. "Ciceronian rhetorical theory in the Volgare: a fourteenth-century text and its fifteenth-century readers." In *Rhetoric and Renewal in the Latin West: Essays in Honour of John O. Ward*, ed. Constant J. Mews, Cary J. Nederman, and Rodney M. Thompson. Brepols, 2003.

Craig, Christopher. "Cicero's strategy of embarrassment in the speech for Plancius," *AJP* 111 (1990) 75–81.

Critchley, Simon. *Infinitely Demanding: Ethics of Commitment, Politics of Resistance*. London, 2008.

Curtis, Kimberley. "Aesthetic foundations of democratic politics in the work of Hannah Arendt." In *Hannah Arendt and the Meaning of Politics*, ed. Craig Calhoun and John McGowan. Minneapolis and London, 1997.

Dagger, Richard. *Civic Virtues: Rights, Citizenship, and Republican Liberalism*. Oxford and New York, 1997.

Dean, Jodi. "Political theory and cultural studies." In *The Oxford Handbook of Political Theory*, ed. John S. Dryzek, Bonnie Honig, and Anne Phillips. Oxford, 2006.

———. "Politics without politics." *Parallax* 15.3 (2009) 20–36.

De Man, Paul. *Blindness and Insight*. Minneapolis and London, 1971.

Dewey, John. *The Public and Its Problems*. Athens, OH, 1927/1954.

Dietz, Mary. "'The slow boring of hard boards': methodical thinking and the work of politics." *American Political Science Review* 88 (1994) 873–86.

Dolan, Frederick. *Allegories of America*. Ithaca, 1994.

————. "The banality of love and the meaning of the political" (review of Elżbieta Ettinger, *Hannah Arendt/Martin Heidegger* and Dana Villa, *Arendt and Heidegger*). *Theory and Event* 1 (1997).

Dreyfus, Hubert and Sean Dorrance Kelly. *All Things Shining: Reading the Western Classics to Find Meaning in a Secular Age*. New York, 2011.

DuBois, W. E. B. *The Souls of Black Folk*. New York, 1982.

Due, Casey. "Tragic history and barbarian speech in Sallust's *Jugurtha*." *Harvard Studies in Classical Philology* 100 (2000) 311–25.

Dufallo, Basil. "Satis/Satura: reconsidering the 'programmatic intent' of Horace's *Satires* 1.1." *Classical World* 93 (2000) 579–90.

Dyer, R. R. "Rhetoric and intention in Cicero's *Pro Marcello*." *Journal of Roman Studies* 80 (1990) 17–30.

Eagleton, Terry. *After Theory*. New York, 2003.

Earl, D. C. *The Political Thought of Sallust*. Cambridge, 1961.

Farr, James. "The history of political thought as disciplinary genre." In *The Oxford Handbook of Political Theory*, ed. John S. Dryzek, Bonnie Honig, and Anne Phillips. Oxford, 2006.

Feldherr, Andrew. *Spectacle and Society in Livy's History*. Berkeley and Los Angeles, 1998.

Flower, Harriet. *Roman Republics*. Princeton, 2010.

Foucault, Michel. *Fearless Speech*. Los Angeles, 2001.

————. *The Government of Self and Others: Lectures at the Collège de France 1982–1983*. New York, 2010.

————. *Hermeneutics of the Subject: Lectures at the Collège de France 1981–1982*. New York, 2005.

————. "What is an author?" In *The Foucault Reader*, ed. Michel Foucault and Paul Rabinow. New York, 1984.

Frank, Jill. "On judgment in Plato's *Republic*." *Political Theory* 35 (2007) 443–67.

Fraser, Nancy. "From redistribution to recognition? Dilemmas of justice in a 'post-socialist' age." *New Left Review* 212 (1995): 68–93.

Freud, Sigmund. "Mourning and melancholia." *The Standard Edition of the Works of Sigmund Freud*, Vol. 14 (1914–1916), 237–58.

Freudenburg, Kirk, ed. *The Cambridge Companion to Roman Satire*. Cambridge, 2005.

Fried, Michael. "Art and objecthood." In *Art and Objecthood*. Chicago, 1998.

————. "New York letter: Kelly, Poons." In *Art and Objecthood*. Chicago, 1998.

————. "Three American painters: Kenneth Noland, Jules Olitski, Frank Stella." In *Art and Objecthood*. Chicago, 1998.

Gagliardi, Paola. *Il dissenso e l'ironia: per una rilettura delle orazioni 'cesariane' di Cicerone*. Naples, 1997.

Galston, William. *Liberal Purposes: Goods, Virtues, and Duties in the Liberal State*. Cambridge, 1991/1996.

Geuss, Raymond. *Philosophy and Real Politics*. Princeton, 2008.

Goodin, Robert. "Folie républicaine." *Annual Review of Political Science* 6 (2003) 55–76.

Gowers, Emily. "Fragments of autobiography in Horace *Satires* 1." *Classical Antiquity* 22 (2003) 55–91.

————. "Horace *Satires* 1 and 2." In *The Cambridge Companion to Horace*, ed. Kirk Freudenburg. Cambridge, 2005.

Grafton, Anthony and Lisa Jardine. "Studied for action: how Gabriel Harvey read his Livy." *Past & Present* 129 (1990) 30–78.

Grant, Ulysses S. *Personal Memoirs*. New York, 1885.

Gruen, Erich. *Culture and National Identity in Republican Rome*. Ithaca, 1992.

Gunderson, Erik. "The libidinal rhetoric of satire." In *The Cambridge Companion to Horace*, ed. Kirk Freudenburg. Cambridge, 2005.

Gyllenhammer, "Phenomenology as an ascetic practice." In *Ethics and Phenomenology*, ed. Mark Sanders and J. Jeremy Wisnewski. Plymouth, UK, 2012.

Habermas, Jürgen. "Three normative models of democracy: liberal, republican, procedural." In *Questioning Ethics*, ed. Richard Kearney, Mark Dooley. London, 1999.

Haker, Hille. "The fragility of the moral self." *Harvard Theological Review* 97 (2004) 359–81.

Hammer, Dean. *Roman Politcal Thought and the Modern Theoretical Imagination*. Norman, OK, 2008.

Heinze, Richard. "The Horatian ode." In *Horace: Odes and Epodes*. Oxford Readings in Classical Studies, ed. Michèle Lowrie. Oxford, 2009.

Held, David and Kevin Young. "Crises in parallel worlds: the governance of global risks in finance, security, and the environment." In *The Deepening Crisis*, ed. Craig Calhoun and Georgi Derluguian. New York, 2011.

Henderson, John. "Be alert (your country needs lerts): Horace *Satires* 1.9)." In *Writing Down Rome: Satire, Comedy, and Other Offences in Latin Poetry*. Oxford, 1999.

Herzog, Don. "Romantic anarchism and pedestrian liberalism." *Political Theory* 35.3 (2007) 313–33.

———. "Some questions for republicans." *Political Theory* 14 (1996) 473–93.

Hölkeskamp, Karl-Joachim. *Reconstructing the Roman Republic*. Princeton, 2010.

———. "Self-serving sermons: oratory and the self-construction of the Roman aristocrat." In *Praise and Blame in Roman Republican Rhetoric*, ed. C. Smith and R. Covino. Wales, 2011.

Honig, Bonnie. "The legacy of xenophobia." *Boston Review*, Dec. 2002/Jan. 2003.

———. *Political Theory and the Displacement of Politics*. Ithaca, 1993.

Honohan, Iseult. *Civic Republicanism*. New York and London, 2002.

Horsfall, Nicholas. *The Culture of the Roman Plebs*. London, 2003.

James, William. "On a certain blindness in human beings." In *Writings 1878–1899*. New York, 1992.

Johnson, W. R. *Horace and the Dialectic of Freedom: Readings in* Epistles *1*. Ithaca, 1993.

Jonas, Hans. "Dialogue with Hannah Arendt." In *Hannah Arendt: The Recovery of the Public World*, ed. Melvyn Hill. New York, 1979.

Kalyvas, Andreas. *Democracy and the Politics of the Extraordinary*. Cambridge, 2009.

Kalyvas, Andreas and Ira Katznelson. *Liberal Beginnings: Making a Republic for the Moderns*. Cambridge, 2008.

Kant, Immanuel. *Critique of the Power of Judgment*. Trans. Paul Guyer. Cambridge, 2001.

Kapust, Daniel. *Republicanism, Rhetoric, and Roman Political Thought*. Cambridge, 2011.

Kaster, Robert. *Emotion, Restraint, and Community*. Princeton, 2005.

Kateb, George. "The adequacy of the canon." *Political Theory* 20 (2002) 482–505.

———. "Freedom and worldliness in the thought of Hannah Arendt." *Political Theory* 5 (1977) 141–82.

Kennedy, Duncan. "'Augustan' and 'anti-Augustan': reflections on terms of reference." In *Roman Poetry and Propaganda in the Age of Augustus*, ed. Anton Powell. Bristol, 1992.

Kraus, Christina S. "Jugurthine disorder." In *The Limits of Historiography: Genre and Narrative in Ancient Historical Texts*, ed. Christina S. Kraus. Leiden and Boston, 1999.

Kymlicka, William. *Contemporary Political Philosophy*. Oxford, 2001.

LaCapra, Dominick and Steven L. Kaplan, eds. *Modern European Intellectual History: Reappraisals and New Perspectives*. Ithaca, 1982.

Lacoue-Labarthe, Pierre. *Heidegger, Art, and Politics: The Fiction of the Political*. Trans. Chris Turner. Oxford, 1990.

Landy, Joshua. "Formative fictions: imaginative literature and the training of the capacities." *Poetics Today* 33.2 (2012) 169–216.

———. *How to Do Things with Fictions*. Oxford, 2012.

La Penna, Antonio. *Sallustio e la rivoluzione romana*. Milan, 1968.

Latour, Bruno and Peter Weibel, eds. *Making Things Public*. Cambridge, MA, 2005.

Leach, Eleanor W. "Ciceronian 'bi-Marcus': correspondence with M. Terentius Varro and L. Papirius Paetus in 46 BCE." *Transactions of the American Philological Association* 129 (1999) 139–79.

Lefort, Claude. *Democracy and Political Theory*. London and New York, 1991.

Leonard, Miriam. "The uses of reception: Derrida and the historical imperative." In *Classics and the Uses of Reception*, ed. Charles Martindale. Oxford, 2006.

Levene, D. S. "God and man in the classical Latin panegyric." *PCPS* 43 (1997) 66–103.

———. "History, metahistory, and audience response in Livy 45." *Classical Antiquity* 25 (2006) 73–108.

———. "Sallust's 'Catiline' and Cato the Censor." *Classical Quarterly* 50 (2000) 170–91.

———. "Sallust's *Jugurtha*: an 'historical fragment.'" *Journal of Roman Studies* 82 (1992) 53–70.

Lezra, Jacques. *Wild Materialism: The Ethic of Terror and the Modern Republic*. New York, 2010.

Lintott, Andrew. *The Constitution of the Roman Republic*. Oxford, 1999.

Long, A. A. "The politics of Cicero's *de Officiis*." In *Justice and Generosity: Studies in Hellenistic Social and Political Philosophy*, ed. André Laks. Cambridge, 1995.

Lowrie, Michèle. *Horace's Narrative Odes*. Oxford, 1997.

———. *Writing, Performance, and Authority in Augustan Rome*. Oxford, 2009.

MacIntyre, Alasdair. *After Virtue*. London, 1981.

Malamud, Margaret. *Ancient Rome and Modern America*. London, 2008.

Markell, Patchen. *Bound By Recognition*. Princeton, 2003.

———. "The insufficiency of non-domination." *Political Theory* 36 (2008) 9–36.

———. "Recognition and redistribution." In *The Oxford Handbook of Political Theory*, ed. John S. Dryzek, Bonnie Honig, and Anne Phillips. Oxford, 2006.

Marx, Werner. *Towards a Phenomenological Ethics*. Buffalo, 1992.

Maynor, John. *Republicanism in the Modern World*. Cambridge, 2003.

Mbembe, Achille. *On the Post-Colony*. Berkeley and Los Angeles, 2001.

McClure, Kirstie. "Disconnections, connections, and questions: reflections on Jacques Rancière's 'Ten theses.'" *Theory and Event* 6 (2003).

———. "The odor of judgment: exemplarity, propriety, and politics in the company of Hannah Arendt." In *Hannah Arendt and the Meaning of Politics*, ed. Craig Calhoun and John McGowan. Minneapolis and London, 1997.

McCormick, John. "Machiavelli against republicanism: on the Cambridge School's 'Guicciardinian Moments.'" *Political Theory* 31 (2003) 615–43.

———. *Machiavellian Democracy*. Cambridge, 2011.

———. "Machiavellian democracy: controlling elites with ferocious populism." *American Political Science Review* 95 (2001) 297–313.

McDonald, Henry. "Aesthetics as first ethics: Levinas and the alterity of literary discourse." *diacritics* 38.4 (2008) 15–41.

McDowell, John. "Virtue and reason." *Monist* 62 (1979) 331–50.

McManus, Helen. "Enduring agonism: between individuality and plurality." *Polity* 40 (2008) 509–525.

Meier, Christian. *Res Publica Amissa: Eine Studie zu Verfassung und Geschichte der späten römischen Republik*. Berlin, 1997.

Merleau-Ponty, Maurice. *The Phenomenology of Perception*. London and New York, 2002.

Meyers, Peter Alexander. *Civic War and the Corruption of the Citizen*. Chicago and London, 2008.

Millar, Fergus. *The Crowd in Rome in the Late Republic*. Ann Arbor, 1998.

———. *The Roman Republic in Political Thought*. Boston, 2002.

Miller, David. "Citizenship and pluralism." *Political Studies* 43 (1995) 432–50.

Mitchell, Richard. "The definition of *patres* and *plebs*: an end to the Struggle of the Orders." In *Social Struggles in Archaic Rome*, ed. Kurt Raaflaub. 2nd edition. Oxford, 2005.

Momigliano, Arnaldo. "Camillus and concord." *Classical Antiquity* 36 (1942) 111–20.

Mommsen, Theodor. *Römisches Staatsrecht*. Leipzig, 1877.

Morgan, Michael L. *The Cambridge Introduction to Levinas*. Cambridge, 2011.

Morstein-Marx, Robert. "The alleged massacre at Cirta and its consequences (Sall. BJ 26–27)." *Classical Philology* 95 (2000) 468–75.

———. *Mass Oratory and Political Power in the Late Roman Republic*. Cambridge, 2008.

Mouffe, Chantal. *The Democratic Paradox*. London and New York, 2009.

———. *On the Political*. London and New York, 2005.

Mouritsen, Henrik. *Plebs and Politics in the Late Roman Republic*. Cambridge, 2001.

Nakjavani, Erik. "Phenomenology and theory of literature: an interview with Paul Ricoeur." *Modern Language Notes* 96 (1981) 1084–90.

Nelson, Eric. *The Greek Tradition of Republican Thought*. Cambridge, 2004.

Noè, Eralda. "Per la formazione del consenso nella Roma del 1 sec. a.C." In *Studi di storia e storiografia antiche*, ed. Emilio Gabba. Pavia, 1988.

Oberhelman, Steven and David Armstrong, "Satire as poetry and the impossibility of metathesis in Horace's *Satires*." In *Philodemus and Poetry: Poetic Theory and Practice in Lucretius, Philodemus, and Horace*, ed. Dirk Obbink. Oxford, 1995.

Oliensis, Ellen. *Horace and the Rhetoric of Authority*. Cambridge, 1998.

O'Neill, Peter. "Going around in circles: popular speech in ancient Rome." *Classical Antiquity* 22 (2003) 135–66.

Orlie, Melissa. *Living Ethically, Acting Politically*. Ithaca, 1997.

Osmond, Patricia. "'Princeps historiae Romanae': Sallust in Renaissance political thought." *Memoirs of the American Academy in Rome* 40 (1995) 101–43.

Pagden, Anthony, ed. *The Languages of Political Theory in Early-Modern Europe*. Cambridge, 1987.

Paine, Thomas. *The Rights of Man*. Oxford, 1791/2009.

Panagia, Davide. *The Political Life of Sensation*. Durham and London, 2009.

Patton, Paul. "After the linguistic turn: post-structuralist and liberal pragmatist political theory." In *The Oxford Handbook of Political Theory*, ed. John S. Dryzek, Bonnie Honig, and Anne Phillips. Oxford, 2006.

Pease, Donald E. "States of fantasy: Barack Obama versus the Tea Party movement." *boundary 2* 37 (2010) 89–105.

Peltonen, Markku. *Classical Humanism and Republican Thought*. Cambridge, 2004.

Pettit, Philip. *On the People's Terms*. Cambridge, 2012.

———. *Republicanism*. Cambridge, 1997.

———. *A Theory of Freedom*. Cambridge, 2001.

Phillips, Anne. "Feminism and republicanism: is this a plausible alliance?" *Journal of Political Philosophy* 8 (2000) 279–93.

Picone, Giusto. "Il paradigma Marcello: tra esilio e Clementia Caesaris." In *Clementia Caesaris: modelli etici, parenesi e retorica dell'esilio*. Palermo, 2008.

Pippin, Robert. *Hollywood Westerns and American Myth: The Importance of Howard Hawks and John Ford to Political Philosophy*. Chicago, 2011.

———. *The Persistence of Subjectivity: On the Kantian Aftermath*. Cambridge, 2005.

Pitkin, Hanna Fenichel. "Are freedom and liberty twins?" *Political Theory* 16 (1988) 523–52.

———. *The Attack of the Blob: Hannah Arendt's Conception of the Social*. Chicago, 2000.

Pocock, J. G. A. *Barbarism and Religion: The First Decline and Fall*. Vol. 3. Cambridge, 2005.

———. "The concept of a language and the métier d'historien: some considerations on practice." In *The Languages of Political Theory in Early Modern Europe*, ed. Anthony Pagden. Cambridge, 1987.

———. "Languages and their implications: the transformation of the study of political thought." In *Politics, Language, and Time*. Chicago, 1960/1989.

————. *The Machiavellian Moment*. Princeton, 1975.

————. "The reconstruction of discourse: towards the historiography of political thought." *Modern Language Notes* 96 (1981) 959–80.

————. "Time, institutions, and actions: an essay on traditions and understanding." In *Politics, Language, and Time*. Chicago, 1960/1989.

————. *Virtue, Commerce and History: Essays on Political Thought and History, Chiefly in the Eighteenth Century*. Cambridge, 1985.

Podlas, Kimberlianne. "Please adjust your signal: how television's syndicated courtrooms bias our juror citizenry." *American Business Law Journal* 39 (2001) 1–24.

Powell, J. G. F. and J. A. North, eds. *Cicero's Republic*. London, 2001.

Putnam, Robert. *Bowling Alone: The Collapse and Revival of American Community*. New York, 2001.

Raaflaub, Kurt, ed. *Social Struggles in Archaic Rome*. 2nd ed. Oxford, 2005.

Rancière, Jacques. "Democracy, republic, representation," *Constellations* 13 (2006), 297–307.

————. *Disagreement*. Minneapolis, 2004.

————. *On the Shores of Politics*. London, 2007.

————. *The Politics of Aesthetics*. New York, 2004.

————. "Thinking between disciplines: an aesthetics of knowledge." *Parrhesia* 1 (2006) 1–12.

Rancière, Jacques and Davide Panagia. "Dissenting words: a conversation with Jacques Rancière." *diacritics* 30 (2000) 113–26.

Rapping, Elayne. *Law and Justice as Seen on TV*. New York, 2003.

Rawls, John. *A Theory of Justice*. Cambridge, MA, 1971/1995.

Rawson, Elizabeth. "The aftermath of the Ides." In *The Last Age of the Roman Republic, 146–43 BC: The Cambridge Ancient History*, Vol. 9. Cambridge, 1992.

Remer, Gary. "Cicero and the ethics of deliberative rhetoric." In *Talking Democracy*, ed. Benedetto Fontana, Cary J. Nederman, Gary Remer. University Park, 2004.

Reynolds, L. D., ed. *Texts and Transmission: A Survey of the Latin Classics*. Oxford, 1983.

Reynolds, Larry. "Subjective vision, romantic history, and the return of the 'real': the case of Margaret Fuller and the Roman Republic." *South Central Review* 21 (2004) 1–21.

Richards, Jennifer. "Assumed simplicity and the critique of nobility: or, how Castiglione read Cicero." *Renaissance Quarterly* 54 (2001) 460–86.

Ricoeur, Paul. *Oneself as Another*. Chicago, 1992.

Riggsby, Andrew. *Crime and Community in Ciceronian Rome*. Austin, 1999.

Rogin, Michael. *Ronald Reagan, the Movie: and Other Episodes in American Political Demonology*. Berkeley and Los Angeles, 1987.

Rorty, Richard. *Contingency, Irony, Solidarity*. Cambridge, 1989.

————. "The historiography of philosophy: four genres." In *Philosophy in History*, ed. Richard Rorty, J. B. Schneewind, and Quentin Skinner. Cambridge, 1984.

————. *Philosophy and Social Hope*. New York, 2000.

Rosanvallon, Pierre. *Democracy Past and Future*. New York, 2007.

Rose, Jacqueline. *States of Fantasy*. Oxford, 1996.

Rudd, Niall. "Horace as a moralist." In *Horace 2000: A Celebration: Essays for the Bimillenium*. Ann Arbor, 2003.

Saramago, Jose. *La Lucidité*. Paris, 2007.

Saxonhouse, Arlene. "Exile and re-entry: political theory yesterday and tomorrow." *Oxford Handbook of Political Theory*, ed. John S. Dryzek, Bonnie Honig, and Anne Phillips. New York, 2008.

Schiesaro, Alessandro. "Horace's Bacchic poetics." In *Perceptions of Horace: A Roman Poet and His Readers*, ed. L. B. T. Houghton and Maria Wyke. Cambridge and New York, 2009.

Schlegel, Catherine. *Satire and the Threat of Speech: Horace's Satires Book 1*. Madison, 1995.

Sciarrino, Enrica. "Putting Cato the Censor's *Origines* in its place." *Classical Antiquity* 23 (2004) 323–57.

Sen, Amartya. *Development as Freedom*. New York, 1999.

Serres, Michel. *Rome: The Book of Foundations*. Stanford, 1991.

Shapiro, Ian. *Democracy's Place*. Ithaca, 1996.

———. *Democratic Justice*. New Haven, 1999.

Shklar, Judith N. *American Citizenship: The Quest for Inclusion*. Cambridge, MA, 1998.

———. *Ordinary Vices*. New York, 1985.

Skinner, Quentin. *The Foundations of Modern Political Thought*. Vol. 1. Cambridge, 1978.

———. *Liberty Before Liberalism*. Cambridge, 1998.

———. *Reason and Rhetoric in the Philosophy of Hobbes*. Cambridge, 1997.

Sklenar, Robert. "La République des signes: Caesar, Cato, and the language of Sallustian morality." *Transactions of the American Philological Association* 128 (1998) 205–220.

Smith, Ruth L. "Morals and their ironies." *Journal of Religious Ethics* 26 (1998) 367–88.

Stiglitz, Joseph. *The Price of Inequality: How Today's Divided Society Endangers Our Future*. New York, 2012.

Strasburger, H. *Concordia Ordinum: eine Untersuchung zur Politik Ciceros*. Amsterdam, 1956.

Stroup, Sarah Culpepper. *Catullus, Cicero, and a Society of Patrons*. Cambridge, 2010.

Swyngedouw, Erik. "Where is the political?" Antipode Lecture, 2008. Accessed online.

Syme, Ronald. *The Roman Revolution*. Oxford, 1939/2002.

———. *Sallust*. Berkeley and Los Angeles, 1964/2002.

Tarnopolsky, Christina. "Platonic reflections on the aesthetic dimensions of deliberative democracy." *Political Theory* 35 (2007) 288–312.

———. "Plato's politics of distributing and disrupting the sensible." *Theory & Event* 13 (2010).

Thurschwell, Review of Simon Critchley. *Infinitely Demanding: Law, Culture, and the Humanities* 4 (2008) 300–304.

Touraine, Alain. "Is sociology still the study of society?" *Thesis Eleven* 23 (1989).

Trenchard, John and Thomas Gordon. *Cato's Letters, or Essays on Liberty, Civil and Religious, and Other Important Subjects*. Ed. Ronald Hamowy. 2 vols. Indianapolis, 1995.

Urbinati, Nadia. *Representative Democracy: Principles and Genealogy*. Chicago, 2008.

van Gelderen, Martin and Quentin Skinner, eds. *Republicanism: A Shared European Heritage*. 2 vols. Cambridge, 2005.

Vasaly, Ann. *Representations: Images of the World in Ciceronian Oratory*. Berkeley and Los Angeles, 1996.

Velleman, J. David. *How We Get Along*. Cambridge, 2009.

Velleman, J. David and Herlinde Pauer-Studer. "Distortions of normativity." *Ethical Theory and Moral Practice* 14 (2011) 329–56.

Villa, Dana. *Public Freedom*. Princeton, 2008.

Viroli, Maurizio. *Republicanism*. New York, 2002.

Waquet, Francoise. *Latin: Or the Empire of a Sign*. New York, 2001.

Webb, Ruth. *Ekphrasis, Imagination, and Persuasion in Ancient Rhetorical Theory and Practice*. Farnham, UK, 2009.

———. "Imagination and the arousal of the emotions." In *The Passions in Roman Literature and Thought*, ed. Susanna Braund and Christopher Gill. Cambridge, 1997.

White, Stephen J. "Contemporary continental political thought." In *The Oxford Handbook of the History of Political Philosophy*, ed. George Klosko. Oxford, 2011.

———. *The Ethos of a Late-Modern Citizen*. Cambridge, MA, 2009.

———. "Post-structuralism and political reflection." *Political Theory* 16 (1988) 186–208.

Wiedemann, Thomas. "Sallust's Jugurtha: concord, discord, and the digressions." *Greece & Rome* 20 (1993) 48–57.

Williams, Gordon. "Libertino patre natus: true or false?" In *Homage to Horace: A Bimillenary Celebration*, ed. Stephen J. Harrison. Oxford, 1995.

Winterbottom, Michael. "Believing the *pro Marcello*." In *Vertis in usum: Studies in Honor of Edward Courtney*, ed. Cynthia Damon. Chapel Hill, 2002.

Wirszubski, Chaim. Libertas *as a Political Idea at Rome*. Cambridge, 1968.

Wiseman, T. P. *The Myths of Rome*. Exeter, 2008.

———. *Remembering the Roman People*. Oxford, 1999.

———. "Romulus' Rome of equals." In *Social Struggles in Archaic Rome*, ed. Kurt Raaflaub. Oxford, 2005.

Wood, Gordon. *The Creation of the American Republic, 1776–1787*. Chapel Hill, 1998.

Wood, Neal. *Cicero's Social and Political Thought*. Berkeley and Los Angeles, 1988.

Woodman, A. J. "Style and attitude: Sallust and Livy." In *Rhetoric in Classical Historiography: Four Studies*. Portland, OR, 1988.

Yavetz, Zvi. *Plebs and Princeps*. Oxford, 1969.

Young, Iris Marion. *Inclusion and Democracy*. Oxford, 2002.

Yuval-Davis, Nira. "Human/women's rights and transversal politics." In *Global Feminism: Transnational Women's Activism, Organizing, and Human Rights*, ed. Myra Marx Ferree and Aili Mari Tripp. New York, 2006.

Zanker, Graham. "*Enargeia* in the ancient criticism of poetry." *Rheinisches Museum* 124 (1981) 297–311.

Zerilli, Linda. *Feminism and the Abyss of Freedom*. Princeton, 2005.

———. "'We feel our freedom': imagination and judgment in the thought of Hannah Arendt." *Political Theory* 33 (2005) 158–88.

Zetzel, James. "Horace's *Liber Sermonum*: the structure of ambiguity." *Arethusa* 13 (1980) 59–70.

Žižek, Slavoj. *Living in the End Times*. London, 2010.

———. *The Sublime Object of Ideology*. London, 1989.

INDEX

accountability. *See* responsibility and accountability

acknowledgment: of human limits, 4, 135–37, 151–53, 167, 172, 176; in oratorical situations, 160n; of others, 131–32, 140–41, 146, 151, 163; of political actors, 33–34, 36, 40–41, 52, 156; through conflict, 40–41. *See also* recognition

active citizenship, 13, 14n30, 20

Adams, John, 3, 9, 61, 62

Adams, John Quincy, 62

Addison, Joseph, 154

Adherbal, 93–94

Ad Herennium (rhetorical treatise), 84

Adorno, Theodor, 193

advocacy, 48, 51–58; dividual, 155–76. *See also* political voice

advocate-orator, as ideal citizen, 55–56

aesthesis (the aesthetic): in Cicero's *pro Marcello*, 185–87, 200; judgment and, 68, 124; oratory and, 158–68, 185; political actions partaking of, 50–51, 204, 206; political imagination and, 174–76, 185–87; Sallust and, 187; and the self, 206. *See also* senses, sensation, and sensibility; the body

aesthetic faculty, 8–9

aesthetic judgment, 67–68, 143, 145, 159, 165, 206

Agamben, Giorgio, 170

agrarian life, republicanism and, 100–101

alienation, xi–xiii, 71

Allen, Danielle, 159n

amnesty, 90

Ando, Clifford, 13

André, Carl, 23

antagonism/conflict: avoidance or diminishment of, 31; channeling of, 47–48; in Cicero's thought, 34, 38–39, 55, 63; class-based, 18, 45–46, 57; cyclical nature of, 45–47; freedom coupled with, 32–34; as one pole of republic's nature, 61–64, 155–56; as oppressive force, 50; oratory appropriate for politics based on, 158–72; politics based on, 22, 27, 42, 58, 81–82, 158–72; republican politics based on, 39; Roman politics based on, 32–34, 39, 45–46; senate-people, 40–41

Antonius, Marcus (cognomen Orator, grandfather of Mark Antony), 164

Antony, Mark, 59, 87, 90, 159

appearance: judgments made in realm of, 68, 78, 163, 165; legitimacy grounded in, 47; Plato's devaluation of, 166; political order maintained through, 50; rhetoric operative in the realm of, 167; in Roman society and politics, 141–42; satire concerned with, 137, 139; vivid narrative details and, 74

Arendt, Hannah, 35; and appearance, 166; *Between Past and Future*, 71, 77; critique of modernity by, 10; on deficiencies of democracy, xii; *Eichmann in Jerusalem*, 65–70, 117, 169; on imagination, 148; influence of, 10; on interpretation of the ancients, 2–4; *The Human Condition*, 117; on judgment and thinking, 65–70, 117, 124, 130; *The Life of the Mind*, 77; on moral action, 169–70; on moral judgment, 144–46; on nature of politics, 110; on Roman philosophy, 77; on self-sovereignty, 117

Aristotle: on human nature, 174; on moral evaluation, 143; political thought of, 4, 17, 155; *Politics*, 47; on power, 47; on rhetoric, 156; and the self, 99, 116

Armstrong, David, 126n22

art: judging as, 148; politics as, 156n; viewers' experience of, 23, 25

Asmis, Elizabeth, 38

auctoritas (personal authority), 33, 111, 167, 180

Augustine, Saint, 117

auxilium (tribune's help), 53

Badian, Ernst, 79

Badiou, Alain, 171

Baebius, Gaius, 95

Baier, Annette, 208

Balibar, Étienne, 165, 165n15

banality of evil, 68

Batstone, William, 79n39, 179

Bauman, Zygmunt, 19

beginnings, historical and political, 83–87

Benjamin, Walter, 89